Blessing and peace,

Doug

ELUSIVE
PEACE

ELUSIVE
PEACE

*How Modern
Diplomatic Strategies
Could Better Resolve
World Conflicts*

DOUGLAS E. NOLL

Prometheus Books

59 John Glenn Drive
Amherst, New York 14228–2119

Published 2011 by Prometheus Books

Cover image © 2011 Media Bakery. Jacket design by Jacqueline Nasso-Cooke.

Inquiries should be addressed to
Prometheus Books
59 John Glenn Drive
Amherst, New York 14228–2119
VOICE: 716–691–0133
FAX: 716–691–0137
WWW.PROMETHEUSBOOKS.COM

15 14 13 12 11   5 4 3 2 1

Library of Congress Cataloging-in-Publication Data

Noll, Douglas, 1950–
    Elusive peace : how modern diplomatic strategies could better resolve world conflicts / by Douglas E. Noll.
        p.   cm.
    Includes index.
    ISBN 978–1–61614–417–3 (alk. paper)
    ISBN 978–1–61614–418–0 (e-book)
    1. Diplomacy. 2. Conflict management. I. Title.

JZ1305.N65 2011
327.1'72—dc22

                                                              2010049899

Printed in the United States of America on acid-free paper

Contents

Introduction

In September 2010, direct talks between the Israeli government and the Palestinian Authority started. As of the close of the first meeting in Washington, DC, there was both pessimism and hope that a sustainable and achievable peace agreement could be reached. The pessimism was based on the history of failure between the parties, the continued violence perpetrated by Hamas, the questionable authority of Mahmoud Abbas to bring the Palestinians to peace, and the dubious ability of Benjamin Netanyahu to stop settlement construction. The hope was based on the fact that the parties are once again talking, that the United States is once again engaged in the process, and that the majority of the people of the region are weary of war.

The news coverage has focused on the external events—the meetings, the phone calls, the consultations—but has not focused on the actual peace work itself. Most people forget that President Barack Obama made peace in the Middle East a primary foreign policy objective. He announced the appointment of former senator George Mitchell as special envoy to the Middle East on January 22, 2009, two days after his January 20, 2009, inauguration. Within twenty-four hours of his presidency, Obama called Middle Eastern leaders to talk about his agenda for peace, and he formally appointed Mitchell as special envoy. Obviously, this was something that had been in the works for some time.

Secretary of state Hillary Clinton has also focused on peace in the Middle East, seeing it as unfinished business from her husband Bill Clinton's administration as well as holding a passion for alleviating the suffering of the people in the region. Secretary Clinton is not afraid to prepare herself, having asked her staff for an exhaustive analysis of all the major peace initiatives to spot trends, sticking points, and areas of agreement. She has maintained her credibility with both sides and has been persistent. More than half of her telephone calls to foreign countries have been to the Middle East.

Senator Mitchell has said many times, "From my experience, I have formed the conviction that there is no such thing as a conflict that can't be ended. Conflicts are created, conducted, and sustained by human beings. They can be ended by human beings."[1] His sentiment reflects wisdom that is often missed by international negotiators and diplomats.

Secretary Clinton and Senator Mitchell are distinguished, highly experienced politicians. How much more effective and powerful might they be if their personal mediation skills and experience matched their political and diplomatic skills? This question has rarely, if ever, been asked because it raises an important and overlooked question: Are the skills of the peacemaker qualitatively different than the skills of the diplomat or the politician? I believe the answer is yes. I also believe that if we truly desire peace in our world, our leaders and their envoys must add an entirely new set of skills and knowledge to their repertoire.

What we know about the causes and resolution of human conflict from both a scientific and practical perspective has grown exponentially in the past twenty years. This has developed as a result of the explosive use of mediation around the world to solve a vast array of human conflicts, from commercial disputes in litigation to public policy disputes to mediations between victims and offenders in criminal cases. In addition, our knowledge about human conflict and peace has benefitted from advances in emerging fields such as social neuropsychology and behavioral economics. The ability to watch the human brain process information through techniques such as functional magnetic resonance imaging, transcranial magnetic stimulation, and sophisticated electroencephalography techniques is demonstrating that the core assumptions of law, economics, and the philosophy of human behavior are incomplete. In addition, as researchers devise ever-increasingly clever means of investigating the source and nature of emotions, beliefs, moral development, and decision making in the brain, mediators are taking the research and applying it to the practical problems of peace. The result is a set of powerful tools that, when used appropriately, can lead us to understand human conflict at a much deeper level. With that understanding, we can approach the problem of peace with a greater degree of subtlety and nuance than has ever before been achievable.

Is peace really attainable or is it merely an elusive dream of tree-hugging liberals? Follow me for a moment to one of the most unlikely places on the planet to find peace, and see for yourself that peace is a not pipe dream.

*　　*　　*

Driving north out of the Los Angeles basin in California requires you to take Interstate 5, the main north-south interstate of the West Coast. For the first forty miles after leaving the San Fernando Valley, Interstate 5 winds through the Angeles National Forest to the east and the Los Padres National Forest to the west. It passes through small hamlets such as Castaic, Gorman, and Lebec before dropping into the San Joaquin Valley. Some twenty miles into the valley, I-5 splits off to the west, and State Route 99 continues up the center of some of the most productive farmland in the world.

Eventually, 99 takes you through the town of Madera, California, and 5 miles north of Madera is the exit for Avenue 20 1/2, 250 miles north of Los Angeles. Take that exit, go to the top of the ramp, and turn right. As you leave the freeway, you are quickly surrounded by almond orchards. In another mile or so, Avenue 20 1/2 curves to the left and turns into Road 22. It's pretty obvious that you are in the center of a huge agricultural district. In a few minutes, on your left, you will pass by the Central California Women's Facility, one of five women's prisons in California. Past the prison is Avenue 24. Make a left turn on Avenue 24, go down one mile, and you arrive at the Valley State Prison for Women, the largest women's prison in the world. Opened in 1995, with a design capacity of approximately 2,800 inmates, it now holds 3,600 women as prisoners of the state of California. Approximately 450 of these inmates are serving life sentences without the possibility of parole.

In August 2009, Southern California mediator Laurel Kaufer received a handwritten letter from one of these life inmates asking if Laurel could provide mediation training to a group of inmates interested in learning to be peacemakers. Laurel asked me if I would be interested in the project, and I immediately agreed. The idea of seeing if we could teach women incarcerated for murder, homicide, and other heinous acts to be effective peacemakers within the prison was a challenge neither of us could turn down.

It took us six months of persistent work to gain the trust of the prison authorities to begin this project. In April 2010, we began a pilot program with fifteen women. All but two of them were serving life sentences or very long-term sentences. They were murderers, drunk drivers who had killed entire families, former drug addicts; in short, the castaways of American society.

We had no idea what to expect. Neither of us had ever been in a prison before, and our first tour was as scary as it was enlightening. We were given a small, dingy conference room as our training space for these would-be peacemakers.

Laurel and I have trained peacemakers and mediators around the world. Laurel was the creator of the Mississippi Mediation Project as a response to the Hurricane Katrina disaster, and through that project she established mediation as a means of resolving postdisaster conflicts. I had taught and trained mediation skills to community mediators, to graduate students, and to the most sophisticated mediators in the United States. I had worked as a trainer in Europe and the Middle East. Neither of us had a clue about what the needs or interests of women incarcerated for life in prison would be.

We started the training within an intense two-day workshop that taught our new peacemakers the essential skills of listening, problem solving, and dealing with high emotions. We had a distinguished trainer from Ridge Associates, and a trainer from the Mississippi Mediation Project. Both trainers volunteered their time to come into the prison. Laurel and I suspected that these women would have little if any empathic listening and communication skills, but over the course of two days, we watched an amazing transformation as these women learned for the first time that they could be effective, empathic listeners.

Every Wednesday for the next three weeks, we drove to the prison and spent three hours coaching, teaching, and listening to the women as they told us how they were progressing with their skills. In week four, we spent an entire day teaching them the principles of restorative justice and how to conduct a process known as peace circles. At the end of that day, we charged them with the task of conducting at least two peace circles in the next week and reporting back to us their results. We had no idea what would happen.

The following Wednesday, we returned for our usual follow-up session and asked the women about the week's experiences. What we heard astounded us. The women told us that as they conducted peace circles, for the first time inmates felt safe to talk, communicate, and express how they really felt. There was one story of a woman who had not spoken in years to anyone, and, upon entering the circle, talked for the first time about her feelings. Our nascent peacemakers were glowing with enthusiasm as they saw how some of the most difficult women they lived with responded in the peace circles.

We returned for the next two Wednesdays, again coaching, teaching, supporting, and listening to the stories. The women continued to convene and conduct peace circles in their prison community, gaining confidence as peacemakers. We watched them grow and transform from shut-down, defensive, emotionally unavailable human beings to articulate, empowered women determined to turn their prison into a place of peace.

In week ten, Laurel and I spent three days teaching these women the skills of mediation. In the beginning, they fumbled, they were nervous, and they were unsure of themselves. By the third day, the process clicked, and they got it. We told them to conduct at least two mediations apiece and observe two mediations in the next several weeks.

The following Wednesday we returned, again wondering what, if anything, had happened. Again, the women astounded us as they told us story after story about how they had prevented fights, violence, and arguments from disrupting their community. And, they were continuing with their peace circle work.

For the next two Wednesdays, we continued our support and training until we felt that they had learned enough and were ready to practice the art and science of peacemaking. By then, we were so amazed by their progress that we nominated them for the Cloke-Millen Peacemaker of the Year award granted annually by the Southern California Mediation Association. The award is named after Kenneth Cloke, an internationally renowned mediator, author, and cofounder of Mediators Beyond Borders, and Richard Millen, one of the first community mediators in Southern California. To our immense surprise, the board of directors unanimously voted these female inmates as recipients of this prestigious award.

Within the prison, word spread fairly quickly that something was happening. Prison guards began to approach our mediators, asking for assistance in resolving disputes with other inmates. Supervisors and prison staff found themselves in mediations when they were in conflict with inmates. Slowly, the women were turning Valley State Prison for Women into a prison of peace.

Today, Laurel and I are training our second group of peacemakers: thirty-two women, all life inmates or long-termers. We have two hundred women on a waiting list, and we are training our first group to become leaders and trainers themselves. Our hope is to have this program self-sustaining within the prison by the summer of 2011. In a time of severe budget cutbacks and funding restrictions in California, the prison authorities have seen that this is a bright spot in an otherwise bleak and gray environment. They'd like us to take on teaching the most difficult inmates some of the skills. We are thinking about it.

What this experience has taught me is that anyone can be a peacemaker. Anyone, if they have sufficient desire, can learn the sophisticated and subtle skills of mediation. If we can teach murderers, baby killers, former addicts, and other social outcasts to be effective peacemakers, why can't the same be done for our international diplomats and negotiators? And, if peace can be brought to a place like Valley State Prison for Women, then I believe peace can be achieved anywhere, no matter how dark the place may be.

I think George Mitchell sees this, as do President Obama and Hillary Clinton. I hope that other people in the international community and readers like you who may have no relationship to peacemaking or international relations will see the possibility too. Peacemaking is the hardest work a human being can be asked to do. It is also the most satisfying work, especially when parties who cannot even stand to be in the same room with each other can eventually find a way to live together without violence.

In the chapters that follow, we will look at some of the most intractable conflicts in the world and show how the modern science of mediation can aid in the possibility of transformation.

Peace is a process, not an event, and it occurs between people, not institutions or governments. Fundamentally, there is no difference between an intense conflict between gangbangers in prison and regional conflicts or civil wars. Fundamentally, peace requires human brains to shift and change, and that is the job of the peacemaker. Peace does not have to be elusive if our leaders and diplomats are willing to up their game. That is what this book is about.

Chapter 1

Eighteenth-Century Diplomacy Will Not Solve Twenty-First-Century Problems

Everyone wants world peace. Miss America wants to work for peace. Churches pray for it. Every Friday afternoon in the beach town of Carpinteria, California, a dozen or so people hold up signs demanding world peace. It is every good person's birthday wish. But how to get there?

The headlines don't give us much hope. Peace talks fail; negotiations over climate change fail; Iran is developing The Bomb. Afghanistan is an expensive mess, and the Sunnis and Shi'a are duking it out in Iraq. There seems to be more war and strife than ever before.

The cost of conflict is high. When you include veterans' obligations, interest on the amount borrowed to finance defense spending, and the cost of the wars in Iraq and Afghanistan, about 54 cents of each US tax dollar pays for the military. The United States spends more on defense than the entire world put together.[1]

International conflicts affect us all, and our inability to solve them threatens our very existence on the planet. The threat is to our personal security, our communities, and to our environment.

Why can't these problems be solved? That's the question I

asked myself. I began to wonder why we can successfully mediate deeply painful conflicts like sexual abuse by clergy members and serious criminal offenses between victims and offenders, but not international conflicts. So I started to study the problem from my perspective as a professional mediator. What I learned was that the people in charge of international mediations and negotiations, though highly distinguished politicians and diplomats, are not always as skilled in the art and science of modern negotiation and peacemaking as they could be. In many cases, they are using old ideas and antiquated assumptions in their efforts to solve twenty-first-century problems.

Imagine sending a board-certified oncologist who specializes in colon cancer into a busy urban emergency room on a Friday night. The oncologist may get through the shift but not nearly as easily or as skillfully as the board-certified emergency room surgeon who has spent ten years working in a major trauma center. This metaphor describes the current practice of using former politicians and diplomats to intervene in international conflicts. We are sending in the oncologist, not the trauma surgeon, to handle the crisis.

In many cases, international mediators lack the experience and knowledge of how to deal with complex conflicts. Very few, if any, international mediators have had much mediation experience measured by the number of conflicts formally mediated. By way of contrast, the average successful US commercial mediator mediates more complex cases in a year than most international mediators have mediated in their careers. That is not to say that quantity is better than quality or that a complex commercial case is equivalent to an international conflict. However, in addition to the lack of formal training, the actual experience of mediating conflicts between people who are at war with each other is quite limited. The trauma center surgeon sees hundreds of medical emergencies, minor and major every week. The oncologist, simply because of the nature of his or her practice, sees none.

In other cases, the processes used to work with difficult conflicts harkened back to white wigs, frocked coats, and silk stockings. Too many diplomats and foreign ministers still believe in eighteenth-century ways of diplomacy and negotiation. Everyone knows that the twenty-first century world is very different than eighteenth-century Europe. The world is a complex place requiring a much more nuanced approach.

These complexities seem to stymie the ability of international negotiators to engage each other constructively when there are huge chasms of difference. When nations do come together, they are often cast into an unwieldy process that is often nonproductive. Not surprisingly, international negotiators often end up angry and disgruntled with each other. The media inflames these failures, making things worse.

Our only hope is to abandon the old processes in favor of approaches to conflict that take into account the knowledge we have gained in a vast array of disciplines around decision making, neuropsychology, and human behavior. It invokes processes that promote collaboration and discourage competition. It is the critical next step in bringing peace to the world.

THE OLD WAY JUST ISN'T WORKING

The old ways of dealing with international conflict are not only failing, they are actually endangering us in ways that we probably are not aware of. Take nuclear nonproliferation as an example. Article VI of the Nuclear Non-Proliferation Treaty says: "[Each of the] states undertake to pursue negotiations in good faith on effective measures relating to cessation of the nuclear arms race at an early date and to nuclear disarmament," and toward a "treaty on general and complete disarmament under strict and effective international control."[2]

For almost forty years, the nuclear weapons states have not fulfilled their mutual obligation to disarm themselves of nuclear weapons. Instead, conflict has arisen between nonproliferation ("We keep our nukes, you don't get yours") and disarmament (the total elimination of nuclear weapons). The nuclear powers conflate nonproliferation with disarmament so that the focus is on preventing North Korea and Iran from developing nuclear weapons, rather than on disarming the United States, China, Russia, France, Great Britain, India, Pakistan, and Israel, among others. The diplomats conveniently ignore this nuclear narcissism, refusing to talk seriously about the possibility of complete, worldwide nuclear disarmament at a high political level. Perhaps disarmament is unrealistic. However, Iran makes a point when it asks why there are not ongoing discussions about global disarmament.

The December 2009 climate change conference in Copenhagen is another example of how old processes have led to impasse. We will look at this conference in greater detail later. Suffice it to say that the 2009 conference was a large political meeting with over forty-five thousand people attending. In addition to diplomats and technical experts from every nation, the conference was observed by dozens of nongovernmental organizations (NGOs), a media mob, environmental groups, and business interests. The critical negotiations took place behind closed doors. Given the adversarial framework in which the negotiations were structured, impasse was inevitable. Kenneth Cloke, the founder of Mediators Beyond Borders, wrote:

> Large political meetings like this one are often arranged hierarchically, bureaucratically and autocratically (even when they adopt a formally democratic official language); around narrow, technical topics that make it difficult for anyone to have authentic, meaningful conversations; entirely in large groups that do not allow for honest inter-personal dialogue; based on formal, arcane procedures that tie conversations in knots; and are increasingly pointless, ineffective, and unnecessary.[3]

The failure to understand and acknowledge the failure of current negotiation processes is systemic. It deeply penetrates the international diplomatic community. While in Copenhagen observing the global warming treaty negotiation process, Laurel Kaufer, a well-known California-based mediator, asked ambassador John Ashe, chair of the Ad Hoc Working Group–Kyoto Protocol, why the parties to climate change conferences do not use mediation when impasse is reached. Ambassador Ashe answered disdainfully, "Why should we do that? Mediation is for human rights issues." Embedded in Ambassador Ashe's answer is the elitist idea, "We diplomats know best. Go away and leave the negotiating to us professionals."[4] The fact is, many diplomats are neither knowledgeable nor professional when it comes to working with deep conflict. The examples I use in the chapters that follow will illustrate this.

The point of this book is to look at these antiquated processes, understand why they are not working, and offer up a more nuanced view of negotiation, problem solving, and conflict resolution that might help us use twenty-first-century technology to solve twenty-first-century problems. I don't suggest that a modern approach will immediately solve all of the complex problems of the world. However, using a scalpel instead of a meat axe to remove a tumor seems like it might lead to a better outcome for the patient. I want to demonstrate the crisis of failure in modern international negotiation. I believe that we have better technology, better knowledge, and better science about negotiation, problem solving, decision making, and human behavior than did eighteenth-century diplomats. Skillfully applied, this technology can help us work more productively on the intractable problems of the modern world.

SOME ASSUMPTIONS OF EIGHTEENTH-CENTURY DIPLOMACY AS APPLIED IN THE TWENTY-FIRST CENTURY

When we have to negotiate for anything, even something as simple as a buying a used car, we want to know the motivations of the people with whom we are negotiating. If we understand the other person's motives, we hope we can strike the right chord to get them to do what we want them to do. To help us achieve this, we formulate assumptions and theories about why people do what they do.

To get a sense about the importance of understanding the assumptions of negotiators, consider what I am doing when I intend to negotiate a used car purchase. First, I generate some fundamental assumptions about the seller. I assume he wants to sell me a car. Second, I assume he wants to sell me a car at the highest price possible because it affects his commission. Third, I assume that he wants to be my newest best friend, but not because of my good looks. He and I both know that affinity is one of the five central elements of effective persuasion. Fourth, I assume he has my best interests in mind only to the degree that it helps him sell me a car. Fifth, I assume he will use sales tricks, tips, and techniques common in car sales negotiations, and that I can expect to be manipulated. Sixth, I will assume some dishonesty. Everyone fudges on something, so I will expect that from him.

I will also assume that he will use the technique of limited authority against me, and that I will have to negotiate with him, a sales "manager," and a finance "manager." I assume that these "managers" are just souped-up salespeople whose purpose is to close the deal at a higher price, with more options, and with a profitable financing deal. That's a lot of assumptions for me to make, but they will guide me in my negotiations so that I am not exploited, manipulated, or overwhelmed by the process. After all, these guys do this for a living every day, while I buy a car every ten to twelve years.

These are all assumptions we implicitly might make in the negotiation over a used car. They guide us in our decision making and help us get what we want without paying too much.

Just like buying a used car, international diplomats have certain assumptions and theories about human nature.

HUMANS ARE EVIL, OR SO THEY THINK

The fundamental assumption in international relations is that human beings are self-interested egoists who tend toward violence, contention, and brutality unless constrained by threat or exercise of violent force. Thucydides expressed this assumption early on,[5] and it was recapitulated later by Niccolò Machiavelli and Thomas Hobbes.[6] This view of human nature is also expounded in the Christian theology of original sin developed by Augustine as a rebuttal to the arguments of the Irish monk Pelagius.[7]

From a gross observational standpoint, the assumption that the other guy is out to advance himself at my expense seems consistent with how the world really works. After all, history and our personal experiences are replete with examples of selfishness and self-aggrandizement leading to misery, violence, and war. We cannot assume that the other guy is altruistic when the evidence points to the conclusion that he wants to smack us down. International relations theory assumes that governments act pretty much like individuals unless they, too, are constrained by a dominant power. Thus, diplomatic negotiation is often conducted through the threat of economic sanctions and the exercise of military power.

Obviously, human beings and their governments have the capacity to act dangerously. However, dangerous behavior is not automatic or inherent. In fact, given a preference, most human beings will choose peace over war. In addition, we have an extraordinary capacity for cooperation, love, attachment, empathy, and altruism. The narrow assumptions of diplomacy do not trust these innate human traits and therefore ignore the enormous power that they may contribute in negotiation, conflict resolution, and problem solving.

Old diplomacy also assumes that human beings are rational players, seeking, in the terms of traditional economics, to maximize their utility. In other words, individuals and governments make rational choices to improve their lives, economic well-being, or security from outside threats.

The assumption of rationality pervades international relations theory. For example, international relations scholars Robert Keohane and Joseph Nye wrote, "Both realism and liberalism are consistent with the assumption that most state behavior can be interpreted as rational, or at least intelligent activity."[8] The language of rational actors, rational states, cool assessments of risk, and so forth are found throughout the literature of international relations.

This concept, called *rational-choice theory*, is the foundation of economics and political science in the Western world. Its greatest flaw is that it discounts the importance of emotions in decision making and therefore fails to predict the actual behaviors of human beings with any reasonable accuracy. New discoveries in behavioral economics, cognitive and social neuroscience, and social psychology have demonstrated that emotions weave through our every thought, decision, and action. To paraphrase neuroscientist Antonio Damasio, we are 98 percent emotional and 2 percent rational.[9] We are not nearly as rational as we think we are. Behavioral economists like Duke University professor Dan Ariely have established that we are "predictably irrational" in most of our decision-making processes.[10] More importantly, rationality may not define what it means to be human.

Our twenty-first-century knowledge paints a picture of a much more complex motivational process. A recent study[11] illustrates the point: A group of people was randomly divided into two groups. Each person in one group was given a two-digit numeral to memorize, such as 12, 20, or 31. The people in the other group were asked to memorize a seven-digit telephone number, such as 3437654 or 7965748. Both groups were told to keep those numerals in their memory and not to forget them. They would be asked at a later time whether or not they remembered the numbers. As they were reminded to keep the numbers in mind, they were offered a snack plate containing apple slices and brownies.

The researchers were interested in whether the groups would

vary in their choice of snacks. Sure enough, more of the people who were required to remember the two-digit numbers picked apples, while more of the people who were remembering the seven-digit number took brownies off the plate. Not everybody picked apples over brownies or brownies over apples. However, the number of two-digit people who chose the apples over brownies compared to the total group, and the number of seven-digit people who chose brownies compared to the total group was statistically significant.

The hypothesis that developed from this experiment, and many others like it, is that when our cognitive capacity is taxed by even a simple task of remember a string of numerals, our ability to manage emotional impulses is dramatically reduced. The two-digit people had an easier time because of the smaller number and therefore had some cognitive capacity left over for impulse control. They could resist the less healthful brownie and make a healthier, if less tasty, decision to eat an apple.

On the other hand, the people remembering the seven-digit telephone number had to use up most of their cognitive capacity to keep that in number in mind. They did not have enough high-level brain bandwidth, so to speak, left over to manage and monitor impulse control. They tended to pick the tastier chocolate fudge brownie over the healthier apple because they had less control over their emotional impulse.[12] The upshot is that we have a very limited rational capacity, and most of our decisions are shaped from emotions, our environment, and by habit.

Nevertheless, old diplomacy assumes that our rational capacity is unlimited. Emotions simply get in the way of good, clear, logical thinking. When people's behaviors contradict rational analysis, they are called "irrational." Unfortunately, we see far more "irrational" behavior in international relations than we see "rational" behavior. In the chapters that follow, we will look at examples of nonrational decisions, such as Pakistan's disastrous decisions to go to war with India, the Bush administration's decision to invade Iraq, and Iran's persistence in pursuing nuclear weapons development. No wonder peace negotiations fail so often.

International mediators persist in assuming that humans are rational in the face of overwhelmingly contrary scientific evidence. If a head of state behaves "irrationally," everyone throws their hands up in the air, not knowing what to do next. Usually, force and coercion are then brought to bear in the hopes of "persuading" the "irrational" person or government to conform to desired behaviors and norms. Little thought seems to be given to the subtleties of information processing and decision making in this "irrational" person. Worse, coercion will often have the unintended effect of making people more intransigent. Cognitive psychologists would tell you that stubbornness in that situation is predictable. As a consequence of their assumptions about human nature, negotiators lose opportunities to build deeper understanding, communication, and trust.

As long as rationalist theories of human behavior are the basis to solve twenty-first-century international problems, emotions will be ignored. Parties to peace negotiations will continue to feel disrespected, mistrusted, underappreciated, misunderstood, and victimized. As long as the emotional nature of humanity is disregarded, international leaders will use outdated negotiation processes that will inevitably lead to impasse, continued violence, and war. Only when we understand that emotions must be treated as at least coequal with rationality will trust, altruism, hope, and empathy will begin to flow, and with them, solutions to complex problems.

SOVEREIGNTY IS NOT WHAT IT USED TO BE

I am about to commit heresy: Sovereignty is not what it is cracked up to be. One of the limitations of modern diplomacy is that it assumes a Westphalian view of the world. In 1648, after thirty years of religious wars in Europe and three years of negotiations, the Peace of Westphalia was signed. It ended the Thirty Years' War, effectively ended the Holy Roman Empire, and instituted the concept of sovereignty in nation-states. The Treaty of Westphalia[13] has been one of the foundations of international diplomacy ever since.

Article 1 of the treaty requires that nations be sovereign entities that work on developing themselves fully, metaphorically like a person. Nation-states became "people" in the new international community and were represented by their "heads of state" and foreign ministers. The idea was that nations would work on their internal affairs and development for the betterment of their citizens, and the nations as a group would work on international matters. For the first time, nation-states agreed that they should not be interfering with each other's internal affairs. This idea arose from the abuses of the Holy Roman Emperor, who had the power to depose princes from their kingdoms. No longer could the pope or some emperor interfere with the domestic politics of a nation-state. It would be another 123 years before the first true democracy was formed in America, but the fundamental concept of international relations between nations was formed in Westphalia.

The Treaty of Westphalia was not the result of a truly international negotiation. Instead, it was limited to European interests. Thus, its underlying cultural, religious, and political assumptions could not possibly represent the state of the world in 1648. Today, the same complaint about the treaty can be made: the concept of nation-states is purely Eurocentric and is inappropriate for many other regions of the world.[14]

Afghanistan is a case in point. As conceived by the Treaty of Westphalia, Afghanistan is not a self-interested, self-developing state. Instead, it is a mixture of rival ethnic and tribal peoples confined within artificially contrived borders, the Pakistan side of which does not even exist except as the Durand Line. While there is a fiction that a central government exists in Kabul, the truth is that Afghanistan is not a nation-state with a distinct "head of state" controlling the rest of the corporeal body of the nation.

Thus, trying to install a democratically elected government that somehow has the consent of the people to govern is an absurdity in a country where such traditions and ideas have never developed. To make the point, consider that the United States has had one constitution since 1793. Since 1923, Afghanistan has had seven separate and distinct constitutions: 1923, 1964, 1976, 1987, 1990, and 2003.

Article 2 of the Treaty of Westphalia is also irrelevant in its application to places like Afghanistan. The literal language of Article 2 says:

> Instead, [the fact that] each and every one, from one side and the other, both before and during the war, committed insults, violent acts, hostilities, damages, and injuries, without regard of persons or outcomes, should be completely put aside, so that everything, whatever one could demand from another under his name, will be forgotten to eternity.[15]

The purpose of this language was to allow the signatory nation-states and principalities to let go of past animosities, war crimes, abuses, and violence so as to move forward with a fresh slate. In essence, the honor codes of vengeance that existed in Europe were to be set aside so that peace could reign. Because of the economic development and prosperity that followed the end of the Thirty Years' War, this was not too hard for most people to swallow. However, the idea that a peace treaty could eliminate honor debts under the Pashtun *Pashtunwali* code is difficult to accept. The only possible way honor feuds can be resolved peacefully within the Pashtun is through the councils of the *jirga* (see chapter 5). In short, eighteenth-century European assumptions about sovereignty do not work in a place like Afghanistan.

PEACE IS NOT A SIX-PACK OF BEER

In his classic text *Diplomacy*, international relations professor Harold Nicolson defines diplomatic negotiation as "essentially a mercantile art. . . . [T]he foundation of good diplomacy is the same as the foundation of good business."[16] Thus, old diplomacy assumes that international negotiations are purely "distributive." *Distributive negotiation* is a fancy term for compromising to get what you want. Basically, it means that, in exchange for a $5 bill, I will sell you my six-pack of beer. If we cannot reach agreement in the transaction, I do not get five bucks, and you do not get beer. It is the metaphor of the buyer and seller, and it transcends cultures and traditions. Since everyone buys and sells stuff (or barters—essentially the same thing) everywhere, international negotiators have made the mistake of assuming that every conflict and problem can be solved through buy-sell bargaining. This Monty Hall "Let's Make a Deal" mentality permeates diplomatic thinking. Unfortunately, the attitude is woefully naive. A moment's reflection will demonstrate the folly of this assumption.

The basic idea of distributive negotiation is that we can compromise and trade so that we can get a better deal for ourselves. However, negotiation is often more subtle and complex than we realize. In the context of cars, for example, it's not only about the price. Buyers are often concerned with emotional things like the color and interior furnishings of the car. Self-image is a critical motivation in a car purchase. Be honest, now: Haven't you asked yourself, "How will I look in this car?" "What will my friends think of me in this car?" "Gee, I really like this Ford 150 pickup truck, but I want to be seen as environmentally conscious"?

I have had this internal conversation, and you have too. This is all emotional stuff influencing our decision making.

In addition, buyers worry about how much money they will have to put down now and how much the monthly payments will be. Then there is the trade-in value of the old car to be negotiated. Pretty soon, price is not such a big issue.

On the seller's side, the salesman is asking himself, "Can I make a profit on the sale of the car?" "Can I make a profit by inducing the buyer to finance the car through me?" "Can I sell a maintenance contract or auto insurance policy?" "Can I make this customer happy enough to make a profit servicing his car?" "Am I going to make my sales quota this month?" "Am I a successful salesman?" Even in the archetypal commercial transaction, buying a car, all kinds of emotions permeate the process.

Now consider the problem of a young urban American couple. They are affluent, well educated, and living in New York City. They come from wealthy families and are each successful financially and professionally. They happily have their first baby and now face a conflict—what religious tradition should the baby be raised under? She's a Jew. He's a Protestant Christian. Each holds deep respect for the other's religious traditions and practices. Each is deeply embedded in his or her religion. They live in a secular society where mixed-religion marriages are accepted as normal. However, their families are putting a lot of pressure on them to conform to the family beliefs. Baptism or bar mitzvah? Christmas or Hanukkah? Temple or church? Priest or rabbi?

Traditional distributive negotiation theory does not give much guidance to this couple on how to solve their problem. They cannot, to quote Solomon, split the baby in half. Divorcing seems like a poor choice, especially because they love each other and their baby very much. In fact, we have just reached the practical limits of distributive negotiation. Something more is called for that cannot be satisfied by our existing notion of bargaining.

That something may be to bring the families together in a meeting to reflect on their deeper values and beliefs. We can expect that emotions will run high. Since most people do not have the skill to manage strong emotions during discussions of difficult issues, this family may bring in a mediator. The mediator may help them resolve the conflict around the baby's religious upbringing by providing a safe container for uncomfortable explorations into very private feelings. A good mediation process will slow the conversation down, allow for reflection, and examine hidden assumptions. Out of this process, solutions will evolve. As the heartfelt emotions are accepted by the group, the families will feel a sense of inner peace at having been heard. After that, everyone will be content with the solutions that honor the couple and the child.

International negotiators often eschew this "touchy-feely" approach. As a consequence, when faced with a problem that is not easily compromised because values and beliefs are involved, diplomatic negotiation generally falls apart. This is the fate of most difficult and complex international problems—when diplomats learn that they cannot forge a bargained treaty, they metaphorically wring their hands, then try again a year later with the same process and end up with the same result. Worse, diplomatic failure gives the hawks of a government the arguments needed to mount up the cavalry and charge in with guns blazing.

Distributive negotiation is efficient and effective in situations where value is easily determined and where a medium of exchange exists that everybody can agree on. So in a commercial negotiation, where somebody is selling widgets, another person is buying widgets, and they are operating under a system of dollars, euros, or yuan, figuring out the value of the widget is pretty straightforward. In those cases, distributive negotiation has the potential to be efficient and economical. Not only that, because the rules around what is being exchanged are reasonably well understood, the level of trust necessary to make a deal is pretty low. Take away the rules, and the need for higher trust levels increases to make the same deal work.

In nearly every other kind of conflict or dispute, where the issues are complex, ambiguous, highly subjective, or emotional, distributive negotiation simply does not work by itself. However, old diplomatic negotiation processes rely principally on this mercantile model of deal making. One side has to give up something in order for the other side to get something. In this view of the world, negotiating peace comes down to bargaining as if for a six-pack of beer. I give up land for peace. Power, authority, money, and resources all become exchangeable commodities at the international bargaining table. You get some land, a little bit of power, some authority, and money in exchange for laying down arms and stopping the bloodshed.

The flaw in this assumption is that conflicts are often not about exchangeable "commodities" that can be traded back and forth. Instead many, if not most, international conflicts are driven by deep-seated beliefs and emotions that are intractable to a buyer-seller negotiation. Thus, international negotiations fail because the basic principles of distributive negotiations are not present: Value is not easily understood by all parties, the items being bartered are highly subjective and emotional, and there is no recognized or accepted medium of exchange.

When there has been civil war, for example, the parties may be negotiating myriad issues ranging from boundaries and human-rights abuses to repatriation of refugees and power-sharing arrangements. The parties often see the negotiation in terms of win-lose.

This type of bargaining fails when demands are made on me to give up things that I cannot or am unwilling to give up. In particular, distributive negotiation is extremely harmful when beliefs and injustices are driving the conflict. It should be common sense, but it is not widely understood, that we resist compromise on deep-seated beliefs, identities, and values. Whether we are a Palestinian or an Israeli Jew or a Hutu or a Serb or a Kosovar, our identity and the stories and beliefs around our identity are who we are. I cannot trade away what creates my sense of self, belonging, and identity in a negotiation. Distributive bargaining will never work with radical fundamentalists of any stripe.

Common sense also tells us that we cannot easily divide up the religious training of our young couple's baby without compromising on values held by one side of the family or the other. Yet the old diplomatic negotiation processes seem to ignore common sense and insist on treating many problems as a deal between a buyer and a seller.

Distributive negotiation has its place. However, there are many other ways of approaching conflicts and problems other than through bargaining, including integrative or interest-based negotiation, polarity management, problem solving, and relationship building. These processes are well known by conflict scholars and practitioners and have shown enormous promise in many types of disputes, yet they seem absent from many international negotiations.

THIS IS NOT A JOB TO TRUST TO CIVILIANS

Another assumption of old diplomacy is that political leaders and diplomats are the experts, and the civilians ought to stay out of the way. There is a certain arrogance that exists in the practice of international relations. In the eighteenth century, there were very few newspapers, and the world population was mostly illiterate. Only the elite of any nation could read or write, and such elites were mostly composed of men (certainly not women) in control of the government, universities, and religious communities. Most governments were autocratic and unresponsive to the general population. People were held in their place by force of arms. What political constituencies did exist were relatively small groups of elites—the noble, mercantile, and military classes.

Thus, diplomats and leaders did not have to worry about broad constituency support. Their diplomacy was not designed to play out in front of world audiences. Discussions and consultations were discreet, private, and confidential. Diplomats sent to foreign states were chosen from the same socioeconomic classes as the leaders who appointed them. Being culturally similar to their colleagues, diplomats stationed far from home had a pretty good idea of what would and would not work during negotiations. Developing and maintaining constituent support was simply not an issue in high-level international negotiations. Although constituent support became more important politically as the twentieth century progressed, the idea that the civilian population could have a voice in international affairs, not to mention mobilize and become active in influencing world events, was distasteful. This attitude has persisted into the twenty-first century.

Diplomatic negotiators could not be faulted too much for ignoring constituency support when communications in the eighteenth and nineteenth century, and the first half of the twentieth century were slow and uncertain. In the eighteenth century, it might have taken two to three months for a letter to make it across the ocean from Great Britain to the United States. It might have taken weeks for a letter to be transmitted across Europe. It might have been impossible to transmit a letter to the Middle East or farther east to Asia. Communication was extremely limited, information was not widely or publicly disseminated, and there was no way to communicate with constituencies who could not read or write. As a result, diplomats were expected to operate within very broad parameters set by their leaders. The diplomatic class grew to believe in their own infallibility when international problems were at issue.

Today, communication is ubiquitous and instantaneous. If you have a Skype account, you can videoconference a buddy anywhere in the world who has access to a high-speed Internet connection. It's free and fast. Want to mount a protest in Tehran against the Grand Ayatollah? Overthrow the Egyptian government? Set up an anonymous Facebook account and give the details. They will come.

International negotiators simply cannot get their heads around the fact that twenty-first-century technology has opened up dialogues and conversations and provided for broad dissemination of information about every event in the world. In the summer of 2010, the web site WikiLeaks published over ninety thousand documents showing the huge military problems in Afghanistan and Pakistan, driving US diplomats crazy. International negotiators are now operating in a fishbowl with everyone watching. They are not used to this and don't seem to like it very much.

ONLY PRESIDENTS CAN NEGOTIATE USED CARS

Another assumption of old diplomacy involves the notion of agents and actors. Old diplomacy has been based on the idea that the primary actors in international relations are the nation-states represented by heads of state. Just as the human head was thought to rationally control the body, the head of state was in "rational" control of the nation-state. What got lost in the metaphor was that the heads of state and diplomatic ministers were human beings with emotions, needs, triggers, and desires, just like you and me. Somehow, being elevated to head of state seemed to imply that a leader's humanity was transcended so that all the richness of his or her emotions was ignored.

One of the major assumptions of this view of international negotiation is that the "head of state" knows how to resolve conflicts. This implies that the head of state is an effective problem solver; knows how to build trust; understands the cognitive, affective, and motivational triangle of cognitive neuroscience; can manage high emotions; knows how to create a deep empathic connection with disagreeable people; has appropriately informed assumptions about human behavior; can effectively de-escalate people; and can close out a negotiation into an agreement that will work. My thesis is that most heads of state and ministers may be highly skilled politicians, but, as a class, they do not have even the most rudimentary of these conflict-resolution skills. They simply are not trained for it. Unfortunately, on-the-job experience does not suffice.

Another characteristic of old diplomacy is its preference for envoys and negotiators who have held a former political or military position. The story is told of the former US ambassador to the Soviet Union, Mac Toon, a crusty career diplomat who went aboard an aircraft carrier in the Mediterranean for a meeting with the admiral who commanded its battle group.

At the end of their discussion, the admiral leaned over to ask, "What's it like being an ambassador? I've always thought that after I retire I might want to try it."

Ambassador Toon replied, "That's funny. I've always thought that, when I retire, I might try my hand at running a carrier battle group."

The admiral said, "That's ridiculous. A naval command requires years of training and experience."[17]

Nevertheless, past political office or high military rank seems to be an imprimatur of competency, power, and subject-matter expertise. These envoys normally have not had significant training in conflict theory, behavioral economics, cognitive neuroscience, social psychology, and a host of other skills. They are asked to "mediate" high-stakes conflicts based on their political experience and common sense. While these attributes are important in any mediator, they fall short of the skills and knowledge about complex problems that can be brought to the table in the twenty-first century.

The problem with having political personalities acting as "mediators" is that they do not know how to design a mediation process, how to engage the parties to the conflict, how to prepare parties for a mediated negotiation, how to facilitate meetings where strong emotions are present, how to deal with prospective impasse, or how to bring a variety of processes and techniques to bear on the normal issues that arise in any complex problem-solving negotiation. In his book *The Truth about Camp David*, author Clayton Swisher describes how President Bill Clinton and his advisers worked with the Palestinians and Israelis over the course of fourteen days in the Camp David talks.[18] Professionally trained and experienced commercial mediators cringe at the rookie mistakes made day after day by the US "mediation" team. Just because you are the most powerful guy in the room doesn't mean that you have a clue how to manage a complex and intractable conflict between two hard-headed opponents. Yet the attitude of presumed mediation expertise persists in international circles.

WHY ARE THESE IDEAS SO OBSOLETE?

In the past twenty-five years, there has been a huge expansion in the knowledge base of conflict resolution, mediation, and negotiation. As a result, there has been a related expansion in our understanding of best practices when dealing with complicated conflicts. When heads of state are the principal negotiators, they are still human beings. Like everyone else, they have emotions and cognitive biases that deeply control their decisions and actions. They respond the same way to situations as any other human being.

Why should diplomats care? Because everything they do is now subject to worldwide scrutiny. Botched negotiations can no longer be hidden or covered up. Peace conferences are subjected to critical analysis as they occur. Climate-change negotiations are broadcast in the moment. Constituencies who, under the eighteenth-century view of the world, were illiterate are now capable of understanding the negotiations. Information about peace negotiations can no longer be spun in a way that makes failure excusable. Furthermore, we have seen in the first decade of the twenty-first century that military intervention is no guarantee of peace.

The good news is that, while extraordinarily difficult problems like Iran and North Korea persist, there are more tools in the toolbox. We have better ways of understanding conflict. We have multiple techniques for engaging our enemies. We have made tremendous strides in understanding the moment-to-moment interactions during negotiations. In the past two decades, commercial mediation as a professional practice has exploded worldwide. Out of that vast experience of dealing with millions of diverse conflicts, a body of knowledge has developed that is directly applicable to international relations. This is twenty-first-century knowledge to be used to solve twenty-first-century problems.

In the chapters that follow, we will look at various conflicts around the world. Some of them are big, complex problems. Others are smaller, regional problems. We will see how the old negotiation processes failed and how use of modern mediation interventions might have made a difference. We will look at an environmental justice dispute between Uruguay and Argentina that has disrupted international trade and relations in the Southern Cone of South America. No one wants to mediate that conflict. We will look at the Palestinian-Israeli conflict from the perspective of the beliefs of the people on the ground. We will look at how fear and anger shape decisions in ways we are not even aware of. We will look at cognitive biases and how they distort decision making in international affairs. The Afghanistan-Pakistan-India mess will be examined from the perspective of social identities. The role of the mediator in the difficult problem of justice will be illustrated in several conflicts. The question of making peacemaking with terrorist groups illegal will challenge the commitment to international peacemaking. Finally, we will ask the question "How do we mediate evil, war, and violence?"

There is never a guarantee of peace. But there is no reason not to be using the very best skills and knowledge available to us. This book should encourage you to start asking some questions and opening a wider conversation about our desire for true peace in our world. Peace is elusive, but it is not unobtainable. We simply have to put better tools to use on the problem.

Chapter 2

Hurricane Chasers and Mediators

HURRICANE CHASERS

On July 27, 1943, the Air Corps command at Bryan Field, about 125 miles inland from Galveston Bay and near College Station, Texas, had learned of an approaching hurricane. Not wanting to lose their training fleet of AT-6 airplanes to storm damage, the commanders ordered the trainers and the flight students evacuated to bases farther north.

A group of experienced British pilots, many of them aces from Europe, were learning the skill of instrument flying under a lead instructor, Major Joe Duckworth. Duckworth was a former Eastern Air Lines pilot who had developed the technique of flying in bad weather by reference to flight instruments instead of looking outside the cockpit. Duckworth had been reactivated in 1940 to develop a military instrument flying program for the Air Corps.

Upon hearing word of the storm and the evacuation order, the British flyers began ridiculing the apparent frailty of the training aircraft. Unfortunately, none of them had ever flown through or near a true hurricane, and they thought that hurricanes were similar to big thunderstorms.[1]

In the mess hall during breakfast, Duckworth finally reached his fill of the ridicule. He defended the AT-6 aircraft, saying it could fly in any weather. The Brits dared him to prove it. Taking the dare, he offered a wager that he could fly an AT-6 into the teeth of the hurricane and return safely. The bet was accepted. A highball to the winner!

This was not a foolish proposition. Duckworth was an experienced and extremely capable instrument pilot, and he knew the limits of both his ability and of his aircraft. He had firmly believed that even the extreme weather of a hurricane was safely navigable when the pilot was competent and the airplane was properly designed and equipped.

Duckworth needed a navigator, so he asked Lieutenant Ralph O'Hair, who was sitting across the table, to volunteer for the flight. O'Hair, although shocked, agreed to accompany Duckworth.

Convinced that their commanders would never clear the flight due to its high risk, Duckworth and O'Hair decided to go without permission. They launched at noon, just as the hurricane came ashore.

Approaching the storm at an altitude somewhere between four thousand and nine thousand feet, the two men felt the scud-filled sky became very turbulent. O'Hair later said they were shaken like a dog with a bone. Flying through the dark storm wall, they fought torrential rain and extreme, turbulent updrafts and downdrafts. They flew through pitch-black darkness and violent wind shears as they approached the storm's eye. Suddenly, they burst through a showery curtain of towering, dark clouds, and light filled the sky. Surrounding them were high cumulonimbus walls—below, the ground; above, fairly clear sky. They had broken into the eye of the hurricane.

Looking down, they could see the countryside. They radioed the Houston weather station reporting the latitude and longitude of the eye. After circling inside the eye a few times, they flew back into the dark overcast and heavy rains, following their radio compass home. Later that evening, they collected on the bet: a highball for each on the Brits.

The year before, a young Harvard student, Roger Fisher, had enlisted in the Air Corps and was assigned to weather reconnaissance. For three years, he flew in Europe and the Pacific, flying into and tracking storms. While Fisher did not replicate Duckworth's flight into a hurricane, the weather observations he and his colleagues developed became invaluable tools to fighter and bomber pilots planning their missions. He lost friends during that violent time and wondered about the necessity of war and conflict.

After the war, Fisher entered Harvard Law School and graduated in 1948. After stints in government service and private practice, he returned to the law school as a professor in 1960. Still curious about the nature of conflict, he began a study of negotiation. Fisher, like Duckworth, was learning how to fly into the eye of the hurricane, only this was the storm wall of international conflict. With his students, Fisher interviewed the best international negotiators he could find, looking for clues about what made them so successful at ending conflict without violence. The result of his research, coupled with his own experience consulting and assisting in international conflicts, was the classic book *Getting to Yes*, published in 1981 with coauthor Bill Ury.[2] In 1991, the book was revised with Bruce Patton added as a coauthor. Thirty years later, *Getting to Yes* still sells about three thousand copies a month.

Getting to Yes introduced the concept of interest-based or principled negotiation as an alternative to the traditional competitive bargaining that typified negotiation up to that point. It sets forth some basic ideas on how to get what you want in negotiation without always making concessions.

The problem was that Fisher assumed negotiators would always act in their own, rational self-interest. In advocating that negotiators separate the problem from the people, he believed that negotiators could separate out their own feelings of injustice, anger, fear, and betrayal—the most common emotions of conflict —from the substantive issues. As anyone who has been in a personal conflict knows, this is often impossible. After all, it is our emotions that drive us into conflict, not the fact that we might disagree over the terms of a deal. This is where mediation enters the picture.

In mediation, a third person assists two or more people to resolve a conflict. If two kids are fighting in the sandbox, a teacher might ask them if they want to resolve what they are fighting about. If they both say yes, the teacher will take the time to have them explain how the fight started, then work with the kids to solve the problem. The teacher won't impose a solution on the kids. Instead, she will help them figure it out for themselves. This is pure mediation.

One way to look at mediation is to remember that the mediator is doing for the parties what they cannot do for themselves. Typically, people or nations that fight are so emotionally caught up that their sense of perspective and their abilities to listen, analyze, and communicate are severely impaired. They have resorted to violence as the only means they believe will help them resolve the conflict. Mediators provide processes and services to help people overcome the cognitive and emotional barriers to good decision making caused by conflict. In *Getting to Yes*, Fisher somewhat naively tells us to separate the people from the problem. In mediation, we recognize the difficulty the parties may have in following that advice. Therefore, the mediator takes on the job of separating the people from the problem. The mediator may lead the parties through a principled negotiation process first described by Fisher after the mediator has de-escalated the emotions in the room. The skills necessary to be a good mediator are extensive and not easily learned.

THE BIG STICK VIEW OF MEDIATION

International mediation as practiced today, like international relations theory in general, is based on the assumption that because people are rational, they will respond to threats and promises. This view of mediation is summed up by a famous quote from Henry Kissinger, "When you have them by the balls, their hearts and minds will follow."[3] International scholars and diplomats believe that through the use of coercive threats and promises, people in a conflict can be led to a negotiated settlement. It is hardball diplomacy, and the mediator should use every tool in his box to drill, cut, rip, gouge, glue, and clamp parties to peace.

This philosophy treats the causes of conflict as objective issues that can yield to negotiation. Peace is only possible when the conflict is "ripe" for resolution. If the parties aren't there yet, a judicious use of force might push them to be more amenable to peacemaking. Even then, these power mediators believe that parties have to be coaxed to the bargaining table through a combination of carrots and sticks. Tactics might include coaching, discrediting, manipulating, legitimizing, making the mediator indispensable, exploring changes in military balance, exploring changes in leadership, and promises of resources or threats of withdrawal.

The problem is that the big stick and bushel of carrots become substitutes for motivation. If parties are induced to come to the peace table because of the promise of an international airport or billions of dollars in foreign aid, their underlying needs and desires are not being addressed. People who come to peace negotiations out of fear of threat are motivated to negotiate not because of their own desire for peace but because of their fear of the consequences if they do not come to the table. As we will see, when the negotiations get tough and emotions begin to run high, parties have a much easier time leaving the table, being intransigent, or agreeing only superficially to peace if their motivation is based on some threat or promise.

For real peace to take hold, the parties must have hope that peace is achievable. They must be motivated to find a peaceful solution, and they must believe that it is possible. They must believe that the other side will be accountable and responsible for keeping promises made in peace agreements. The mediator is responsible for creating, nourishing, and bringing these beliefs to blossom.

Sometimes the big stick and bushel of carrots approach to mediation is useful because it provides political cover for leaders. Leaders can approach their constituencies and say, "What else are we to do? If we do not appear at the table, we will be pounded into rubble." In fact, the leadership may be looking for a face-saving way to negotiate a peace agreement, and the big stick or big carrot may be just what is needed for that purpose.

Carrots may also provide evidence of tangible benefits to constituencies. Peace by itself may not have enough immediate economic or political effects to motivate agreement. A peace agreement may mean giving up something of value, such as a military advantage. Carrots become replacements for concessions so there is less sense of loss.

In August 1975, Henry Kissinger mediated the Israeli-Egyptian interim peace agreement known as Sinai II. Kissinger induced Israel to make territorial concessions to Egypt in exchange for US aid. Both the Israeli and Egyptian negotiators returned to their constituencies with tangible benefits of an otherwise odious peace agreement. As a result, in 1976, annual aid to Israel rose to $2.2 billion, and economic aid to Egypt grew to nearly $500 million.[4]

Carrots have limits, however. Generally, you can't buy peace with increased aid. Money does not defuse a crisis or substitute for basic political will. The lesson for mediators is that deep engagement with the parties resulting in a commitment to peace is essential. During the Oslo years, the Palestinians were not fully engaged with Washington. While much is made of President Clinton's visit to Gaza and Yasser Arafat's many White House visits, the relationship between them was so thin that Arafat was willing to walk away from it at Camp David, and Clinton was willing to cast it aside afterward when he blamed Arafat and the Palestinian leadership for the summit's failure.[5]

Sticks don't work so well either. Economic sanctions are often ineffective as instruments of peace. In his study of five major cases of US sanctions, Ernest Preeg concluded that sanctions "have been almost entirely ineffective in achieving their intended foreign policy objectives while having a substantial adverse impact on other US foreign policy and commercial interests."[6] Margaret Doxey has argued that sanctions can achieve modest gains of the "slap on the wrist" variety but that "a major change in policy is . . . harder to come by."[7] The definitive empirical work in the field, conducted by Gary Hufbauer and his colleagues at the Institute for International Economics in Washington, concluded, "Sanctions are seldom effective in impairing the military potential of an important power, or in bringing about major changes in the policy of the targeted country."[8]

In addition, using sticks avoids the important work of understanding the complexity of the conflict. People enmeshed in conflict make choices independent of the mediator and will hold intense feelings of hatred, frustration, fear, and mistrust. These feelings lead to decisions that do not resemble the prudent cost-benefit outcomes one might expect with the cold calculus of rational choice. Power mediators consistently underestimate the resolve of groups whose members are willing to kill and die for their cause. Their visceral hatred for negotiations cannot simply be dismissed as stubbornness or a ploy for a bargaining advantage.

In intense conflicts, the disputants have good reason to resist pressure to make peace. In civil wars, the belligerents are bent on destroying each other politically and physically. Avoiding defeat is an absolute imperative, and settlement is viewed as synonymous with defeat. The parties are therefore highly motivated to thwart efforts to impose an outcome on them, whether those efforts come from the enemy or a mediator. Thus, the concessions usually necessary for peace will not only be unpalatable, but may also pose considerable personal danger. Moderate leaders may be ousted or assassinated by militants. A party that disarms under a ceasefire agreement may be destroyed if its opponent reneges on the agreement. A minority community that surrenders power may be marginalized or persecuted. A party may be so out-negotiated that settlement becomes a resounding political defeat. Imposing outside will on these parties may coerce a peace agreement on paper, but as soon as the international community turns to the next conflict du jour, the parties will be back in the fight.

Even if threats eventually make negotiation attractive, the targeted party will view the mediator who applied such pressure as allied to its enemy. In contrast to the power mediator, the truly skilled professional mediator's job is not to push the parties to the brink of disaster but to talk them off the precipice by raising their confidence in mediated negotiations.

WANTED: EMINENT PERSON TO MEDIATE— NO EXPERIENCE NECESSARY

Not only does international mediation suffer from the counterproductive idea that power is good and more power is better, its practitioners for the most part have shown little interest in raising their mediation skills to a professional level. Generally, international mediation is seen as the dashing special envoy swooping in to save the day. It is an ad hoc service practiced in an ad hoc manner.

The international community has a fascination with mediators who are political "Names." They are called Eminent Persons and are usually senior retired politicians or military generals. Fame seems to be the only qualification for being an international peace mediator. Nick Grono of the International Crisis Group tried to justify this when he said, "The dynamics of the conflicts we deal with will often require someone who has a 'standing,' and not one who has mediation expertise per se."[9] Grono, along with many other international relations experts, believes that parties to a conflict are not interested in the mechanics of the process but in the status of the mediator. "You could have the world's best mediator and the best mediation network, and that would make no difference whatsoever."[10] From this perspective, the eminence of the mediator is seen as leverage to get parties to the table.

Fame is not all bad. Any mediator will have to seek the support and confidence of international sponsors, including the United States, Great Britain, and the European Union, to name a few. Frequently, this requires a high degree of political notoriety so that people are comfortable they are entrusting the problem to the hands of a known quantity. For the same reason, fame may make acquiring the trust of the conflict parties easier. On the downside, as we will see in example after example in the chapters that follow, eminent persons generally lack the most rudimentary technical skills demanded of professional mediators. As a result, they often cause more long-term harm than they create with their short-term "successes."

The international diplomatic community seems to have a hard time grasping that mediation is a practice that empowers parties, rather than an activity that burnishes the image of the mediator. The fact that parties choose their mediator and drive the mediation process reduces—at least in the eyes of the uninformed—the role of the mediator to nothing more than a facilitator. Where is the sexiness in that? The idea that "the mediator is nothing, but the parties are everything," explains one difficulty of professionalization. Famous people want to be at the center of the stage, not in the wings. They want to control and direct the process, telling everyone what to do. This is the antithesis of a professional mediator, who should be seen but not heard in the media. EU Special Representatives are a case in point. They are chosen because of political interests, not because they are qualified as mediators. As a result, they attempt to impose their quick solution on the conflict because they want to get rid of it and go to the next conflict. Patience, persistence, and comprehension of the nuance of conflict are simply not in their game bag.

SOME SKILLS OF THE MEDIATOR

The skills and services that a professional mediator provides to people in conflict are significantly greater in number than most people realize. From convening to accountability, the mediator is, in the words of Erica Ariel Fox, creator of the Beyond Yes project, "the Prophet, the Sage, the Lover, and the Warrior"[11] for the parties throughout the process.

Convening the Mediation

Bringing people who hate each other together to talk is the process of *convening* and is many times the most difficult work of the mediator. In some conflicts, the mediator will intervene without the request of the parties to see if a mediated negotiation or dialogue might be useful. In other conflicts, people outside the conflict might persuade the parties to mediate and nominate potential mediators. In still other conflicts, the parties will decide on mediation and select the mediator themselves. In each of these situations, the mediator is responsible for convening the mediation. Convening can be as simple as securing agreements about the time and place of the mediation conference. Usually, however, convening is a laborious, time-consuming process that includes studying the underlying history and dynamics of the conflict, developing a strategy, designing a process, determining who should be present, securing funding from donors, dealing with the media, assembling a team of experts, considering whether observers will participate, deciding on the presence and role of co-mediators, and a myriad of other details. The convening process will usually require the mediator to meet privately with all the participants many times to get a flavor of the issues and emotions and to secure agreement on the process details.

If the parties had to decide these matters themselves, the likely result would be a series of procedural disputes and wrangling over petty details that more often than not derail or delay the peace process. As a classic example of this problem, in the late 1960s, the US and North Vietnamese negotiators spent months negotiating over the shape of the conference table.

In May 1968, US and North Vietnamese representatives agreed that peace talks should be convened to discuss a settlement in Vietnam.[12] US negotiators declared, however, that a meeting would not be possible unless South Vietnam participated as a separate delegation. North Vietnam accepted this proposal on the condition that the National Liberation Front would also be included in the peace talks. North Vietnam viewed the forthcoming talks as a four-sided conference to be attended by four independent delegations. The United States saw the talks as a two-sided conference with the United States and South Vietnamese on one side and the North Vietnamese and anyone else they wanted on the other side.

This created a dispute over the seating plan and the shape of the table. The United States and South Vietnam wanted a seating arrangement that would not recognize the National Liberation Front as one of the parties to the talks. The North Vietnamese argued that the Saigon government was the puppet of the United States, but were willing to meet with South Vietnam as long as the National Liberation Front had full delegate status.

The United States proposed two long rectangular tables facing each other. The North Vietnamese countered by alternative proposals: a single four-sided conference table; four separate tables arranged in a square pattern; four separate tables arranged in either a circular or diamond pattern; or one round table with the delegations seated in such a manner that there would be visible, distant, and equal spaces between each of the four delegations.

The United States countered with the idea of two separate arcs of an oval, two separate semicircles facing each other, or two separate semicircles facing each other with two rectangular working tables in the spaces between the two semicircles and a space on each side of the rectangular tables.

The North Vietnamese rejected these ideas because they were still based on the idea of a two-sided conference. The North Vietnamese negotiators proposed that the semicircles not be split and that the North Vietnamese and National Liberation Front be seated next to each other. The United States rejected this proposal because it called for the dreaded four-sided arrangement, giving the National Liberation Front equality with South Vietnam. A number of other proposals were made, including an oval table with a rectangular working area cut from its center, two parallel tables with half circles at each end forming a continuous table, a doughnut-shaped table with a singular rectangular table beside it, a doughnut-shaped table with two small sunken working areas at opposite points of the circle, a doughnut-shaped table with two small secretarial tables placed against it at opposite points of the circle, a solid round table bisected by a strip of baize separating the sides, and a doughnut-shaped table with narrow strips of baize or with narrow painted or scratched lines separating the ring into two sides.

Finally, after nearly a year of negotiating on the shape of the table, the parties agreed on a solid round table with two separate rectangular tables placed at right angles to the round table at opposite points of the circle giving the appearance of the separation of two sides. Each rectangular table would be separated from the round table enough to permit walking distance between it, and the side tables were to be used for clerical purposes. Whew!

This was a classic convening dispute that probably would have been resolved much faster with a mediator helping the parties work out an acceptable physical and symbolic seating arrangement. By paying careful attention to the convening aspect of the mediation, a mediator can put the parties into a frame of mind necessary for a successful outcome. Meeting individually with each side (including counsel), discussing the mediator's philosophy and experience, explaining the mediation process, and obtaining each side's input into the design of the process can build familiarity and trust. Many times peace talks falter simply because the parties cannot agree on how to proceed. The mediator's convening skills are therefore critical to bringing people to the table for productive conversations. This process takes time and patience that famous, busy people may not always have.

Offering Compassion and Empathy and Acknowledging Injustice

Many conflicts arise because someone feels that he or she has not been heard. Each story in mediation is a tale of perceived injustice, and it is important for the parties to express how they feel about it and have their story acknowledged.

Professional mediators are trained to listen at multiple levels of conversation, which allows them to hear the parties' stories at a deeper level. Mediators not only listen to the words, they listen to the symbolic meaning of the words, the emotional data field supporting that meaning, the body language, and the reactions of everyone else to those words. And, they pay attention to what is *not* being said. This is a learned skill that takes years of practice to develop.

Mediators may also provide emotional support through expressions of compassion and empathy without compromising neutrality, since the mediator does not have to agree with the merits of either side. Providing this kind of support is particularly important to parties in emotionally difficult cases; for example, those involving war crimes, deep social injustice, and human rights abuses. The mediator's compassionate ear is open to all sides. Sometimes, the mediator is the only source of emotional support for a party.

Mediators can also teach the parties how to listen and see the adversary's point of view. This can lead them to be more compassionate and empathetic. When the parties want to salvage peace out of violence, learning to listen to the other side can lead to reconciliation. Sometimes, this is not possible or practical. However, mediators must look for opportunities to help the parties reconcile, if they so desire, and restore sundered relationships.

Providing Leadership

Mediators provide the services of leadership in mediation. The parties, the observers, and the media look to the mediator as the leader of the process, to set the agenda and the rules, control the process, and keep the negotiation moving forward. The leadership function is vital to an efficient, constructive mediation process. The mediator should exercise this leadership in a firm, but nonthreatening way. Although the mediator is not the arbiter of the dispute (and the parties should understand this), being the leader of the mediation should make the parties want to work with rather than against the mediator. Professional mediators have a bundle of leadership models that they bring forth as the mediation develops. Most eminent persons have never studied or practiced different leadership theories or models and work off of instinct and experience. Sometimes this works; most of the time it doesn't.

De-escalating Conflict

After convening, the mediator's most important and challenging job is to de-escalate the conflict. Conflict escalates in an inverse relationship to the parties' psychological integration. The higher the level of escalation, the less psychologically integrated the parties are. In other words, as conflicts become more intense, the parties show behaviors indicating regression of their emotional development. As a conflict escalates, the parties go through five stages of emotional and cognitive regression:

Stage 1. The parties still have a good relationship even though there is a conflict.

Stage 2. If the conflict is not resolved at stage 1, the parties fluctuate between cooperative and competitive positions. They know they have common interests, but one side's wishes become more important than the common interests. The preferred method of conversation is persuasion, but without much listening.

Stage 3. The parties become more irritable and hostile to each other. They may start to think about taking more direct action. The typical method of conversation is argument, usually with loud voices and no listening or empathy. Insults and disrespect typify this level of escalation. People become angry, frustrated, and anxious. Peacemaking is seen as weak and is rebuffed in favor of a demonstration of resolve through displays of military strength.

Stage 4. Each side feels that his or her core sense of identity has been attacked or threatened. The executive function of the brain is overridden by dominating emotions. The parties are likely to see no way out other than through violent coercion. The adversary is demonized into stereotypes, there is no room for moderates, and dogmatic positions become entrenched. All hope for peace is lost.

Stage 5. The parties feel that their sacred values and convictions are at stake. The conflict assumes mythical dimensions as the parties dehumanize each other. War and violence typify stage 5 conflicts.

Here is a deep mediation secret: A conflict can be successfully negotiated only when the parties are at stage 1. Parties might reach agreements at stage 2 or 3, but unless there has been serious de-escalation back to stage 1, the agreements will not hold. Therefore, the bulk of a mediator's work involves de-escalating the conflict and returning the parties to a psychological place in which they are able to resolve their dispute. One of the great challenges in mediation is managing the de-escalation process of not only the parties, but also of the parties' various constituencies. In the two-day talks in early September 2010, President Obama and Secretary of State Clinton had not considered how to de-escalate the Palestinian and Israeli populations over the issue of Jewish settlements. It did them no good to talk only with Abbas and Netanyahu and their advisers. If the people at home were not de-escalated, there would be no hope for acceptance of a peace agreement. To add further complexity to the de-escalation problem, leaders sometimes do not want their constituencies de-escalated because the conflict provides the emotional energy and political cohesiveness to keep the leader in power.

Providing a Fair Process

People in conflict often want justice, but this term has different meanings to different people. However, there are findings from social science research about people's perceptions of procedural fairness. These findings revealed that parties believed that they were fairly treated if the process was fair, regardless of the outcome. They considered the process to be fair if the following elements were present: they had the opportunity to tell their story in their own words to a respected, impartial authority figure in a setting in which they were treated with respect. To the degree that a mediator can allow stories to be told and listen respectfully, while keeping the process on track, people will experience a fair process. This nuance alone has escaped the notice of many international mediators.

Assisting in Decision Making

Ultimately, the parties must make a series of decisions, for example, when and how much to offer or demand up until the other side decides whether to accept a particular offer. Frequently, they must decide between bad choices that are emotionally, politically, financially, and pragmatically difficult to accept. During these difficult stages of the negotiation, the mediator helps each side examine the available choices and the present and future consequences of each one.

Some people have a more difficult time making decisions because of fear or because of cognitive biases (more about these in chapter 5). They may need to bring trusted advisers to the mediation to help them decide. The mediator must ensure that the parties bring the necessary "stakeholders" to the mediation so that decisions can be made to move the negotiation along. Sometimes there are spoilers that must be managed. *Spoilers* are groups or parties who will not see the benefits of a peace agreement and therefore do what they can to stop or delay the process.

Typically, extremists on both sides are spoilers because peace will remove their cause and reason for existence. The mediator may have to help them make decisions as well.

Coaching

Mediators also serve as coaches and teachers. There is no limit to what mediators can teach the parties in mediation. They coach the parties through the mediation and see that they adhere to the ground rules, which include being civil and respectful to one another, despite intractable differences. Mediators teach disputants many things, including how to communicate more effectively, negotiate, identify needs and interests, understand their best and worst alternatives to a negotiated agreement (BATNAs and WATNAs), brainstorm, and devise possible solutions that could resolve the dispute. As we will see in chapter 7, where the parties are contemplating a political power–sharing agreement, the mediator should be coaching them on how to work together despite their initial mutual mistrust. Parties that distrust each other are not going to magically transform into cooperative political allies because of a peace agreement. This assumption has been the cause of failure for many negotiated power-sharing agreements. A political solution is just the beginning of the work for a professional mediator. Essentially, the mediator must teach the parties how to be peacemakers rather than adversaries, which may take years of continuous work after the initial peace agreements have been signed.

Managing Information

In any negotiation, at least some information must be exchanged for the parties to be in a position to negotiate. The parties need to be able to understand the facts and issues involved in order to decide how to find peace. Frequently, parties in conflict understand only a part of the story and have made mistaken assump-

tions about the rest. One of the most important services mediators perform is as a receiver, manager, and conveyer of confidential and nonconfidential information. Mediation is about
different kinds of information, and peace cannot be achieved
without it.

Ideally, mediators would like the parties to make full, honest,
and complete disclosures of information to each other because
that is when the best decisions in mediation are likely to be made.
But such complete disclosures do not happen very often. People
naturally resist an honest and open exchange of information
because they do not want to give any advantage to their opponent, who might exploit the information in some way. When you
hate the other side, you are not likely to confess your secrets to
them. Mediators play an invaluable role in helping people
exchange information when there is mutual mistrust.

To obtain information, the mediator will ask questions,
probing deeper into the story of the dispute, and seek clarifica-
tion of ambiguous information. The mediator will often
"reframe" what the parties say in order to better understand their
stories. The parties may find the mediator's reframed statement
to be enlightening. They may hear information that they have
unconsciously filtered out. As a result of disclosing their stories
and their feelings, the parties may lessen the anger they feel
toward each other.

The mediator will also discuss each side's negotiation strategy
in private meetings. This may enable the mediator to intuit their
next move and perhaps predict if the conflict will end in a peace
agreement or if an impasse will occur.

The mediator can use the information learned in private
meetings to send signals to each side in order to advance the
negotiations, without disclosing confidential information. When
authorized to disclose confidential information, the mediator
will do so in a way that is most likely to evoke a positive rather
than a negative response.

Eliciting Interests and Injustices

As Fisher explains in *Getting to Yes*,[13] most people bargain from their positions. A *position* is nothing more than a suggested solution to a problem. However, because people know they will have to make concessions, that is, give up stuff to make a deal, they tend to start from extreme positions. They give themselves room to negotiate so that they can induce the other side to make concessions as well. This positional bargaining works when emotions are not in play but is otherwise disastrous.

Interest-based or principled negotiation calls for the identification of the interests that underlie the positions. Imagine a dispute over a boundary line. One party wants the boundary line to follow a river in a valley while the other wants the boundary a quarter mile away up on a ridge top. The mediator wants to know if the boundary line were to be set along the ridge top, what would be all of the interests satisfied for the party taking that position. Going through a carefully orchestrated process, a mediator might have the parties discover that the ridge line has symbolic meaning, is important for security reasons, and is a logical dividing line because of infrastructure issues like canals and power lines, and so forth. Identifying what the parties are really needing rather than focusing on their positions is a powerful process. Unfortunately, while *Getting to Yes* talks about the power of interest-based negotiation, Fisher does not tell us how to do it. It has taken thirty years of mediation practice and scholarship to design processes and procedures that turn the theory into a viable, effective mediation tool. This again is a skill that is learned and is not in the eminent person's intuitive toolbox.

Managing Proposals

While the parties go through the process of developing solutions, the mediator will anticipate how the other side of the room might reasonably react to the proposal (for example, he or she might feel highly insulted and inclined to walk out of the conference) and alert the party who is contemplating the making of this offer. Whatever is proposed, the mediator will convey and explain the basis for the offer. The mediator will go through the same process with the receiving party with regard to its proposal. All the while, the mediator will keep both parties focused on moving the negotiation forward. The mediator may have to deal with a party with unrealistic expectations or with a party who will not make an offer out of fear. President Clinton inartfully managed Yasser Arafat's unrealistic expectations at the Camp David talks in 2000, resulting in impasse and renewed violence. The mediator is a model of patience, encouragement, and hope for the parties even when they think that a peace settlement seems improbable and distant.

PEACEMAKING IS ABOUT PEOPLE

Institutions do not mediate and do not make peace. People mediate and people make peace.

The peacemaking process is hard work for the parties and for the mediator. It can be some of the hardest work any human being can be asked to perform, whether as a person in conflict or as a person intervening in the conflict. While big ideas about democracy, power sharing, political control, and sovereignty are interesting, the real work of the skilled mediator is in the moment. Listening to the hidden messages in the tone of voice, working at the largely unconscious, nonverbal level of human communication, experiencing the fleeting emotions second by second and interpreting their meanings, and considering what to do in the next microsecond is where the real work of peace is conducted.

Most people manage their personal relationships on an intuitive and relatively simple basis. Their relationship tools can be piled into the back of a little red wagon and pulled behind them wherever they go. When conflict arises, the little wagon is often overloaded, and the wheels fall off. The tools that worked for everyday conversations become inadequate and even counterproductive in fights.

Mediators are trained to tune in to the nuances of every moment and to respond to them in the most effective way possible. The amount of information that a mediator must pay attention to is staggering. In the middle of the peacemaking process, every facial expression, every gesture, every lifted eyebrow, every movement, every spoken and unspoken word is important. The mediator must pay attention to the speaker, to all the listeners, and to the mediator's own emotional and cognitive responses simultaneously. In addition, the mediator has to pay attention to the sponsors, to the observers, to the secondary political leaders, to the media, and to the millions of people who have a keen interest in the outcome. Experienced mediators often enter into a state of hyperconsciousness in which they are acutely aware of everything going on around them. This is the state of flow described and studied by psychologist Mihaly Csikszentmihalyi.[14]

THE INTERNATIONAL MEDIATOR AS HURRICANE CHASER

Joe Duckworth was the first pilot to fly into a hurricane. But he knew exactly what he was doing. He knew how to fly an airplane on the instruments so that he could fly blind. He knew where he was, his altitude, and his direction of flight at all times. He knew his airplane could handle the G-forces inflicted by heavy turbulence. He knew he would come out on the other side. Professional mediators are the same way. They know exactly what they are doing and why they are doing it. They have a plan in mind and follow it as long as it works for them. They are flexible enough to change their plan as the situation calls for it. They have a skill set that allows them to anticipate and deal with the heavy turbulence of conflict, including high emotions, intractability, and the aftereffects of violence. However, like Duckworth's instrument flying into the hurricane, none of this is intuitive, seat-of-the-pants work. Had Duckworth been the garden-variety visual pilot, who literally does fly by the seat of his pants, and had thought to himself, "Well, I'll just show those uppity Brits who's top gun around here," he would have lost control of the AT-6 and undoubtedly death-spiraled into the earth. International mediators can avoid catastrophe by understanding the complexity of the practice of peacemaking. The following chapters will look at some of this complexity to understand better why peace can be so elusive.

Chapter 3

A Backyard Dispute Goes International

"We don't like it, but this is our only possible solution,"[1] argues one of the protesters. He has just told an Argentine family returning from Uruguay that they will not be allowed to drive across the Libertador General San Martín international bridge. The bridge is the main international crossing point for sixty miles along the river in either direction.

"There is no other way for us to impose our wishes," another protester continues. "If we leave the highway, from Uruguay's point of view, the conflict is over."

"Our blockade will be lifted when the plant is removed," says the protester.

He is referring to the pulp mill recently placed in operation across the bridge in Fray Bentos, Uruguay. At the heart of the conflict is a classic environmental dispute with international repercussions.

In the open countryside of Arroyo Verde, a solid, tin-roofed wooden building now stands, complete with electricity supplied for free by the local power company, along with a well, a water storage tank, and three environmentally friendly latrines. All of this infrastructure supports the blockade and the *piqueteros*, participants in a unique form of Argentinean social protest who block roads or streets to call attention to a particular issue or demand. The practice started in Buenos Aires in the mid-1990s to protest policies of then-president Carlos Menem and quickly became a popular form of social action. It has been adopted by a local group, the Citizens' Environmental Assembly of Gualeguaychú, formed to protest the construction and operation of the paper pulp mill across the river in Uruguay.

Uruguay seems like an unlikely place for a major diplomatic conflict to erupt. Nevertheless, Fray Bentos, a small cattle town on the Uruguay River, which separates Uruguay from Argentina, has been the focus of a unique environmental dispute that has made its way to the International Court of Justice in The Hague and has disrupted diplomatic relations in the Southern Cone, the geographical area of South America comprising Argentina, Uruguay, Chile, and Paraguay. This conflict presents us with an interesting opportunity to see how old diplomacy has failed to solve a common twenty-first-century problem.

Fray Bentos is a small, poor community of twenty-three thousand that borders Uruguay and Argentina. It is home to the largest deep-river port on the Uruguayan side of the Uruguay River. The local tourism authority optimistically promotes Fray Bentos as offering the "romance of the sun, the cliff, and the river."[2] This belies the hot, humid summers and cold winters typical of the interior regions in this part of South America.

The early economic and social history of Fray Bentos was based on the local cattle industry. Because of its deep-water port, cattle from the Uruguayan interior could be shipped to market along the Uruguay River.

In 1899 a company called Anglo began making corned beef in Fray Bentos, a product that was exported and quickly became a staple of the British diet. Over the years, the Fray Bentos meatpacking plant diversified, producing soups, meatballs, and canned fruit. In the 1990s, the Campbell Soup Company acquired the plant and shifted production to meat pies and puddings. The economic fortunes of Fray Bentos have risen and fallen on the meatpacking business, and it has suffered through business cycle after business cycle without much success at more permanent economic development.

Across the river, in the Entre Rios province of Argentina, the town of Gualeguaychú sits on the Gualeguaychú River, a tributary of the Uruguay River. Gualeguaychú is thirty-three kilometers northwest of Fray Bentos, and the two cities are connected by the international bridge that crosses the Uruguay River.

Like Fray Bentos, Gualeguaychú is a cattle town of approximately seventy-six thousand people. In addition, it is a popular vacation area for Argentineans. It has developed a tourism industry based on its hot springs, beach resorts, a casino, and vacation homes. During the months of January and February, Gualeguaychú offers the Carnival of the Country, similar in its bawdy party atmosphere to Mardi Gras in New Orleans.[3]

THE PULP PLANT CONFLICT

Beginning in the 1980s with the decline of the cattle business, local Fray Bentos businessmen began planting eucalyptus groves for pulp harvesting. By 2004, twenty years of forest industry development had created a sufficient supply of renewable raw material, and the Finnish company Botnia decided to build a paper pulp plant in Fray Bentos.

The company received its environmental authorization to build in February 2005. In 2007, the paper pulp factory began operations, converting eucalyptus from the growers to cellulose and paper products for export. While the Botnia plant, which employs over three hundred people, has been an economic boon to Fray Bentos, it has been the source of an emotional and highly polarized conflict between Argentina and Uruguay.

The Uruguay River, which forms the natural border between

Argentina and Uruguay, is protected by a 1975 bilateral treaty,[4] which establishes joint management and protection of the natural resource of the river. The treaty requires each party to inform the other of any project that might affect issues such as water quality or navigation. In the event of disagreement, the treaty calls for a technical advisory group to be established to examine and report on the issues. If the parties are dissatisfied or cannot reach agreement through that process, the treaty provides for a 120-day period to resolve the issues by negotiation. After the 120-day period, either party may file a proceeding in the International Court of Justice requesting appropriate judicial relief. The treaty does not require or provide for mediation, facilitation, or other consensual dispute resolution processes.

In this case, Uruguay notified Argentina of its plans for the pulp mill plant in Fray Bentos. Since the plant was located on the river, the treaty provisions were invoked. Argentina asked for a technical group, staffed by Argentinean and Uruguayan specialists, to examine the project.

When the proposed plant was first announced, Jorge Busti, then governor of the province of Entre Rios, Argentina, mobilized the citizens of Gualeguaychú against the project.[5] His motivation was apparently political: the plant was the perfect bogeyman to rally voters to support his reelection. His assertion that the plant would cause acid rain, water contamination, air pollution, and other environmental horrors spoke to provincial fears that valuable second homes would be damaged and tourism in the area would be destroyed.[6] Busti, of course, had no authority or power to stop development in Uruguay. However, he saw a perfect political opportunity. He could create a conflict without having to provide a solution. He could be a hero without any accountability.

In the meantime, the technical advisory committee formed under the Uruguay River Treaty could not come to agreement on the effects of the project on the river. Accordingly, Uruguay and Argentina had 120 days to negotiate an agreement resolving the issues.

When the technical group called for negotiations, the entire town of Gualeguaychú mobilized in defense of its land, water, air, and economic prosperity. The Citizens' Environmental Assembly of Gualeguaychú was created as a grassroots protest against the Uruguayan plant. Those Uruguayans were not going to destroy their lives! From the beginning, these community fears, inflamed by political rhetoric, made Gualeguaychú unwilling to engage in conversations about how to resolve the conflict. In the collective mind of the community, the only solution was to prevent the pulp mill from being built.

In April 2005, two months after Uruguayan president Tabaré Vazquez and his government took power, a large group of Gualeguaychú residents blocked the Libertador General San Martín Bridge connecting Gualeguaychú with Fray Bentos. This was the start of a series of civil protests against the pulp mills. The strategy was to disrupt traffic between Uruguay and Argentina as much as possible, bringing attention to the claims of the Gualeguaychúvians that the pulp mills would be environmentally and economically disastrous.

The Citizens' Environmental Assembly of Gualeguaychú rebuffed attempts at mediation. The archbishop of Montevideo offered to mediate and was ignored. Nobel Peace laureate Adolfo Pérez Esquivel offered to mediate if the protesters agreed to a temporary end of the blockade. Because the protesters perceived the blockade as its only leverage, they refused Esquivel's offer to mediate. Catholic church leaders in both countries vowed to facilitate dialogue, but declined to act as mediators. Their offers were ignored. Likewise, the government of Finland, home to the company that was constructing the plant, declined to intervene in what it perceived as private business concerns.

Uruguayan president Vázquez spoke privately to Argentine president Néstor Kirchner, searching for a solution to the conflict, while stating publicly that the construction of the mills would not be halted by the Uruguayan government. The conflict was growing into a hot potato that no one wanted to catch.

A few weeks later, the protesters suspended the blockade to give the Uruguayans a chance to stop construction. Botnia agreed to a ninety-day suspension, but when faced with pressure from its European investors, it suspended construction for only a week. As a result, the blockade was put back in place.

On May 4, 2006, Argentina filed a formal complaint with the International Court of Justice arguing that Uruguay breached the Uruguay River Treaty. Argentina requested an injunction to stop construction of the pulp mill, claiming it would suffer irreparable harm if construction and operation of the mill continued while the case was being decided before the court.

On July 13, 2006, in a 14–1 ruling in Uruguay's favor (the only vote against Uruguay was cast by the judge appointed by Argentina), the International Court of Justice denied the injunction, ruling that Argentina had not demonstrated that Uruguay's actions were enough to stop the construction of the pulp mill.[7] This decision did not, however, settle the question of whether Uruguay breached its treaty obligations to Argentina. The next day, the Gualeguaychú Assembly organized a protest demonstration, with cars, bicycles, and people on foot along National Route 14 finishing with a rally in the city.

Later in the year, at the Ibero-American Summit in Montevideo, Argentinean president Kirchner asked King Juan Carlos of Spain to facilitate the renewal of negotiations between the two countries. The proposition was accepted by the Uruguayan government. Trinidad Jiménez, Spanish secretary of state for Ibero-America, explained that the monarch would not be a mediator, but would facilitate the easing of tensions. The Uruguayan government reiterated its position that it would not agree to presidential meetings while a road blockade was in place. And, while expressing support for facilitated discussions, José Pouler, a member of the Citizens' Environmental Assembly of Gualeguaychú, said that construction of the mills on the river was "not negotiable."[8]

THE MERCOSUR TRIBUNAL

Mercosur is the South American trade bloc comprising Argentina, Brazil, Paraguay, Uruguay, and, more recently, Venezuela. It has established an arbitral tribunal to hear complaints about trade restrictions, flow of goods, and barriers between the member countries.

In June 2006, Uruguay appeared before the Mercosur Tribunal asking that Argentina be punished for the blockades and forced to pay reparations. The claim was made under the Treaty of Asunción, which guarantees the free circulation of goods and services between Mercosur members. Uruguay also demanded that the Argentine government be forced to stop any future blockades.

The tribunal was an ad hoc assembly composed of three arbiters, one Argentine, one Uruguayan, and one Spaniard. It gathered in Asunción, heard the allegations, and, on September 7, 2006, decided that Argentina had acted "on good faith." The tribunal rejected Uruguay's request for sanctions, while noting that the blockades had caused "undeniable inconveniences to both Uruguayan and Argentine trade, in addition to the violation of the free circulation right."[9] Typical of litigants in a hotly contested dispute, both governments cited the tribunal's report as supporting their respective positions.

Beyond the arbitral tribunal, Mercosur has been unwilling or unable to address the local conflict and the diplomatic breakdown between Argentina and Uruguay. Some fear that Mercosur's impotence to manage this conflict indicates a wider inability to solve trade and commercial conflicts that may arise in the future between member nations. Thus, confidence in the trade and diplomatic structure of the Southern Cone is weakened by the pulp mill dispute.

POLITICAL EFFORTS

No one in Uruguay or even in the higher reaches of the Argentinean government imagined that the social protest movements of the Entre Rios province and the town of Gualeguaychú would gain the momentum the protests demonstrated. When Entre Rios governor Busti lost control of the conflict, he turned to President Kirchner for help. On the principle that social movements should not be suppressed, Kirchner did not ask the protesters to lift their blockade of the bridge, despite its international repercussions. He was afraid that they would refuse, leaving him with the politically unpalatable solution of removing them physically from the bridge.

Nevertheless, in March 2006, Governor Busti, at the apparent request of President Kirchner, tried to have the blockade removed. The local movement was losing some legitimacy because it was not being supported by similar environmental justice movements in Fray Bentos. Obviously, the people most likely to suffer environmental injustice would be those living closest to the plants in Uruguay rather than those living in the wealthier districts on the other side of the river. In spite of this, the local support for the *piqueteros* rebounded, and Busti quickly backed off from his attempt to stop the blockade.

The Uruguayan officials' assessment of the social situation was also badly off the mark. Believing the demonstrations were purely the work of Busti's bid for reelection in October 2005, they ignored Argentina's request for discussions and negotiation. They assumed that once the elections were over, everything would return to normal. By the time they realized their enormous miscalculation, the protest had gained too much political energy to dissipate by itself.

In August 2009, the World Bank, which participated in the financing of the pulp mill, received a complaint from the Citizens' Environmental Assembly of Gualeguaychú. After conducting interviews with members of the assembly and the sponsors of the project, the World Bank determined that joint fact finding, mediation, or other alternative dispute resolution processes were not feasible. This assessment was based on the assembly's apparent lack of interest in any dialogue or conversations with the Uruguayans, and the Uruguayan's belief that it would prevail in the matter pending before the International Court of Justice.[10]

In 2010, Uruguayan president-elect José "Pepe" Mujica attempted to intervene in the seven-year-old conflict. Ironically, when the Argentineans first questioned the environmental effects of the project, Mujica, then minister of economic development, essentially told them to pound sand. As president-elect, however, he sought an end to the blockades. Mujica met with President Kirchner and with the new governor of Entre Rios, Sergio Urribarri. No progress was made.

Bloggers and journalists reflected and inflamed the polarized positions. The conflict excited emotions in Uruguay and Argentina, heightening already strong nationalist feelings.

THE INTERNATIONAL COURT OF JUSTICE GIVES ARGENTINA A PYRRHIC VICTORY

On April 20, 2010, the International Court of Justice handed down its final decision.[11] The court decided that Uruguay had breached some of its procedural obligations under the treaty. However, the court was not persuaded that the plant was an environmental hazard to the river or to Argentina. In other words, there was insufficient evidence to prove that the Botnia plant was polluting the air or the river in violation of the statute. In effect, Uruguay won and Argentina lost. However, the underlying conflict remains.

WHAT MAKES THIS CONFLICT DIFFERENT?

This conflict was about more than the pulp mill. Many factors underlay and contributed to it. Among these factors were:

- The political aspirations and manipulations of the regional governor standing for election,
- The inflammation of local self-protective interests,
- The conflict-avoidant behaviors of the Argentinean national authorities,
- The minimal and desultory attempts to gather people to the table,
- The staking of positions and refusal to retreat from them,
- The resort to litigation to vindicate perceived violations of rights and to deflect political accountability,
- The use of nonviolent, but unlawful, social action to protest with the concomitant disruption and inconvenience to tens of thousands of people,
- The failure of those asked to mediate to take any active steps to design and implement an effective process,
- The refusal of potential mediators to accept the reputational and political risk of failure,
- The absence of any professional, experienced mediators available to work with the conflict, and
- The fact that this was an international environmental dispute with important commercial and trade issues and there was not an adequate international process to contain the conflict.

In a nutshell, a local protest action blocked an international crossing point to affect commerce between two countries. While the blockade was illegal, the government of Argentina saw a great political risk in stopping it solely for the benefit of a controversial commercial project in a neighboring country. The government of Uruguay could do nothing to stop the blockade because it occurred on the Argentinean side of the bridge. Thus, Uruguay had no sovereign jurisdiction to solve the problem on its own. And, it supported the pulp mill project because of the economic benefits to the region and to the town of Fray Bentos.

A characteristic typical of social justice and environmental disputes in general is that the protesters do not wish to negotiate. Typically, in these disputes, they take an early inflexible position. They see mediation and negotiation as a compromise of sacred, nonnegotiable values. These emotional responses to conflict are grounded deeply in the psyches of the local citizens. The idea of even having a dialogue with the enemy is conceptually difficult because there is no solution to the problem other than that conceived of by the citizens. The Citizens' Environmental Assembly of Gualeguaychú felt that the only power it had was the *piquetero*. Since the assembly cast the dispute as a clash of values, it does not see any advantage in negotiation. Even the mention of a dialogue process is met with obstinate resistance because to the protesters, the only conceivable solution is to stop the pulp mill operation and tear down the factory. Thus, the assembly has focused on a position that has been transmuted into an ideology of belief common in the twenty-first century. In later chapters, we will look at these social-identity and belief-based conflicts in depth to understand how they evolve and how they must be managed.

In this conflict, many people have heard the words, "We will not negotiate!" and there is little perceived motivation to resolve the conflict through consensual dispute resolution. Although the president of Argentina and the regional governor of Entre Rios acknowledge that the *piquetero* violates local, national, and international law, the political consequences of enforcing the law seem too great to bear. Everyone seems locked down into immovable positions.

This raises several questions. First, why does the Citizens' Environmental Assembly of Gualeguaychú not want to engage with the Uruguayans? How much time, energy, and effort can the community continue to expend on the protest? How long will their support last, locally and nationally? What will be the effect of losing the case before the International Court of Justice?

Second, why do the Uruguayans think that the favorable decision from the International Court of Justice will actually resolve the conflict? What confidence does Uruguay have that the protests will abate or that there will not be further efforts at a political and civic level to stop or impede operations of the plant?

Third, what are the implications if this conflict is not resolved? Will confidence erode in Mercosur's ability to resolve trade disputes? Will the inability of the national leaders to engage in fruitful processes continue to be an irritant in diplomatic relations? What would be the long-term consequences of strained relations between highly interdependent neighboring nations?

This intractable conflict will not be solved by simply offering mediation, or by trying to entice the assembly to negotiate a solution to the problem. Although the stubbornness of the assembly may be frustrating to some, an experienced professional mediator will see it as normal and expected behavior in this type of conflict. What is most surprising is that no one seems to recognize that this kind of intractability is a common problem throughout the world. Further, the political leaders do not seem to understand that more subtle and nuanced approaches will be required to move the parties toward resolution.

Here, we see the limitations of the "rational choice." If people are not "rational" and do not want to "negotiate," we cannot deal with them. The old diplomacy is simply incapable of dealing with local leaders who stir up the populace for their own political advantage and are not controlled by the national government. The assembly is an ad hoc group operating under loose democratic principles with no apparent hierarchy, few spokespeople, and no leaders. It has the support of the local community, the regional government, and, tacitly, the national government. As a group, the assembly has created an identity around itself based on local, regional, and national pride and in defense of sacred values. The assembly essentially controls the public and political dialogue around the pulp mill dispute. However, it is not controlled by a political leader, and, under the eighteenth-century diplomatic model, Uruguay really has no one to negotiate with over the issues.

Historically, in international relations, nations did not have to deal with protesting residents blocking international bridges. If there were civil uprisings or protests, they were addressed by national leaders, usually by force or coercion. The old diplomacy assumes that nation-states are able to control their own citizens through an internal police force and compel them to follow local and international law. This follows from the rational choice assumption—member states sustain law and order within their own boundaries because that's the rational thing to do. When Argentina refused to enforce its laws against the *piqueteros*, traditional diplomacy became unworkable. No one wanted to intervene or tell Argentina what to do for fear of interfering with Argentina's sovereignty.

But a different political reality exists in the twenty-first century. First, local citizens have enormous visibility through the Internet and other media, with the power to bring awareness to perceived social and environmental injustice. Second, politicians may see little advantage in reining in civil disobedience and protests that only interfere with commercial enterprises in neighboring countries, when doing so erodes popular support at home. Enforcing the rule of law is worthwhile as long as it perpetuates the power of local vested interests. The rule of law is counterproductive when those interests are not furthered and only the interests of a foreign government are benefited. This view of the rule of law as a matter of convenience rather than a duty has repeated itself throughout the world.

With globalization, increased international trade, media exposure, and relaxed border crossings, conflicts not amenable to traditional diplomatic negotiation are rapidly increasing. Agreeing to engage in diplomatic negotiation can be seen by protesting local citizens as caving in to the demands of foreign powers—and this is politically unpalatable.

There is a positive side to this. The rising power of local groups that in the past might have been suppressed by internal authoritarian violence or threats indicates a deeper sense of democratic empowerment that can only be good in the long run.

With this grassroots power, however, comes responsibility. Local groups asserting their autonomous power, whether political or economic, will fail if no effort is made for consensual dispute resolution. The challenge is to help groups balance their need for a voice with processes that engage opposing ideologies. That will not happen under old models of diplomatic relations.

Because of the amorphous nature of the parties and the high emotions of the conflict, potential political mediators are often as fearful of risking harm to their reputations as they are of the conflict itself. In the case of the citizens' assembly and the pulp mill, representatives of the Catholic Church declined to mediate, although they saw the need for consensual dispute resolution processes. King Juan Carlos of Spain was willing to lend his good offices but was clear that he did not want to mediate the dispute. Finland, the factory's home country, wanted nothing to do with the conflict, and Mercosur, the relevant international trade organization, did nothing. Apparently, for all these potential intermediaries, the political risk of damage to reputation outweighed the potential benefits of success.

WHAT ARE SOME
TWENTY-FIRST-CENTURY STRATEGIES?

Assume you were asked to intervene in this conflict. What are some of the strategies you might consider?

First, solving this international dispute will require much more than convening ministers and heads of state at a pleasant place hosted by a neutral government for a negotiation conference. If this conflict is to be resolved, it will require a well-designed and well-executed intervention at multiple levels of society, by mediators skilled in working in high-conflict situations. The national governments will have to consent to and support the process. For example, if Argentina resisted the idea of mediation, the focus would first have to be at the national level to gain commitments to support a broader process. This might be time-consuming, and the difficulty in achieving success will depend on the political situation in the country. However, it is a necessary first step.

The idea of *multitrack diplomacy*,[12] a term coined in 1992 by peacemaker Louise Diamond and Ambassador John D. MacDonald, comes to mind here. Multitrack diplomacy includes the unofficial efforts made outside the governments to help resolve conflicts in the world. The concept expands the original distinction made by retired career State Department Foreign Service officer Joseph Montville, between track one (official, governmental action) and track two (unofficial, nongovernmental action) approaches to conflict resolution. Diamond and MacDonald have identified nine different tracks that could be used to further peace.

Sometimes diplomatic professionals resist multitrack efforts because they do not want civilians interfering with what they—the experts—think they know best. But we are interested in strategies based not on traditional diplomatic expertise, but on our current knowledge of human cognition, motivation, and emotion.

We might engage the Argentinean national government by pointing out how its national interests are advanced by resolution of the problem. The ability of a group of well-intentioned local citizens to block an international bridge with impunity creates the perception that international law and commerce are not respected in Argentina. This perception cannot advance trade and economic growth in the Southern Cone.

At a personal level, overcoming the negative media coverage will require some courage. It might be possible to show how engaging as a statesman can be a good political move. Politicians worldwide like to be seen as problem solvers, but only when they see little risk of failure. Carefully crafted political statements could support the concerns of the Citizens' Environmental Assembly of Gualeguaychú while signaling an end of tolerance for the *piquetero* action.

At the next level, the regional leaders in Entre Rios could be engaged in the same process with the persuasion of the Argentinean national government. Since this is essentially a political question for the governor, what are the advantages and disadvantages of supporting a mediation process? What if some of the economic benefits from the Uruguayan project could flow to Entre Rios? What if the process could be used to strengthen protection of the river and surrounding regions in Argentina and Uruguay? What if the project could further economic development in Entre Rios? Asking questions that open up new possibilities might, in the words of Notre Dame peace professor John Paul Lederach, excite the moral imagination of the regional political leaders.[13]

The next step, and the most delicate, is to build a relationship with the Citizens' Environmental Assembly of Gualeguaychú. Since the group is ad hoc and democratic, identifying and engaging the local thought leaders will be a key tactic. That is, they must be seen as influencing the beliefs of their community. Every group has thought leaders, and they are not necessarily the political leaders. Usually, through their opinions and beliefs, these people lead the minds of their community. We need to examine the local situation carefully. The assembly seems to be the most radical group, but does it really have the complete support of the local citizens? Are there others who may support different strategies yet are remaining silent for fear of social reprisal? Are the "leaders" of the assembly personally popular or have they simply hijacked the conflict by cloaking themselves in sacred values that no one wishes to question? These are difficult questions to consider. A confrontational, takeover attitude will not work. However, if a small meeting might be arranged for a curious outsider, what might that look like? Here's how we might imagine a conversation with a group of local thought leaders. Our hypothetical conversation might go like this:

"Thank you for meeting with me. I'm interested in learning more about you and the problems you are facing with the pulp mill. Tell me a little of the history."

"The pulp mill has been a terrible blight on our community," says Gustavo. Gustavo has been an outspoken opponent of the pulp plant. "It is poisoning our air and our waters, making our children ill, and hurting us economically. It has to be stopped."

"Yes. You are deeply frustrated and angry."

"Yes, yes. No one is listening to us. They do not believe us. But it is true. All of it is true."

"So, you feel disrespected and ignored. No one is listening to the truth."

"Yes. No one is listening to the truth," Gustavo agrees, nodding his head. Others around the table are sipping their maté and agreeing with him.

"I am wondering how this all started?" I ask, inviting the stories. For the next three or four hours, I listen to the stories as the men and women around the table begin to unburden themselves. I have no agenda other than connecting, listening, and learning with these people. Finally, the stories wind down, and the conversation is ready to move on.

"So," I note, "the International Court of Justice decided that the treaty was violated, but it refused to shut down the plant."

"Yes. We won. We are right. The Uruguayans violated the river treaty and the court upheld our rights."

"Have you ever been able to share your concerns with the Fray Bentos people or anyone in Uruguay?"

"No. They have no interest in talking to us, and we have no interest in talking to them!"

"What if some Fray Bentos people were interested in listening to you? Would you be open to sharing your story with them?"

"They don't want to listen to us. They just want to continue polluting our air and injuring our children!"

"Would you be willing to have a few Fray Bentos people come over here to see for themselves the problems you face?" I ask.

"They are not interested in coming over here. Otherwise, they would have been here years ago."

"Perhaps. But the problem for you is not going away at the

moment. So maybe telling the Fray Bentos people about your concerns firsthand might be useful."

Gustavo and the others raise objection after objection explaining why the Fray Bentos people would not, could not, will not listen. These objections are normal, expected, and perfectly understandable in these conflicts. My job is to plant the seed that being heard by the other side might be possible and might be a good thing. The objections actually constitute a deeper level of processing around the possibility of confronting the enemy—what that would feel like, be like—the total emotional experience.

This invitation process takes patience and time, but it almost always works eventually. After all, everyone wants to be heard, needs to be listened to, and needs to be validated. In addition, I am being very careful not to create any sense of commitment, or demand anything other than telling a story. The Gualeguaychú people must not feel like they are being asked to negotiate about the underlying conflict. All we are seeking is an opportunity to meet and listen. Just like I am doing now.

This is not how traditional negotiation works with the old diplomacy. Rather, I am beginning a very subtle engagement in a highly escalated conflict. The dance is prickly and time-consuming. The Gualeguaychú people are suspicious, especially of a Norte Americano outsider. They have already rejected any peace overtures. They are not interested in any solution to their problem short of the closure and demolition of the pulp mill. If one is looking for a fast, bottom-line negotiation, this is not the place to be.

Let's assume I am successful at securing an agreement to tell stories to some Fray Bentos people. What next?

First, I have to go talk to the Fray Bentos people and find two or three men and women whom I can coach on how to listen and engage with the Gualeguaychú leaders. I need people who can be peacemakers without being obvious about it. They need to be comfortable in a high-conflict environment and take some personal abuse. Most importantly, they need to be able to listen to a disagreeable story without becoming reactive. My listeners also need to be seen as the thought leaders in their own community. They need to have equal status with the storytellers in Gualeguaychú. People of higher status, like politicians, might be seen as patronizing. People of lower status might seem insulting. Like meets like whenever possible.

The process of recruiting those people is again, a process of building relationships. I will start in the usual places: local businesses, the parish, and the schools. I will try to convene a group of likely candidates and listen to their stories just as I did in Gualeguaychú. I hope that the feelings, while intense, will at least provide a favorable opening to present my ideas. I know that stories are powerful, and I am rarely disappointed by people's desire to engage when given the right opportunity.

Since Fray Bentos is small, with a population of only twenty-three thousand, finding people should not take too long.

Once they are engaged, I will need to prepare the group for the meeting in Gualeguaychú. Preparing people is a large part of the process. We talk about the meeting, describe problems that might be encountered, and engage in some role-playing. In the beginning, I am gentle, but as we progress, I become tougher. I know how the Gualeguaychú people may act at their worst, and the preparation includes setting up situations that are even worse. If my Fray Bentos peacemakers are prepared for anything and everything, the meeting might work.

Finally, after a few days or perhaps a week of preparation, the Fray Bentos people are ready. In the meantime, I have also been maintaining contact and building the relationships in Gualeguaychú. I have been careful not to engage in much substantive discussion, and have tried to become a friend. It's been a great opportunity to play tourist and let the locals show me around.

Meeting day arrives in Gualeguaychú. We have a large room with some privacy. I arrive well before the appointed time to prepare the room and make it comfortable and informal. I don't want a conference table between people because that would signal negotiation and bargaining. I decide that I will let people decide for themselves where to sit and how to arrange themselves. I will just make sure that I am sitting in a physical location that suggests that I will be leading the meeting without me having to say so.

Coming to this type of meeting creates anxiety that may trigger anger. Clear leadership, without domination, provides an important psychological service to everyone. People feel safe when someone they know and trust is in charge. People are willing to confer social power on a capable leader in exchange for relieving their anxiety. The danger is that if the leader loses control and people feel unsafe, that social power will be retracted immediately, and the meeting will be over. My job will be a high-wire act. Falling off would not be good.

The Gualeguaychú contingent arrives first. There are five people, and they all know me. We exchange greetings, and they help themselves to maté. The Fray Bentos people arrive, and as they come into the room, the tension and temperature shoot up. I welcome them and introduce everyone around. As the group sorts itself out and settles down, I invite people to pull up chairs around me.

"Welcome, and thank you for coming. As you know, I have been interested in the problems here and have found the stories you have shared with me to be powerful and compelling. I thought so much so that I received your permission for us to come together so you could hear each other's stories firsthand. I hope you find them as interesting as I have during my meetings with you.

"I want to share in a way that is respectful and useful, so there are a few ground rules. I have talked about these rules with all of you, and I want reiterate them again so everyone is on the same page. First, let us allow stories to be told without interruption. If you have a question or disagree with something, write it down. Everyone will have a chance to be heard.

"Second, let us be civil and respectful with our words, tone of voice, and body language.

"Third, let us tell our truths from our hearts and our minds.

Finally, let us be fair to each other. If anyone feels that he or she is being treated unfairly, you have my permission to bring it up at once so we can deal with it. What would be unfair would be for someone to leave this meeting and say 'You know that guy Doug Noll was really unfair.' That would be unfair to me. Is everyone in agreement?"

I watch and listen to make sure that everyone says yes or sí.

"Good. Let us begin. Gustavo, if you don't mind, I would like to you to start with your story and share with us your problems and concerns." I have already asked Gustavo privately if he would go first, and he agreed. I carefully prepared the Fray Bentos group to hear what he had to say.

Over the next two hours, Gustavo tells us his story. At times, he is angry, frustrated, and sad. At times, he blames the Fray Bentos people and is even a little insulting and disrespectful to them. This is normal and expected. The Fray Bentos people graciously take his words in stride. I gently ask him about his commitment to civility, and he apologizes. Everyone sees that he is speaking from both his heart and his mind, and he sets a good example for what I am hoping for. When he concludes, we take a break, allowing the group to mix and talk socially. This is critical to the process.

As the day goes on, others of the Gualeguaychú group tell their stories. The Fray Bentos people listen respectfully. They engage with questions that ask for deeper information rather than to make argumentative points. They acknowledge the feelings in the room. They are terrific. I can feel a sense of calm and hope descending into the group. This is good.

Finally, the stories are told, and the Gualeguaychú people look to the Fray Bentos people. They are silently asking, "What are you going to do about all of this?"

The Fray Bentos people expect this. Oscar, their leader, says, "Thank you for taking so much time to share your stories and your hospitality. This has been very moving and meaningful for me and my friends. We would like you to consider coming across the river for another meeting and allow us to share our stories with you. We do not need your answer right away—we know that you must think deeply about it. But we would be honored if you would allow us to extend our hospitality to you as you have to us."

With that, the meeting begins to break up. People are smiling and shaking hands. They are civil, if not warm. Progress has been made.

Who knows where these small meetings will lead? Experience has shown that when people are able to share their stories and truly listen to each other without any commitment other than to be civil and respectful, conflicts between them naturally and gracefully de-escalate. UCLA neuroscientist Matthew Lieberman has shown that when feelings are expressed and validated, the brain functions associated with fear and high emotions are inhibited while the executive function of the brain is activated.[14] Thus, having people tell their stories and label their feelings is a powerful way to de-escalate conflicts. While rational-choice diplomats would dismiss this idea as "touchy-feely," the empirical evidence and deep experience suggest that storytelling is the only way through the conflict maze.

That does not mean that peace is around the corner. Many peace talks have failed because the people talking to each other failed to bring their constituencies along with them. Like surfers who get too far out over a wave, many peace negotiators have been wiped out by the disapproval of their supporters. With the foundation of this meeting, however, the participants can go to their communities and report what happened. With help, they can think about how to engage a few more people and, little by little, create a slightly larger bridge. This is not a speedy process, but it is not slow either. Connecting with people's feelings is the only way to find peace.

But the assembly members have strong beliefs about their cause. How we recognize and manage stubborn beliefs in mediation is next.

Chapter 4
Beliefs

From a distance of a mile or so, it's a white dot that stands out against the rocky hillside as something not natural. The intense blue sky of the desert is a reminder that the dot will be seared by the sun in the superheated Middle East summer. As places go, it is not aesthetically appealing.

The speck does not look like much, but it represents an enduring problem for peace in the world. The white dot is a trailer owned by an Israeli settler. He and his family have set the trailer on a hilltop, for better security, claiming a piece of land forever. Electricity, when there is any, is provided by a small generator. There are no amenities or municipal services, other than an Israeli Defense Force military presence to protect the family. No utilities, no water, no garbage collection. It is bleak indeed.

The settler might be a recent émigré from Europe or Russia or Ethiopia, looking to set down roots in Zion. He might be an ultraorthodox *haredi* who is committed to following traditional conservative Jewish practices. He may have suffered from oppression in his country of origin because he was Jewish. In other places, he might be called a squatter or trespasser. In some Israeli circles, he is a hero.

If we were to talk to this settler, we would learn that legal and international niceties do not matter to him: this land is the sacred land of the Bible. We would learn that he believes that the manifest duty of every devout Jew is to occupy the biblical lands of Ysrael. This white spot carries a deep sense of holiness. This is the land of Abraham. Now, it is the settler's turn to experience the transcendence of living on the land given by God. The land is hot, bone-dry, and rocky. Nothing grows there easily, and even the lizards struggle to eke out an existence. Yet the land is sacred and must be protected. That is the settler's deep and abiding belief.

In a few weeks, like a cellular growth, the dot may grow to two dots as word spreads about this new stakeholding. Over a few more weeks or months, the dots will continue to grow until a small outpost is settled around the hilltop. The settlers may find a spring or drill a well. If not, they have to truck in water. But, it does not matter to them how harsh living on the hillside might be. It is God's land, and it is now their land as well.

The problem is that this piece of sacred land is in the West Bank, the regions formerly known as Judea and Samaria on the west bank of the Jordan River. Palestinians have lived on this land for a thousand years as subsistence farmers and herders. Because the land is harsh, many hectares or acres are needed to support even one goat and her kid. Olive orchards might be planted where water is available, and every task is performed by hand. No fancy tractors, tree shakers, drip irrigation systems, or modern agrieconomic principles are used here. It is much the same as it was five hundred years ago. The Palestinians have lived here generation after generation, and their hard work has been steeped into the land. Babies are born and grow into children, teenagers, and then adults who have their own babies as the cycle of life moves with the seasons through the generations. The Palestinians have put down deep roots into the dry soil and seek a life of peace for themselves.

Richard Boudreaux, a journalist for the *Los Angeles Times*, captured the essence of this situation in a December 27, 2007, story about the legal battle of a Christian Palestinian farmer against Israeli interests focused on seizing his farm.[1] As Boudreaux reports, Douad Nassar and his family have spent twenty years fighting a legal battle to retain land that Nassar's grandfather, a Christian from Lebanon, bought in 1916 when it was part of the Ottoman Empire. For more than ninety years, the Nassars have worked the land, growing almonds, figs, grapes, olives, pears, and pomegranates.

The struggle over the Nassars' hundred acres has consumed Nassar's adult life.

"It is our land, and our land is like our mother," he said. "I cannot abandon or sell my mother."

Most West Bank Palestinian families do not have land titles because formal recording systems typical in Western nations simply do not exist. In theory, Israeli law allows these families to keep rural land acquired without title before 1967 as long as they keep it cultivated. In practice, cultivated land is often seized by the Israeli government, and the burden of proof is on the Palestinian to prove he is the rightful owner.

Until 1991, there had been no hint of trouble between the Nassar family farm and the Israeli authorities. That year, after some Israeli settlers moved onto the property, an Israeli military tribunal ordered three-fourths of the Nassar farm to be taken by Israel, claiming it was neither privately owned nor actively cultivated. The Nassars challenged the order with land ownership papers dated and stamped 1924. The military judge rejected the challenge, ruling the hand-drawn map inadmissible as evidence. This was despite the fact that the ownership papers had been honored by Turkish, British, and Jordanian rulers for nearly one hundred years.

The Nassars returned to military court with a new survey map and scores of witnesses to support their land claim. The case languished until 2002, when the judge without explanation ruled against the family.

Nassar tapped his family's modest wealth and appealed the

decision to the Israeli Supreme Court where, eventually, the family received a fair hearing. The Supreme Court demanded an explanation of the military court's ruling and ordered a halt to the settlers' incursions onto the property.

The Israeli state attorney's office argued that the farm's land boundaries did not precisely match those in the 1924 land documents. The Nassars countered with testimony from a leading Israeli surveyor who they had sent to London and Istanbul to research colonial land records. His testimony was so convincing that, rather than risk an unprecedented loss, the Israeli state attorney's office dropped the case. That, however, has not ended the conflict.

As Boudreaux reports, Shaul Goldstein, mayor of the adjacent Jewish settlement, Neve Daniel, rejects the Nassars' claim to any land except the patch its farmhouse occupies.

"That is state land," he said, pointing to a steep, uncultivated stretch. "Douad Nassar went to court and tried to claim it, but he has not proven a thing.

"The state will decide what to do with that land," Goldstein continued, predicting that the family would not be allowed to register all one hundred acres it claims. "If the state wants to give it to me, for my settlement, they will give it to me. All the land belongs to Israel. We can build wherever we want."

Depending on your perspective, the West Bank has been either administratively controlled or illegally occupied by the Israeli government since the 1967 war. It is hotly contested by both the Palestinians and the Israelis. More important, both sides' attachment to the land is deep and wide. The clash of these beliefs constitutes one of the major sources of ongoing conflict in the Middle East.

*   *   *

Backspace 1,891 years. In 118 CE, Publius Aelius Hadrianus became emperor of Rome. By most historical accounts, he was one of the most competent men to hold the position and wanted to strengthen and unify the Roman Empire. He arrived in Jerusalem in 130 CE and saw a poverty-stricken, off-the-beaten-track city that was a poor excuse for a provincial Roman capital. He also saw a great opportunity to gain political support. His proposal: To rebuild the wreck of Jerusalem into a modern city and rename it Aelia Capitolina.

The resident Jews were horrified. The ruins of Jewish Jerusalem would be buried under an urban renewal project ordered by an imperial power? Zion would be destroyed! The remains of Solomon's Temple would be destroyed! The holy sites that were central to the identity of Judaism would disappear forever!

Hadrian was puzzled by the vehement protests of the Jews. He wanted Jews and Romans to put the enmity of the past behind them and work toward lasting peace. Ostensibly to this end, he issued edicts to abolish the practice of the Jewish religion—circumcision was forbidden, and ordination of rabbis, the teaching of the Torah, and public Jewish meetings were made illegal.

The Jews revolted and were led into a guerilla war by Simon Bar Koseba. Bar Koseba and his soldiers fought against the Romans for three years. They avoided pitched battles, picking off Roman troops a few at a time. Some might call it an early form of asymmetrical warfare against a superior force—that is, terrorism. Eventually, the Romans wiped out Bar Koseba's army and laid Judea to waste. The Jews were evicted from Jerusalem and banned from living in, traveling through, or otherwise occupying space in Judea.

It seems that Middle East building and construction has been a weapon in the hands of the victors for nearly two thousand years. Although Jerusalem has changed hands from Jews to Christians to Muslims to Christians and so on, each victor has erected structures designed to declare its final domination.

Fast-forward. In July 1999, Ehud Barak formed his Israeli government, a shaky coalition of parties with widely divergent views on the central issues of the Palestinian conflict—the status of Jerusalem and the expansion or retraction of settlements in the West Bank. From July until December 1999, Barak's government issued 3,196 new invitations to tender bids for settlement construction. The Jewish settler population on the West Bank expanded from 177,000 in 1999 to 203,000 in 2000. Included in this expansion were the construction of Jewish-only bypass roads, houses, trailer parks, and even luxurious beachfront homes in Gaza.[2]

Barak, who was elected on a platform of peace with the Palestinians, made a well-publicized visit to the large West Bank settlement of Ma'ale Adumim in September 1999. He promised the settlers that the government would strengthen their presence.

"Every house you have built here," Barak said, "is part of the State of Israel—forever—period."[3]

*   *   *

The modern history of the Palestinian-Israeli conflict has been recounted many times in many places. In the late nineteenth century, the region known as Palestine was inhabited by Palestinians for hundreds of years under the rule of the Ottoman Empire. At the turn of the century, along with the rise of European nationalism, the Zionist movement began in Europe, and many Jews began to think about, then act, on a desire to return to Israel.

After World War I, the Ottoman Empire was dismantled, and Great Britain took over governance of the area. In November 1917, Great Britain issued the Balfour Declaration stating British support for the creation of a Jewish state in Palestine. This declaration was received with dismay by the Arabs, as it appeared to be a course reversal of British policy. The British had previously promised that Palestine would be included in the Arab national lands. It now appeared to be reneging on that agreement. To quell Arab dissent, Great Britain imposed strict rules against further Jewish immigration. Nevertheless, Jews clandestinely and illegally moved into Palestine in ever-increasing numbers.

As the horrors of the Holocaust became known at the end of World War II, international sentiment shifted in favor of a Jewish state in Palestine. The British government, however, continued to resist this idea. In 1947, bowing to internal political pressure and international public opinion, Great Britain turned over its official mandate of Palestine to the United Nations. In November 1947, the United Nations voted on a partition plan that would divide Palestine in half, creating a Palestinian state and a Jewish state. The Jewish leadership accepted the plan, but the Arabs rejected it, viewing the entirety of Palestine as their rightful land.

In May 1948, the British Mandate over Palestine officially expired, and British troops withdrew from the region. Israel declared itself a state, the Arabs protested, and war erupted. The Israelis won that war, and the state of Israel was created. The cease-fire resulted in the division of Jerusalem such that the old walled city, including the most sacred Jewish land, the Temple Mount, as well as the third most sacred site in Islam, the Al-Aqsa Mosque and Dome of the Rock reliquary, were given to Jordan to administer. In addition, the lands of Judea and Samaria, formerly part of British Palestine, were controlled by Jordan. The remaining land that had formerly been reduced to Palestine remained with Israel. Jordan did nothing to organize self-rule or create an autonomous state from the Palestinian lands it controlled. Over seven hundred thousand Arab Palestinians were displaced from their homes, now located in the new state of Israel, and turned into permanent refugees living in camps in neighboring Arab countries. And hundreds of thousands of Jews from Europe, America, and the rest of the world began to immigrate to Israel.

In 1967, the Israeli Defense Force preemptively struck the Egyptian, Jordanian, Syrian, and Lebanese armed forces that were massing on all Israeli borders to annihilate Israel. The Israeli forces soundly defeated the Arabs in six days. As a result, Israel occupied the Egyptian Sinai peninsula, the Golan Heights in Syria, and the Palestinian territories to the west of the Jordan River that had been administered by Jordan. Those territories have been collectively called the West Bank. Israel never annexed the region, and it immediately became a source of deep conflict because it included east Jerusalem and the sacred sites of three religions, and provided Israel with the opportunity to expand into what it considered to be the traditional holy lands of the Jews, lands that were also the ancestral homeland of the Palestinians.

But international law did not recognize Israel's right to occupy the West Bank. Numerous UN resolutions, which Israel ignored, opposed Israel's continued occupation and settlement. Since the United States, as Israel's protector and principal benefactor, refused to support any form of international sanctions against Israel, the United Nations was powerless to enforce its resolutions. All this was taking place in the context of the Cold War, when Israel was seen by the United States as a beachhead against the incursion of communism in the Middle East and a bulwark against Soviet interests in the region. These same interests led the United States to support Sadaam Hussein in Iraq and Shah Rezi Pahlavi in Iran, although both were well known as despots and tyrants. We have seen how this backfired on the United States rather spectacularly.

Since 1948, the Palestinians have claimed that Israel stole their land, and since 1967, they have claimed that by occupying the West Bank, Israel has continuously violated UN Resolution 242, which essentially forbids an occupying nation from unilaterally appropriating or annexing land.[4] In addition, the Palestinians claim that east Jerusalem is the true capital of Palestine because it is the home to the Al-Aqsa Mosque (*al masjid al-aqsa*) and the historical center of Muslim rule for nearly 1,500 years.

It's useful to remind ourselves of the sacred importance of the Al-Aqsa Mosque. The Al-Aqsa Mosque (the "Remote Mosque") is the third most sacred site in Islam, after Mecca and Medina. When Muhammad was evicted from Mecca and lived in Yathrib (Medina), he turned his followers' attention to Jerusalem as a holy city. From that time, Muslims never forgot that their first direction of worship, or *qiblah*, was toward Jerusalem. Jerusalem helped them form a religious identity against the pagan traditions of their enemies and had been crucial in the formation of the Islamic faith community.

As time went on, an increasing number of Muslims began to believe that Islam had superseded the older traditions of Judaism and Christianity. This is a particular flaw of monotheism—since each faith assumes that it alone embodies the truth, the proximity of others who make the same claim poses an implicit challenge to belief. The early Jews believed their faith was transcendent. They were followed by the Christians, and finally by the Muslims, each in turn, proclaiming the one true way. As members of all three traditions lived within the walls of Jerusalem, conflict was predictable and inevitable.

*   *   *

We humans tend to seek out information that confirms our beliefs and ignore other contradictory facts.

As Francis Bacon observed:

> The human understanding when it has once adopted an opinion . . . draws all things else to support and agree with it. And though there be a greater number and weight of instances to be found on the other side, yet these it either neglects or despises, or else by some distinction sets aside or rejects.[5]

Social psychologists call this the *confirmation bias*. For example, suppose that two parents are fighting over the custody of the children. Parent A has moderately good parenting skills, abilities, and resources. Parent B is emotionally close to the children, and has good parenting skills, but, because of job responsibilities, has to travel and be away from the children.

How do you pick the parent with the most positive attributes for child custody? Most people, including judges, would probably pick Parent B. If I asked you which parent was least suited to have custody, you would probably also pick Parent B.

Huh? That makes no sense, does it? How can Parent B have the most positive attributes for child custody and yet be the least suited?

It makes sense when you understand our tendency to seek information that confirms a statement or belief. In the first question, we seek information that confirms that Parent B is a good parent. Emotional bonding with the children is a good thing. Since we have no comparable information for Parent A, we are biased toward Parent B. What about the travel schedule? Well, according to the confirmation bias, we look for confirming information. We essentially ignore information that is inconsistent with what we are searching for and thus discard the travel schedule. It's not relevant to our search for confirming information that Parent B is good.

We can see how this reverses when the question is posed in the negative. When I ask you which parent is less suited to be the custodial parent, you look for information that confirms that statement. Now, the travel schedule looms as a major negative, and you tend to ignore the close emotional bond. Since Parent A has no negative information attached, we decide that Parent B is less desirable.

The important thing to know about confirmation bias is that it is a preconscious process. Basically, our brains use shortcuts and rules, called *heuristics*, that allow us to process information and make quick decisions. While, most of the time, these rules and shortcuts work, they are very poor at dealing with complexity. When emotional beliefs become involved in decision making and negotiation, many of our heuristics betray us. A group of brain researchers wanted to know exactly why this is, and the timing for their project could not have been better.

The 2004 United States presidential elections pitted the incumbent George W. Bush against Democratic senator and Vietnam War veteran John Kerry. The nation was at war in Iraq and Afghanistan, and the memory of September 11, 2001, was still fresh. National politics in the United States was as polarized as it had ever been; the nation was deeply divided on many issues. When the election result came down to a few districts in Ohio, John Kerry conceded rather than take the country through a painful repeat of Bush vs. Gore four years earlier.

At Emory University in Atlanta, Georgia, research neuroscientist and psychologist Drew Westen became interested in the polarization of American politics. Westen, both a clinician and researcher, put together a research team to look at how the brain processes political beliefs. In particular, he was interested in exploring the actual mechanics of the confirmation bias in the brain.[6]

The team used brain scanning technology to study highly partisan Democrats and Republicans during the three months before the 2004 US presidential election. During the study, the partisans were given eighteen sets of statements, six each regarding President George W. Bush, his challenger, Senator John Kerry, and politically neutral male control figures such as actor Tom Hanks. For each set of statements, partisans first read a statement from the candidate (Bush or Kerry). The first statement was followed by a second statement that contradicted the candidate's words and deeds, generally suggesting that the candidate was dishonest or pandering. Here are some examples:

Sample Statement Set—George W. Bush

Initial: "First of all, Ken Lay [former CEO of Enron] is a supporter of mine. I love the man. I got to know Ken Lay years ago, and he has given generously to my campaign. When I'm President, I plan to run the government like a CEO runs a country. Ken Lay and Enron are a model of how I'll do that."—Candidate George Bush, 2000

Contradictory: Mr. Bush now avoids any mention of Ken Lay and is critical of Enron when asked.

Sample Statement Set—John Kerry

Initial: During the 1996 campaign, Kerry told a *Boston Globe* reporter that the Social Security system should be overhauled. He said Congress should consider raising the retirement age and means testing benefits. "I know it's going to be unpopular," he said. "But we have a generational responsibility to fix this problem."

Contradictory: This year, on *Meet the Press*, Kerry pledged that he will never tax or cut benefits to seniors or raise the age for eligibility for Social Security.[7]

Next, the partisans were asked to consider the discrepancy, and then rate the extent to which the candidate's words and deeds were contradictory.

Finally, they were presented with an exculpatory statement that might explain away the apparent contradiction, and asked again to rate the extent to which the candidate's words and deeds were contradictory. Here are the exculpatory statements used in the previous example:

Bush Exculpatory: People who know the president report that he feels betrayed by Ken Lay, and was genuinely shocked to find that Enron's leadership had been corrupt.

Kerry Exculpatory: Economic experts now suggest that, in fact, the Social Security system will not run out of money until 2049, not 2020, as they had thought in 1996.[8]

During the task, the partisans' brains were scanned to see where the blood flowed. Functional magnetic resonance imaging (fMRI) technology works by detecting the iron in blood, extrapolating the quantity of blood in a given brain location, and assumes that increased blood flow correlates to which parts of the brain are active. Researchers generally accept fMRI data as a reasonable representation for what is happening real time in the brain.

When the Republicans rated the consistency of the two statements for George Bush, their brains acted in very strange ways. First, the parts of the brain engaged in reasoning, logic, and problem solving were shut down. Second, the parts of the brain responsible for emotions lit up like fireworks. Third, the dopamine centers of the brain, involved in pleasure and reward, became unusually active. It was as if the Republicans' brains had turned off all reason and were reacting emotionally to the inconsistency between President Bush's words and actions.

Guess what? When the Democrats rated the consistency between the two statements for John Kerry, their brain activity was just as strange in exactly the same way. The reasoning, logical, and problem-solving parts of their brains shut down. Their emotional circuits lit up, and the dopamine circuits fired to provide a blast of pleasure.

What Westen and his group found was striking. "We did not see any increased activation of the parts of the brain normally engaged during reasoning," said Westen. "What we saw instead was a network of emotion circuits lighting up."[9]

Once the partisans had come to completely biased conclusions—essentially ignoring information that did not confirm their opinions—not only did circuits involving negative emotions like sadness and disgust turn off, but their brains rewarded them in a manner similar to the reward addicts receive from their fix. In other words, the partisans got a brain high for holding onto beliefs in the face of objectively truthful, yet contradictory information. It was if they were being rewarded for being stubborn!

Here's another critical point. The partisans were completely unconscious of their decision-making processes. All the information processing was performed outside of conscious awareness. In other words, structures in the brain massively reinforced preexisting beliefs and rejected information contrary to those beliefs—without the partisans even being aware of it. "None of the circuits involved in conscious reasoning were particularly engaged,"[10] reports Westen.

The decision-making process did not involve rational thinking; instead, it was purely emotional. And, the more inconsistent the facts were with the beliefs, the more the neocortex, the reasoning part of the brain, shut down. The idea that we look at information inconsistent with our beliefs in a cold, calculated, and logical manner just got crushed by Westen's research. So much for the rational man assumptions underlying economic theory and Western legal systems—hard science was now saying those assumptions do not hold water.

By the way, it didn't matter whether the partisan was a Republican or a Democratic. Both rejected apparent contradictions and inconsistencies in their own candidate that they had no problem seeing in the opposing one.

Westen hypothesized that emotionally biased reasoning leads to the "stamping in" of a defensive belief, associating the participant's "revisionist" account of the data with positive emotion or relief and elimination of distress.[11]

"The result is that partisan beliefs are calcified, and the person can learn very little from new data," says Westen.[12]

*   *   *

In researching his book *Planting Hatred, Sowing Pain*,[13] professor Moises F. Salinas recruited Israeli and Palestinian college students to interview cross sections of their respective cultures. Two interviews of extremists, one Jewish and one Palestinian, are striking.

The Jewish man is Itamar and was twenty-six years old at the time of the interview. He lives in a West Bank settlement and reports that he is an active member of the extreme right wing in Israel. Hussein, a thirty-year-old professional working for an international company, lives in Nazareth. Hussein was a former member of the radical Peoples' Front for the Liberation of Palestine and still supports their positions. Here is what they believe:

"I'm Itamar, born in 1980. I'm twenty-six years old, and as you see, I am a resident of Bat-Ayin, which is considered a legal settlement. . . . I was born in Israel and my parents were also born in the Israeli . . . the Holy Land, let it be built Amen. . . . I am the son of the King of Kings, the Holy One Blessed Be He, a father in heaven. . . . I maintain a small farm, in which I grow goats, and from them I do milk and cheese.

"I'm a man who defines himself as the extreme right. . . . I don't believe in all these stupid agreements that our army and state try to do with the Arabs. . . . I will tell you unequivocally that I don't think that the Arab people has a right to exist at all, let alone exist and live in the State of Israel, and even more, they don't deserve a piece of land of the Holy Land . . . because . . . according to the Holy Torah, this state belongs to the people of Israel. . . . We Jews will receive the Land of Israel, and much more, the entire Land of Israel with all its different parts, as it is stated in the Torah. . . . This land was promised to Abraham our ancestor, and [he] was our, and not the gentiles', father.

"I hold my views because I see myself as the son of Father in Heaven, the Holy One Blessed Be He, and in his Sacred Torah he had given us the land. And he said to Abraham our ancestor that 'To you I will give the Land of Canaan, your own land when you were a small people.'"

"What do you think will eventually be the solution?"

"There is no solution. . . . They are fanatics, these Arabs. . . . They would lynch you worse than the Nazis did to us. . . . There is no one to make peace with. . . . Like it was in 1948, they want to throw us into the sea."

Hussein expressed similar views from the extremist Palestinian perspective:

"My name is Hussein. I was born in Al-Quds (Jerusalem) in the year 1976. . . . Today I am married, and have a two-year-old daughter who we named 'Philistin' (Palestine). Today I work in Nazareth and work as a manager in an international company.

"About twelve years ago, I became a member in an organization called the Popular Front for the Liberation of Palestine. It is an organization that calls to the end of the Palestinian-Israeli conflict in a 'comprehensive' way. That means the liberation of the complete land of Palestine from the Jordan River to the Mediterranean Sea. To this day, I support any organization that calls for the destruction of the State of Israel. Because this is Palestinian land, and it will remain Palestinian.

"I see that Palestinian actions, the attacks inside the State of Israel, as heroic actions resulting from a natural reaction of any person subjected to repression, torture, and humiliation. . . . I am sure that all the Jews are murderers. Just because they conquered my land, I hate every Jew."

"What do you think will be the ultimate solution to the conflict?"

"Solution! I don't think there is a solution because [there] is not a middle point between good and evil. The Palestinian lands are our right, and the Israelis have to return to where they came from. And what is called 'peace,' it's a lie that the world has supported to promote the Israeli interests at the expense of the Palestinians. . . . The Israeli-Palestinian conflict is an existential conflict and not a conflict about money that you can divide between the two parties. Nobody has the right to give up our land and the blood of martyrs, what Israel planted is death and violence and there, that is the only thing it will get back from us."

Suppose that Itamar was the prime minister of Israel and Hussein was the president of the Palestinian Authority. Imagine that you have to negotiate a peace agreement between Itamar and Hussein as the duly appointed representatives of Israel and the Palestinians. How might you go about the process, considering their extreme beliefs?

Jumping into the substantive issues might be a big mistake. As Drew Westen learned in his neuroimaging study of Democratic and Republican partisans, emotionally biased reasoning strengthens defensive beliefs, associating the participant's version of information with positive emotional relief and elimination of distress. Partisan beliefs become calcified, and "the person can learn very little from new data." In all likelihood, Itamar and Hussein will not be moved by rational, logical, objective arguments for peace. Instead, as information that conflicts with their beliefs is presented to them in an attempt to convince them to give up land for peace, they probably will become more rigid and extreme in their positions.

This is exactly what happened at Camp David in 2000 between Israeli prime minister Ehud Barak and Palestinian Authority president Yasser Arafat, and it may well continue to be one of the major blunders of every peace attempt since then.

In the evening of July 24, 2000, after weeks of grueling and generally unproductive discussions at Camp David, President Clinton and his advisers presented Arafat with a plan for Jerusalem that gave Arafat a sovereign presidential compound inside the Muslim Quarter of east Jerusalem for his exclusive use.[14]

To Arafat, the offer was another perceived insult and sign of disrespect. His reality was that the Palestinian people and the larger Islamic world would never consent to an agreement that would grant Israeli sovereignty over an Islamic holy site.

Arafat is reported to have stated, "So there will be a small island surrounded by Israeli soldiers who control the entrances. This is not what we are asking for. We are asking for full Palestinian sovereignty over Jerusalem occupied in 1967."[15]

Clinton reportedly went ballistic. "If the Israelis can make compromises and you can't, I should go home. You have been here fourteen days and said no to everything. These things have consequences; failure will mean the end of the peace process. . . . Let's let hell break loose and live with the consequences," he angrily said to Arafat.

Later in the conversation, Arafat said, "Do you want to come to my funeral? I would rather die than agree to Israeli sovereignty over the Haram al-Sharif."

The summit was over. It had ended in complete failure. The Al-Aqsa intifada started later that year.

What could have been done differently?

*   *   *

The one thing I have learned in mediating thousands of conflicts and disputes is that when people fight, emotions dominate reason. If the people in the fight cannot work through their emotions, negotiating an agreement or solution is generally impossible. Impasse is almost always due to the emotions and feelings of the parties. No amount of cajoling, threatening, or persuading will move a mind if it is emotionally locked into a strong belief. That is why Drew Westen's study strikes such a deep chord—the brain phenomena he discovered play out tragically time after time in conflicts around the world. It sometimes seems that diplomatic negotiators, mediators, and heads of state are oblivious to the fact that deeply held beliefs cannot be bargained away.

What is needed when two or more belief systems collide into deep and intractable conflict is a mediator willing to help the parties look at their belief systems with each other—something they are extremely resistant to doing. The mediator must have courage because the usual first reactions from the parties in conflict are anger, fear, blame, and accusation directed at the mediator. Simply raising the possibility of talking to the enemy about beliefs may be very threatening. As a result, the mediator must often invest significant time in preparing the parties to meet. Preparation includes lengthy individual meetings in which the mediator listens, asks questions, gently probes for self-reflection, and builds trust. The mediator must become the impartial and neutral trusted friend of each side so that when the parties come together, they can look to the mediator for psychological safety and soothing.

This sounds like a lot of psychobabble to many professional diplomats who prefer to imagine they can put feelings aside and jump right into the substantive issues.

"Why should we waste time with this feeling crap when we have to negotiate a deal?" is the common reaction of the political Type-A personalities responsible for sensitive conflict negotiations.

As a mediator, when I hear people say they are not into "touchy-feely" or that feelings are irrelevant, I know that the feelings are most important. What is really being said is "I am afraid of my feelings. I am not interested in the other person's feelings. I want to be safe. I want to be in control."

My job as mediator is to ignore this resistance, to not worry about my reputational interest, to recognize the underlying fears, and to create a safe container to hold them.

So what might a mediated conversation look like between Hussein and Itamar or between President Abbas and Prime Minister Netanyahu in 2010? How, in the context of high-stakes international mediation, can two extreme beliefs intractably opposed to each other come together with the help of a skilled mediator?

One technique is to ask for the story to be told indirectly: "President Abbas, you represent many people with many different perspectives on this conflict. Tell us about the people who are most angry about the settlements." We are not asking Abbas for his personal story, although it will naturally come out. We are asking him to tell the many stories of his people, the stories that support his belief structure and make him feel good about his cause.

We can expect his Israeli counterpart, Prime Minister Netanyahu, for example, to roll his eyes and reflexively dismiss the stories. Even if Netanyahu is well schooled in masking his emotions, that is how he will be emotionally reacting under the surface. Count on it. The upshot is that Netanyahu will not and cannot listen to Abbas's stories. Listening thus becomes the primary job of the mediator. Through the presence of the mediator, Netanyahu hears the stories, and they actually penetrate slightly into his belief systems.

During the storytelling, Abbas will undoubtedly become emotional. The mediator's role is to validate those emotions, to help Abbas clarify them, and to implicitly grant Abbas permission to feel those emotions in the presence of the archenemy.

When Abbas is finished, the question is asked of Netanyahu, "Tell us the stories of the settlers." Again, we are not asking for

Netanyahu's personal story. We are asking for his beliefs to emerge in the stories and narratives of the people he represents. The stories become metaphors for the conflict. They will not be reconcilable, nor should they be. As Netanyahu tells his stories, his emotions will be validated, acknowledged, and clarified. The mediator has to contain these explosive feelings by creating a safe space. As long as the emotions are directed at the mediator and not so much at the other side, the other side can listen, hear, and absorb the feelings.

The next step might be to ask each side about the values that underlie the stories. "President Abbas, what are the most important values your people hold as expressed by their stories?" Typically, values are layered and complex. With persistence, however, fundamental values emerge: hope, peace, honor, economic opportunity, security, certainty, and freedom.

When Netanyahu is asked the same question, the same values will eventually appear. Now common ground is being discovered. The mediator will play a powerful role as an observer as he looks for and comments on the possibility of shared values.

In this case, the mediator might reflect on the deep injustices experienced by the people in the stories—the Palestinians have lost their ancestral land; the Israelis have sought a homeland free from persecution and close to God.

Sometimes, the beliefs are so intensely held that nothing further can be achieved. However, the fact that each side has been willing to be present as the other side shares deeply held feelings is a critical step toward peace.

This process also contains within it a great danger. Because the process invites some honesty into a relationship previously characterized by posturing, insensitivity, and lack of authenticity, participants may experience personal transformation. The danger is that they will transform themselves faster than they can bring along their constituencies. Any mediator engaging in this work must be prepared to help the parties face the arduous work of convincing skeptics in their respective communities of a new relationship. The conversation will have to be repeated through the layers of the political establishments and constituencies. The goal is to engage the participants in thinking about how such conversations can occur across their respective societies.

This may seem a waste of time. After all, there has been no bargaining over hard issues like boundaries, cease-fires, disarmament, political succession, transitional governance, and the rest of the meaty subjects of international negotiation. But that is the point! The substantive issues *cannot* be resolved in the face of deep-seated beliefs without first participating in some process that allows for a deeper penetration into those beliefs. I have personally witnessed days of mediation passing without any apparent progress on a single substantive topic, only to see a complete agreement come together in less than an hour. The substantive agreement was easily achieved once the parties had finally heard each other at a deeper level. They did not necessarily agree with each other, but they had had the time and space to tell their stories, to be listened to, and to reflect on the meanings implicit in the stories. This is the core of a twenty-first-century approach to international negotiation.

*   *   *

Douad Nassar has turned Daher's Farm into a center for nonviolent activism. With help from volunteers in Germany, Nassar and his wife, Jihan, have started a summer camp called Tent of Nations (www.tentofnations.org), where children twelve to sixteen years old, from war-torn countries, are invited to come learn about cross-cultural understanding and reconciliation. The center hosts visiting peace groups and sponsors talks, workshops, and retreats on peace and peace building.

"We have to move out of this circle of blaming others," Nassar said to reporter Boudreaux. "Frustration is a power. It can prompt us to react violently, or to despair. We need to invest it creatively, building something, even if it is small."

Mayor Goldstein and Nassar live about half a mile apart, but the two have never met. That is why Nassar proposed a dialogue with his Jewish neighbors, as long as they meet him unarmed.

"We have to change the picture we have of each other—the enemy picture, radical settlers and radical Palestinians," he said. "If we talk face to face, we could lay a foundation for peace, a peace that cannot be dictated by our leaders."

Our beliefs sustain us and guide us. Until international diplomats are willing to engage with beliefs deeply and authentically, without seeking to change, challenge, or reconcile, only reaching out to understand, peace will remain elusive.

Chapter 5

Biases

Imagine it is 250,000 years ago. You are a male hominid standing on an African savannah, and a pride of lions is out there. They spot you. Rationally, you have no chance. If you run, they will give chase and cut you down. If you freeze, they will attack. So what do you do? You invoke the mystical gods of your tribal fathers, your ancestors, and the spirits of the nature kingdom. Thus fortified with the knowledge and belief that you are protected and will overcome, you charge the lions, yelling, screaming, and waving your spear. The lions, somewhat full from their last meal of antelope, take one look at this large thing running at them aggressively and take off in a dead sprint. No way do they want to be around something that crazy. You survived. Your faith in yourself, your connection to the nature spirits, your ancestors, and their gods is reinforced, and you feel pretty damn good about yourself. You go back to the extended family that is your tribe and tell the story, with a few embellishments. The children listen with wonder and absorb your lessons. You mate with your female, and sure enough, she becomes pregnant again. Your genes, full of optimism, self-confidence, and belief in your mastery of the universe are passed on to the next generation.

Evolutionary biologists, psychologists, neuroscientists, behavioral economists, and a host of other scholars and researchers have concluded that human beings are full of themselves as a matter of hard fact. We could not have survived the harsh environment we evolved within unless we were overconfident, optimistic, and felt in control. While this is a good thing for individual success and happiness, it is devastating to humans in groups larger than an extended family and as a species. For the inherent biases that work in small groups to overcome adversity and maintain optimism lead to tragic decisions regarding war, violence, climate change, and the environment. These biases make mincemeat out of the rational-choice theory of human behavior and, more importantly, make successful negotiations difficult to achieve.

So, what are cognitive biases?

Psychologists tell us that cognitive biases are distortions we create for ourselves. It is not that we fail to see what is in front of us. It's that we process what we perceive with predictable slants.

Our biases usually have a strong emotional content associated with them. Our biases help us manage our anxiety by creating a slightly altered reality. This private reality, which is mostly subconscious, is one in which we, for example, see ourselves as above average. By interpreting events through this positive bias, we can explain away our failures and protect our self-esteem. A healthy dose of overconfidence, tempered with common sense, can often get us through a tough situation. In conflicts, however, our cognitive biases seem to go into overdrive, distorting reality to the point that to outsiders it seems like the people in conflict are in a different universe.

I AM SMARTER THAN YOU

The typical international negotiator, and every other human being, unconsciously believes the following:

- Thinks she is more talented than she is.
- Thinks her side is more likely to win than is objectively the case.
- Is willing to take a huge future risk to avoid taking a small loss today.
- Tends to reject any ideas from her opponent simply because the idea originates with the other side.
- Thinks her land, settlements, status, and so on are worth more than they are simply because she owns them.
- Believes she can control future events by force of will.
- Believes she will win because she is right and just and holy.
- Believes she has studied all the relevant facts objectively and carefully, and believes they support her view of the situation.
- Cannot evaluate uncertainty because she does not understand probability analysis.
- Is reluctant to do anything to interfere with the way the gods have ordered the universe.

Reams of journal articles document the evidence of these biases. Since the 1960s, controlled experiments have demonstrated that language, memory, and thought are all biased. We consistently overrate our health, leadership ability, competence, athletic ability, and our integrity. We believe we are more intelligent, more attractive, more just, and more skillful than others. We believe that we are more likely than others to have gifted children, succeed at work, and do well at future tasks. These biases exist within each of us regardless of our culture, language, or context. In short, they are hardwired into every human brain. Researchers are uncovering the neurological mechanisms underlying these biases and are finding gating mechanisms in our brains that control the flow of information from the "unconscious" to the "conscious" centers. These gating mechanisms appear to be associated with many of our cognitive biases. It seems that we simply filter information in certain predefined ways that lead us, in the right contexts and circumstances, to poor negotiations and decision making.

The research also shows that people overestimate ideological differences between their groups and opposing groups, seeing opposition viewpoints as more extreme than they really are.[2] Groups with high levels of self-esteem demonstrate higher levels of hostility and violence, and group violence seems to be linked to beliefs in the superiority of the group.[3] Nearly all our modern tyrants, terrorists, and war makers have believed in their own cultural superiority. Osama bin Laden believes in the superiority of Wahabism, a fundamental form of Islam, in the same way that former president George W. Bush believes in the superiority of democracy and unfettered capitalism. Each believes his culture is superior to the other, and each has been willing to unleash violence to prove the point.

In addition to these powerful cognitive biases, there are motivational biases at play. Motivational biases protect us emotionally from conflicting, unfamiliar, or unpleasant information. *Groupthink*, a term created by twentieth-century social psychologist Irving Janis, is a form of motivational bias.[4] In his social psychological study of disastrous decisions made in the twentieth century by international political leaders including Presidents Kennedy, Johnson, and Nixon, Janis identified characteristics of groupthink that systematically prevent cogent analysis and evaluation:

- A shared illusion of invulnerability
- An unquestioned belief in the group's inherent morality
- Collective attempts to maintain shaky, but cherished assumptions
- Stereotyping out-groups as too evil for negotiation or too weak to be a threat
- Self-censorship of debate or counterarguments to conform to the group
- A collective illusion of unanimity in the majority viewpoint based on a faulty assumption that silence means consent

- Direct pressure on dissenters to maintain group loyalty
- Self-appointed mind guards (thought police) to protect the group and leader that might threaten the group's resolve[5]

The problem with groupthink is that it closes the door to possibilities that could actually promote the goals of the group. Because groupthink is self-reinforcing, it is extremely difficult to work with in negotiations. If the negotiations are not mediated, the side facing the groupthink can become cynical about the intentions on the other side of the table.

Cognitive and motivational biases lead us to interpret new information to fit our ideas of how the world is or to justify our preferred courses of action. These biases are important to healthy, functioning human beings. They lead to higher motivation, greater persistence, more effective performance, and greater success. People who lack these cognitive and motivational biases are generally unsuccessful in life.

The dark side is that these biases create closed-mindedness. In conflict, we literally filter out negative information. The more we are threatened, the greater the effect of the biases on our decision making. This leads to an insight missed by many world leaders: threats of sanction or war have the unintended consequence of shutting down clear decision making. Instead of creating a cool calculus of risks and benefits, threatened decision makers see themselves as more likely to win, not less. The conflict over Kashmir is an illustration of this problem.

INDIA AND PAKISTAN—BIASES RUN AMOK

The history of the troubled relations between Pakistan and India demonstrates how unconscious cognitive and motivation biases lead to war rather than to peace. Few other conflicts, with the possible exception of the Palestinian-Israeli dispute, have proved to be as intractable.

Over the years, Pakistani decision makers have overestimated the desire of Kashmir to be a part of Pakistan and have underestimated Indian military power and its likely responses to force. The biases leading to these poor decisions have been rooted in Pakistan's political and social structure. Without open public debate, Pakistan has been unable to consider alternative assessments of Indian motivations and capabilities. While the same strong nationalistic tendencies exist in India against Pakistan, India's democratic institutions and practices have permitted alternative viewpoints to be aired and discussed.

The first example arose in 1947 when Pakistan decided to invade Kashmir. Looking at the situation objectively, one has to wonder at the Pakistani self-deception. Under the terms of the transfer of power from Great Britain, all movable military equipment, supplies, and troops had been divided 30/70 between Pakistan and India. The Pakistani army was desperately short of officers and manpower, most of which were helping civilian authorities with the refugee crisis caused by partition. In addition, the vast majority of military bases, weapons factories, and training camps were located in India. Objectively, Pakistan was undermanned and ill equipped for any serious military action outside its borders, yet it decided to provoke a war with India. To no one's surprise except the Pakistanis, Pakistan promptly lost.

There are a number of cognitive biases that appear to have been active in Pakistani decision making. Pakistani decision makers seemed to be under the influence of what is called the *Lake Wobegon effect*. In the mythical town of Lake Wobegon, created by Garrison Keillor, all the women are strong, all the men are handsome, and all the children are above average. In other words, the Lake Wobegon effect describes the positive affirmation bias that "I am better than average." The Pakistani military was caught by this bias when it mistakenly believed that its superior skill and fortitude was greater than that of India's military and therefore would overcome India's military advantages.

The *endowment effect* occurs when we overvalue what we

own. This is a robust effect, meaning that it cuts across cultures and gender. We tend to place more value on what we own than what is realistic. The Pakistanis fell prey to the endowment effect when they believed that they "owned" Kashmir and were therefore unwilling to give it up for any price.

Self-deceptive overconfidence arises when we, without empirical justification, believe that we can overcome adversity. Pakistani decision makers deceived themselves into thinking that they could wrest control of Kashmir from India.

The *false consensus effect* is particularly insidious. It comes into play when we assume that who and what we are represents what is normal. It's a false consensus because it is based on an inference drawn from a statistical sample of one. In Pakistan's case, its decision makers believed that Pakistan represented the norm of Islam, and that all of Kashmir was of the same Islamic belief. Therefore, the decision makers wrongly believed Kashmir would support annexation by Pakistan.

The *self-righteous bias* is another positive illusion that arises when we believe we hold a higher moral ground than everyone else. It is a particular application of the Lake Wobegon Effect to matters of values and morality. The Pakistani decision makers held a firm belief that God was on their side and saw themselves as more righteous than their Indian counterparts and therefore certain to win the war.

Similar to the self-righteous bias is our innate belief in a *just world*. This bias operates to cause us to believe we are entitled to justice as we subjectively define it. In fact, the world is neither just nor unjust, and we have no objective reason to believe otherwise. The Pakistanis believed that their world was just, which required a smashing victory over India.

These biases are exquisitely captured by Pakistani Major General Akbar in his book about the war with India:

> In the remotest of our villages, the humblest of our people possess a self-confidence and ready willingness to march forward

into India—a spirit the equivalent of which cannot be found on the other side. It may take many generations to create such a spirit [in India]. . . . In India, the absence of homogeneity, a penetration in a direction can result in separation of different units geographically as well as morally because there is no basic unity among Shudras, Brahmins, Sikhs, Hindus, and Muslims who will follow their own different interests. At present, and for a long time to come, India is in the same position as she was centuries ago, exposed to disintegration in emergencies.[6]

The second war, in 1965, was instigated again by Pakistan. Despite being outgunned and outmanned again, the Pakistanis believed that the Indian military was not prepared to defend against an attack in Kashmir. The Pakistani leadership drew a flawed inference that India lacked the courage and heart for battle. They also believed, without objective basis, that the population in Kashmir supported annexation to Pakistan. In addition, the Pakistani military leadership had confidence in what it perceived as the inherent martial qualities of Muslim soldiers compared to the nonmartial Hindu counterparts in the Indian army. Finally, Pakistani leaders incorrectly interpreted from one intemperate public speech by a Chinese leader that China would support and assist Pakistan in the event of war with India.

Expecting a quick victory, the Pakistanis were surprised by the fast and resourceful response of the Indian military. By September 1965, the war was at a stalemate, and Pakistan gave up the fight. The United States had no interest in resolving the dispute, which enabled the Soviet Union to step in as mediator. Soviet premier Alexei Kosygin persuaded the two sides to reach a superficial settlement that included a cease-fire, a return to the status quo ante, and an agreement not to use force to resolve future disputes. The underlying causes of the conflict remained undiscussed and unresolved.

In the background, both countries were racing to develop nuclear weapons. In May 1998, to the horror of the international community, both countries tested nuclear weapons, demonstrating their newfound capacity to annihilate each other and everyone around them.

India and Pakistan were pressured to reduce their tensions. As a result, the prime ministers of the two countries met in Lahore to sign an agreement reiterating their countries' desire for peaceful relations. During this visit, Prime Minister Vajpayee of India visited the Minar-e-Sharif memorial and affirmed Pakistan's right to exist as a country. This was an important political and deeply symbolic gesture that created the opportunity for further reductions in hostilities and tensions. Unfortunately, elements in the Pakistani government interpreted this symbolic visit as a weakness, and began another military operation in Kashmir. Again, the Pakistanis were stalemated by a superior Indian force.

How might a mediator deal with these types of cognitive biases?

As of the time I am writing this, in September 2010, Pakistan is in an undeclared state of civil war. The Pashtun Taliban in the west and northwest of Pakistan are rebelling against the central government. At the same time, the Pakistan intelligence service, the ISI, is supporting the Afghan Taliban in hopes of destabilizing the pro-India Afghanistan government. Meanwhile, India and Pakistan spent two days in July talking about their differences with no results. To complicate all of this, the Indus River has flooded 25 percent of Pakistan, displacing over twenty million people. Pakistan is out of money and resources to deal with this natural catastrophe. The Pakistani Taliban is claiming that the flooding demonstrates the wrath of God against nonbelievers and has threatened to kill any foreign aid workers who attempt to assist Pakistani refugees. Whether Pakistan can survive as a functioning nation-state is highly questionable right now.

Assume you are mediating between Pakistan and India in a quiet, behind-the-scenes peace process. How might you help Pakistan overcome its perennially poor decision making caused by its cognitive biases? How do you get people to see things differently when they already think they are right, that they are smarter, holier, more righteous, and better aligned with God against India?

Sometimes mediators have to reality check the parties. Reality checking is the subtle tightrope of asking people to examine their assumptions about the conflict without challenging their self-esteem. If the mediator is too timid, the reality is not sufficiently checked. If the mediator is too aggressive, people will feel threatened. Sometimes, a mediator may help people question their assumptions, only to face deeper intransigence as the new logic chain leads to an unhappy result. As we saw in the previous chapters, trying to change beliefs with logic is difficult at best, making reality checking challenging when people are not open to considering alternative perspectives. In addition, reality checking only works if the mediator is seen as a trusted friend. No one likes their position to be challenged, so it helps if the questions are coming from someone who is respected and who has no dog in the fight.

One of the phrases we use when training mediators is "You have to earn your turn." This means that mediators have to invest in personal relationships and build up a savings account of trust. During the peace process, there will always be difficult phases when you will draw down that trust account. There is no overdraft protection in mediation, and a bounced check in mediation is usually disastrous because it means the mediator's trust and credibility is gone.

Deposits to the trust account are made from listening to stories, creating empathic connections, building friendships, sharing food, problem solving on smaller issues, and just spending time together. The mediator's job is to understand, not to be understood.

When cognitive biases seem as embedded as they appear to be in the Pakistani leadership, a mediator may take months or even years to create a trusted relationship. This is not the time frame under which diplomats or their governments think, which is one reason why the practice of mediation should be left to highly skilled professionals. Common sense tells us that Ambassador Do-Good cannot blow into Islamabad, conduct a series of high-end meetings over the course of a few weeks, and expect to influence any change in fundamental decision making. Considering the fragmentation of Pakistani civil society, relationships will have to be built with the military, the intelligence service, the government, and the members of the civil society. In fact, a mediator assigned to the India-Pakistan dispute may spend more time building consensus and peace within Pakistan than mediating between Pakistan and India.

In Pakistan, power is uneasily shared between the military, the civilians, and the intelligence service. These groups share common biases. They believe in the superiority of Islam. They believe that Pakistan is foreordained to be a pure Islamic state in South Asia. They believe that Kashmir rightfully belongs to Pakistan. They believe that India is a corrupt bed of mongrels.

Ideally, the world would like to see Pakistan and India coexist in peace. If Pakistani leaders were not enmeshed in the belief of their moral superiority over India, they might be more pragmatic about peace. How might you go about reality checking the Pakistani leaders? Here's an example of how it might be started:

"Tell me about India. What do you think are its motivations around Pakistan?" the mediator asks the Pakistani negotiator.

"Ever since partition, they have wanted Pakistan. They believe Pakistan should have never come into existence."

"What do they believe today?"

"The same, of course. They want Kashmir, and they want to control Afghanistan."

"Who do you think the Indians fear more, China or Pakistan?"

Silence.

"Well, why do you think India fears China?"

"China and India have large populations. They are competing for resources and economic development. China is much larger than India. India feels that it may not be able to compete with China for resources and technology."

"Does India compete with Pakistan for resources?"

"Yes, of course, in Kashmir."

"Does Kashmir have sufficient resources to drive India's economy?"

"No, of course not."

"Other than Kashmir, does India see Pakistan as a resource competitor?"

"No, we are too small to be a competitor with India."

"So there may be some competition for resources in Kashmir, but otherwise not much."

"Yes. I think so."

"How long is the border between India and Pakistan?"

"About 1,200 kilometers."

"And how long is the border between India and China?"

"About 3,500 kilometers."

"Might the Indians have more concern over the Chinese border than your border?"

"Probably."

"Does any of this suggest that India is focusing on issues dating back to 1947 with Pakistan?"

"Well, probably not."

"So if India is more focused on China than Pakistan, what does that say about Pakistan's obsession with India?"

"Perhaps we have been focusing too much inward and not enough outward."

"Perhaps."

The inquiry is intended to open up new perspectives while challenging Pakistani conventional wisdom. This is what reality checking is all about.

Another line of questions might go as follows:

"I know you are convinced that your military can defeat India. But let us imagine the unthinkable for a moment. How could India defeat you?"

Focusing the decision makers to examine how they might lose may be painful. The decision makers may respond aggressively with something like, "That is impossible! It could never happen!"

Or, "How dare you question our military strength. You know

nothing about our capability. You are a mediator and not a military analyst!" Whenever a mediator is the target of a personal attack, he knows he is facing a deep-seated cognitive bias. The decision maker would rather insult the mediator than face the reality check.

The mediator can often circle back behind the cognitive bias by creating a new logic chain:

"So let us say you win this time? Then what?"

"We have triumphed. Islam has triumphed. God has proven to us the righteousness of our cause."

"Do you think that winning will end the conflict with India?"

"Yes, of course. We were superior."

"Is it possible that India will amass an overwhelming force to throw you out of Kashmir?"

Silence.

"And then you will have to fight to defend your gain. How many generations do you expect this conflict to last before it is over? What are the prospects of a final peaceful settlement for your grandchildren or great-grandchildren?"

Persistent questions that poke people to rethink their assumptions can be effective. Sometimes, the decision maker can see multiple perspectives but faces a constituency that suffers from cognitive biases. The mediator can support the decision maker in thinking about how to shift the political dynamics to a broader perspective.

IRAN AND NUCLEAR POWER— MORE BIASES AT WORK

The problem involving Iran's development of enriched uranium and its refusal to answer questions about nuclear weapons development is another classic example of how cognitive biases deeply affect international negotiations. This issue is particularly dangerous because of the conflict between Iran and Israel, carried out in Gaza and Lebanon by Hamas and Hezbollah, Iran's proxies. Should Israel feel sufficiently threatened by Iran's development of nuclear weapons, it could launch a preemptive conventional or nuclear attack on Iran. The resulting chaos would be devastating to the people of Iran and Israel, not to mention its effect on long-term international political stability. Negotiations with Iran concerning its compliance with the Nuclear Non-Proliferation Treaty therefore have a special urgency and importance.

Suppose you are negotiating with Iran about its nuclear development issues. You don't trust the Iranian government any farther than you can throw it, for a number of reasons:

- The current regime is undemocratic, and you don't trust undemocratic regimes.
- The current president has made inflammatory statements that indicate his personal aversion to the West and to Israel.
- Iran "protesteth too much" about its civilian intentions for nuclear enrichment. It simply fails to answer some basic questions that an honest nation would be happy to answer.
- Iran has insisted that it has the right to an enrichment program to replenish its medical isotope reactor. The problem is that even with enriched uranium, Iran cannot manufacture the fuel rods necessary to refuel its nuclear plant. That can only be done by France or Argentina, the original nuclear power plant contractors.
- If Iran can enrich to 20 percent, what will stop it from enriching to 90 percent, which is weapons grade?
- Iran's statements are inconsistent with its actions.
- Iran supports Hamas and Hezbollah, which are actively engaging in warfare against Israel in Gaza and Lebanon.
- Iran supports a monotheistic Islamic theocracy to the exclusion of all other ideas.
- Some of Iran's leaders have expressed a strange apocalyptic vision of the end of time and return of the Mahdi, which they believe will be hastened by nuclear destruction.

- Iran abuses human rights. It denies basic freedoms to social outliers, women, and dissidents, while accusing the developed world, and especially the United States, of the same thing.

What are some of the cognitive biases that could be influencing Iran's decision makers?

First, there is the framing effect. Essentially, we are hardwired to reject choices framed as losses. Benedetto De Martino and his colleagues at University College London set up a simple experiment to see what happens to the brain when facing these kinds of choices.[7]

Volunteers were placed in a scanner and told that they had just received $40. They were then given one of two choices:

> Keep $20 or gamble for $40, or
> Lose $20 or gamble for $40.

In either case, had they chosen not to gamble, they have $20.

Volunteers told that they could keep $20 or gamble tended to keep the money. They took the safer choice, and their brains showed little emotional activity coupled with significant reasoning activity. The volunteers told that they could lose $20 or gamble for $40, tended to choose the gamble. In other words, when presented with the choice between an immediate loss and an uncertain future, they avoided the immediate loss by making the riskier future decision. When making this decision, the emotional centers of their brains activated, while the reasoning part of their brains shut down. It seems that when a choice is framed between a sure loss and risky, uncertain future, emotions take over and the riskier choice tends to be made.

Consider this in the context of Iran's leaders. Their decision has been framed by the international community as "Give up your nuclear ambitions or face severe economic sanctions." The choice is between an immediate loss—no nuclear weapons development—and an uncertain, future outcome—the potential negative effects of economic sanctions. This type of choice activates the emotional centers and inhibits the reasoning centers of the brain. It should be no surprise that Iran's leaders will tend to avoid the immediate loss of nuclear weapons.

Phrased another way, the benefits of future economic trade and development are not seen as equal to the immediate loss of prestige associated with being a nuclear power. Most likely, Iran's leaders will accept economic sanctions in lieu of giving up nuclear weapons. Internally, they will use the hardship of the sanctions to generate political support for their continued intransigence, thus creating the unintended consequence of strengthening Iran's resolve not to abandon nuclear weapons development.

Could reframing help? Maybe or maybe not. Perhaps the choice could be framed as "We will help you modernize your nuclear reactors for medical isotope production, or you can choose to continue with nuclear weapons development and face severe economic sanctions, including a complete embargo on modernization of your current plants. Your choice." Framing the choice this way opposes the gain to the risky choice and activates the reasoning part of the brain.

In addition to the framing effect, the Iranian leaders are suffering, like the Pakistanis, from an implicit belief in a just world: We need to see the world as an orderly, rational, fair place. Goodness, especially mine, is rewarded. Evil, especially yours, is punished. This cognitive bias has skewed Iranian perceptions to favor its leaders' views of reality. For example, the Iranian leaders believe that their refusal to abide by the International Atomic Energy Agency (IAEA) demand for inspection and disclosure of the Iranian nuclear program is justified by Iran's higher moral stance.

Iranian president Mahmoud Ahmadinejad has said:

All problems existing in our world today emanate from the fact that rulers have distanced themselves from human values, morality, and the teachings of divine messengers. Regrettably, in the current international relations, selfishness and insatiable greed have taken the place of such humanitarian concepts as love, sacrifice, dignity, and justice. The belief in the One God has been replaced with selfishness. Some have taken the place of God and insist to impose their values and wishes on others.[8]

Mr. Ahmadinejad's public statement suggests that he believes in a just world controlled by the "One God" and, implicitly, that "One God" favors Iran over others. These cognitive biases will distort decision making.

Iran's leaders also seem to suffer from the false consensus bias because they see themselves as representative of all countries oppressed by developed countries. Iran clearly is not representative of all the countries its leaders claim to represent. The Iranian decision to oppose the IAEA is, however, consistent with the false consensus bias.

Mr. Ahmadinejad has said:

The main question is this: What was the role of the previous ruling system in America and its allies? Were they the representatives of the world nations? Were they elected by the world nations? Do they have representation by the world nations to interfere in the affairs of all parts of the world and especially our region? Don't these actions, the occupation of Iraq and Afghanistan, count as examples of selfishness, racism, discrimination, and violating the dignity and independence of other nations?[9]

In placing Iran as the accuser of America and its allies, Mr. Ahmadinejad believes that Iran is representative of nations other than America and its allies. He is demonstrating a classic example of false consensus effect.

The Iranian leadership, in deciding to resist the IAEA and the UN Security Council, seems overconfident in its assessment of world opinion, the effect of economic sanctions, and the potential of military action to eliminate its nuclear program. Like the Pakistani leadership, the Iranian leadership has displayed unwarranted self-confidence in its ability to stand against all threats.

Furthermore, the greater the threat of sanctions or military action against Iran, the stronger the illusion of self-confidence to make the right decisions grows within the Iranian leadership.

Iran also seems be influenced by the endowment effect, which causes us to overvalue that which we believe we own. President Ahmadinejad has said:

> The Iranian nation's right to nuclear energy is nonnegotiable. No one can ever force us to back down an inch from the path that we are currently treading.[10]

If Iran believes it has a sovereign right to develop nuclear weapons, even if covertly, its leaders will overvalue it. Pressure from the international community will only add to the reactive devaluation of potential alternatives, such as supplying enriched uranium for Iran's medical isotope reactors. Outside pressure threatens Iran's freedom to select what it wants and its sense of autonomy, which it perceives as a threat to its existence. This pressure typically will incline Iran's leaders to choose an opposing course of action.

In summary, there are a number of cognitive biases that create a specific Iranian worldview. The biases are evolutionary adaptations to challenging and dangerous environments. As they are confronted with threats, Iranian leaders tend to become more self-confident, to have a greater positive illusion about their ability to control outcomes, and to more strongly believe in their own self-righteousness. They will ignore or discount any information that is inconsistent with their worldview. Furthermore, these biases become more pronounced as the threat of sanctions grows. This is, of course, exactly the opposite of what one would expect under a rational-choice theory of human behavior.

What might a conversation be like with an understanding of these biases?

"So let's say that your country has a nuclear weapon capability. What then?" a mediator might ask.

"We will be listened to. We will no longer be dismissed. They will have to listen to us. We will take our rightful place at the table of the superpowers."

"Respect, having an important voice, being influential, having the power to back it up. . . . Those are all important goals. Is there anything else along those lines that would benefit your country?"

Silence.

"Why do you think there is so much resistance to your country's nuclear weapon development?"

"They are trying to stop the rise of Islam. They are frightened of us and the sword we are forging. They want to keep us under their imperialistic thumbs and impose their sick, secular values on the One True Faith. We uphold the Light of Islam by resisting them and by becoming their equal."

"What do you think would happen if an Iranian-made nuclear weapon was detonated in Los Angeles and that fact was discovered? How much restraint would you expect the American people to show toward your country?"

Silence.

"What if you were in America's shoes? How much restraint would you show? What about the Israelis or the Europeans?" continues the mediator.

Silence.

"It is said that power flows in many directions in Iran. How unified are the various factions in a desire to control your country's nuclear weapons for purely defensive purposes?"

Another way to overcome these biases is to ask the question, "Why shouldn't Iran be allowed to develop nuclear weapons, if that is what it wishes to do?" The knee-jerk reaction is one of horror. "Let those crazy people have a weapon of mass destruction? No way!" But let's look at some of the follow-up questions that might be asked.

First, what is the real likelihood that Iran would use a nuclear weapon preemptively? I suspect that there is always a chance of a preemptive strike. However, Iran would surely expect a devastating reprisal by a number of different countries from which it could not expect to recover. In other words, starting a nuclear war would be a guarantee of national annihilation. Iran simply does not have the capacity to take out all its perceived enemies and therefore is left with the prospect of massive retaliation. The twentieth-century rubric Mutually Assured Destruction contained the United States–Soviet Union conflict in a series of low-level brushfires and proxy wars instead of a nuclear holocaust. The United States and the Soviets tacitly agreed to avoid direct confrontation because they each knew they would be destroyed in a nuclear war. What is the likelihood that, cognitive biases and all, Iran will be able to make the same assessment?

Second, what is the real likelihood that Iran will deliver nuclear weapons to its terrorist proxies in the Middle East? Maybe Iran would take this risk if supplying a nuclear weapon to Hezbollah was plausibly deniable. Still, the risk of discovery of that secret, which would eventually be uncovered, would also result in deep retaliation, loss of power and prestige, and probable war crimes indictments.

Neither of these questions is comforting because each is essentially unanswerable. However, by asking the questions and working through the various possibilities, decision makers can overcome some of the effects of their cognitive biases. This might lead to a conversation, through intermediaries or through secret direct talks, along the following lines:

"Give us assurances and prove to us that your intentions are defensive only."

"How do you think we should respond if you ever release a nuclear weapon preemptively?"

"Under what conditions do you think we would show restraint if one of your weapons got into the hands of Hezbollah and was detonated in Israel?"

"Do you think the Israelis would show the same restraint that we might be inclined to exercise?"

These questions might provoke silence, bitter outburst, or perhaps reflective dialogue. However, the questions might cause some Iranian leaders to reconsider their opinions and decisions in a new light.

There is a situation in which none of these questions will work. Certain elements of the Iranian government appear to follow an Islamic messianic prophecy. In this prophecy, the Fourteenth Imam, the Mahdi in the Shi'a faith, will appear at the end of time. As with many apocalyptic beliefs, these Iranian leaders have convinced themselves that the time of the prophecy draws near and that they are paving the way. Their delusions, if sufficiently strong, could compel them to believe that launching nuclear weapons to destroy Israel, the Persian Gulf oil fields, and European cities within reach of the Shabat 3 missiles will accelerate the coming of the Mahdi. They would gladly see the destruction of Iran in exchange for the chaos they create. The confluence of beliefs, biases, and social identities make any kind of intervention with these people extremely challenging. All that can be hoped for is that other political elements within Iran stop these people before they have the capacity to launch effective nuclear weapons.

In many negotiations, people are entrenched in cognitive and motivational biases that prevent them from listening to reason, from objectively evaluating evidence, from seeing other perspectives, from constructively problem solving, or from collaborating to find workable solutions. Threats only entrench and magnify these biases. In addition, the mere presence of antagonists will exaggerate the effects of cognitive biases. Behaviors such as grandstanding, outbursts, manipulation, insincerity, and disrespect should be expected.

Dealing with cognitive biases requires that decision makers receive objective information about the potential consequences flowing from the choice of war. The source of the information is as important at the messenger. If the Pentagon has run simulations on various Pakistani invasions of Kashmir showing a devastating Pakistani loss, is the United States the right messenger?

What if the conclusions were corroborated by a respected neutral nation? What if the messenger were a respected Islamic leader? Our knowledge of cognitive biases suggests that the information will be filtered no matter what. However, a subtle choice of messenger may create a greater chance that it will be heard and evaluated. In addition, conversations should be structured by skilled interveners who are as culturally acceptable as possible. In addition, the interveners must be impartial to outcomes, have experience in moderating high-conflict, high-emotion situations, and be deeply educated through practice, life experience, and formal education in the nature of human conflict.

As Nazee Moinian has written, "Change is slow to occur in the Middle East, where the past is very much a part of the present, and traditions are not only kept, but revered."[11]

All of this is certainly not guaranteed to succeed. However, these ideas work at the core of the problem, not at the periphery. Thus, solutions, if they can be found, will tend to be deeper and more durable.

Chapter 6

Family, Friends, and Not-Friends

AN ALBANIAN BLOOD FEUD

On the afternoon of August 3, 1998, forty-three-year-old Shtjefen Lamthi was walking through one of the main streets in Shkoder, Albania. As he passed a small tobacco kiosk, a man in his mid-thirties stepped into Lamthi's path, brought up a Kalashnikov assault rifle, and shot him. As Lamthi fell, the murderer shot him twenty-one more times, emptying the rifle's ammo clip. The assailant walked away, and none of the two hundred people who witnessed the murder came forward to identify him. As war correspondent Scott Anderson reported in a *New York Times Magazine* article in 1999,[1] this was a classic example of an honor killing based on the Albanian notion of *kanun*. The *kanun* is a book of rules and oaths that, if you live in the Albanian outback, require you to give your complete allegiance to your family and community. Blood vengeance by murder can become a sacred duty to defend the honor of your family. Shtjefen Lamthi's murder, by Leka Rrushkadoli, was such a murder, avenging a death occurring thirteen years earlier.

At its core, the *kanun* is about defending honor, since a man who has been dishonored is considered dead. Small offenses and dishonors can be settled through more peaceful means, while greater offenses require vengeance killings. Under the *kanun*, murder is the ultimate dishonor to a family. The family lives in disgrace until it can obtain revenge by killing the killer. Of course, once this is done, the killer's family is in disgrace, and the cycle must repeat itself. Occasionally, these conflicts are mediated to peace, but not very often.

The rules of *kanun* vividly illustrate an important, yet seemingly ignored aspect of international conflict and of international negotiation: social identity. *Social identity* is the idea that people define themselves by their groups. In essence, they see themselves as having a social identity. Social identity theory is supported by a huge amount of empirical evidence, both psychological and anecdotal.

People categorize and attach themselves and others into groups as a way of describing attributes, including their own. Since we each have a basic need to see ourselves positively compared to others, we tend to exaggerate our similarities with our groups and differences with other groups. This group identification provides us with a sense of security and increases self-esteem. It also helps us simplify a complex world by organizing people into groups.

We have multiple social identities, which become active depending on the group and context in which we find ourselves. Social identities regulate our behaviors as members of groups. These behaviors may include conformity, stereotyping members of out-groups, favoritism toward members of in-groups, and discrimination against members of out-groups. For example, the typical religious fundamentalist movement demands strict conformity to a set of shared beliefs; the group benefits from the cohesion resulting from that conformity. Members remain obedient to the group and gain higher self-esteem from the group's singular identity. The preconscious processing goes something like "I feel good because I am a member of this group." A religious fundamentalist member regards himself as uniquely blessed and is able to treat out-group members as damned. We can see examples of social identities everywhere once we know what to look for. We'll get there, but first let's follow the story in Albania.

As Anderson reports in his story, the incident that led to Lamthi's murder in 1998 occurred on the night of January 13, 1985. Noue Rrushkadoli stopped by Preka Lamthi's house to visit. Preka's younger brother Shtjefen was present, along with a few other neighbors. As was the custom, the men started drinking heavily. At one point, Noue became angry—apparently he was a belligerent drunk—and overturned the dining room table. This was not mere spite, as Noue knew that toppling the host's dining table was one of the gravest of insults to be committed by a guest in an Albanian home. Preka ordered Noue from the house. Noue pulled a knife and stabbed Shtjefen six times before he was overpowered. Then someone stabbed Noue in the heart, killing him instantly. The authorities determined the killing was justified self-defense and no criminal charges were filed. However, the law of *kanun* was not so dismissive.

Noue left two teenage sons, Leka and Angelo. To them, Preka Lamthi had not only escaped justice, he had violated another one of the most sacred covenants of the *kanun*: guests in a house are under a seal of protection by the householder, and the householder is expected to lay down his life to protect the guest. By allowing Noue to be murdered in his house, Preka had committed a deep crime of honor that mandated execution of the Lamthi family, burning of the house, and expulsion of the family from the country.

Years passed. In April 1997, the Albanian economy collapsed around a huge financial pyramid scheme. The ensuing riots destroyed civil order, and thousands of weapons in armories were loosed onto the streets. In August 1998, Leka, unemployed with a young son to care for, bought himself a Kalashnikov assault rifle and went hunting for any Lamthi he could find. Shtjefen Lamthi happened to be the first one he encountered, even though Shjtefen was a victim himself, having suffered six stab wounds by

Leka's father Noue. Thus, Shjtefen was the next to die in this Albanian blood feud.

In his article, Anderson reports on his meeting with Leka:

When I suggested that [Noue's overturning of the table] made [Noue] more culpable in the fight, and the Lamthis less so, Leka simply shrugged.

"That does not matter in the kanun," he replied. "By the kanun, the very worst crime is to kill someone inside your house, no matter the circumstances or how it started."

"That's right," Angelo chimed in. "For this, the Lamthis would have left Thethi. By the kanun, Preka should have been executed, his house destroyed, and all his family made to leave the valley and never show their faces again."

Leka nodded, "But we did not ask for that. All we wanted was for Preka to come to us and ask for our forgiveness. But he was the big party boss for the district; he knew he could not be touched, so he treated it like nothing. For 13 years we waited for them to come to us, and finally I could not wait any longer."

"Rather than kill Shtjefen, why didn't you wait for the chance to kill Preka?" Anderson asked.

Leka pondered. "But it made no difference," he said eventually. "By the kanun, any of the Lamthis are equal, just so long as one of them paid. I saw Shtjefen first, so he paid."

Later, Anderson sat across from Preka Lamthi, who feigned amazement about an ongoing blood feud.

"Blood? But we have no blood with them. That is all in the past now." As he said this, Anderson saw Preka's two sons smirking at each other.

When Anderson left the Rrushkadoli brothers, Angelo said to him, "The Lamthis should give us peace now, because technically they still owe us. We are not asking for anything more but, by the terms of the kanun, for killing our father inside their house, and they owe us three deaths."

"That's right," said Leka. "Three of theirs."

The social identity in rural Albania is defined, in large part, by the *kanun*. The *kanun* requires that honor be given, be received, and be avenged, even if the terms of interpretation are loose. The Lamthi family and the Rrushkadoli family are loyal to themselves first and define themselves in terms of blood relationships. By the *kanun*, those relationships create debts of honor that must be repaid. The likelihood of ending the blood feud is very low as long as this powerful social identity defines who the Lamthis and Rrushkadolis are and what is meaningful in their lives. Understanding the power of social identity and negotiating in the context of social identity therefore becomes very important.

It does not take much for a social identity to form. People living thousands of miles away from Oakland, California, can identify as a member of the Raider Nation and become quite fanatical about all things involving Raider football. In fact, the NFL, and every other professional sports league, counts on this social identification as a key to financial success.

Social identity is extremely powerful and unconscious in its effects. In one early study, researchers divided school boys into two groups.[2] The researchers told the boys that they were being chosen on the basis of their preference for one modern artist over another or on the basis of their judgment about how many dots were being presented on the screen. In fact, this was a pretext, and the assignments were completely random.

Each boy was given the task of assigning points to an anonymous member of the in-group and to a member of the other group. The boys never met any of the boys in either group in person. So this was an individual being assigned to a random group with whom he had no previous association and having no contact with his own group or the out-group. The created identification was purely fiction, although the boys did not know that.

There was no reason for a boy in one group to discriminate against a boy in the other group. Yet the boys did discriminate, awarding more points to members of their own group than to members of the other. When they had a chance to be fair to both groups at no cost to themselves or their group, the boys never-theless chose to be unfair to the out-group members. The impli-cations are considerable. These boys never met any of their cohorts. They were simply told that they were a member of a group. That statement was sufficient to create a social identity that caused each boy to treat his own cohorts better than others. It was sufficient to cause persistent unfair treatment even when there was no reason to be unfair. These were eleven- and twelve-year-old boys in the 1960s. Extrapolate this effect to the myriad groups in the twenty-first century that have far more cohesion and identities, and imagine the challenge to negotiating peace.

We have many social identities, some of which are more dom-inant at times than others. We might be a lawyer in a courtroom in the morning, a law partner at a partner's lunch, a golf club member in the afternoon, and a parent and spouse in the evening. These are all social identities because the groups with which we associate create meaning for us, tell us who we are, inform our behaviors, reduce our anxiety, and raise our self-esteem.

Which of our social identities is active in the moment is dependent on several conditions. First, a given social identity must be strongly internalized within us. I am not a Raider foot-ball fan, so the Raider Nation identity is meaningless to me. I am a lawyer turned peacemaker, so the identity of peacemaker and problem solver resonates deeply within me.

The more complex or ambiguous the social situation, the more internalized the social identity must be in order to become active. For example, in a classically Western, liberal culture in which many beliefs and values may be tolerated, a conservative social identity will be activated only if the conservative is deeply committed to that identity. The ambiguity may, however, ignite a deep conservative's social identity as she finds an affinity to the "family values" espoused by the conservative rhetoric. A fiscal conservative may not feel the same affinity to "family values" because social conservatism as a social identity is not deeply embedded within him. In either case, social identities that define us at our core will tend to be more active than peripheral social identities. Again, by way of personal example, my social identity as a civic leader is far more active than my social identity as a fly fisherman. On the other hand, my close friend Michael Maloney, one of the greatest fly-casting instructors in the world, defines himself in terms of the sport more deeply than I.

Which of our social identities is active at the moment is also dependent on our social environment and the existence of other groups. In other words, social identity becomes active when there are other groups against which the identity can be compared. A fundamentalist Christian may construe a social situation such as being at a party or at work as one in which other people present are unsaved sinners. In these contexts, the centrality of faith defines identity in the context of two groups: the saved and the unsaved. On the other hand, when at church, the same person is unlikely to compare himself on the basis of saved versus unsaved. At church, another social identity most likely becomes active to create a differentiation with others. The greater the contrast between one's own group and another group, the more social identity is activated. We have to be as like each other as possible and as different as possible from them. Social identity is therefore a context-determined process that is highly sensitive to relative differences between groups.

Whenever there is a threat to the in-group's social identity, the group experiences insecurity. In addition, if the boundaries around an in-group are sharply defined and difficult to penetrate, in-group members may find it difficult to leave. Insecurity and impermeability are likely to cause the in-group to scapegoat an out-group and start fighting.

PROTOTYPING AND STEREOTYPING

Our brains have enormous power to make social categorizations. We pay very close attention to the characteristics of people in order to determine whether or not they are part of our group. In addition, we tend to attribute the beliefs, values, and norms of our group to each member of our group. These commonly held characteristics of the in-group are called *prototypes*. Characteristics attributed to an out-group are called *stereotypes*. Prototypes minimize differences within a group to build cohesion and reduce anxiety. Stereotypes maximize differences with out-groups and allow for depersonalization and discrimination.

Prototyping is important because it emphasizes the importance of conformity. Those who wish to become members of the in-group must embrace the new norms, often through symbolic or ritual process. They may have to change their appearance, language, and habits to signal that they are now members of the in-group. Prototypes are also fuzzy in that some members will demonstrate the characteristics of an in-group more than others. Leaders are typically very prototypical, thereby gaining respect as a model member of the in-group. Interestingly, the more general and inclusive the out-group becomes, the more extreme the in-group's prototype. As the out-group expands to include more and more people, only an extreme prototype will differentiate the in-group from all out-group members. Typically, in-group leadership is more extreme and seeks to define the out-group with even greater differentiation. We see this prototyping in scholarly Muslim clerics who increasingly become more militant to overthrow mainstream and more inclusive Muslim governments. America becomes the great Satan because its cultural appeal casts a broad net around the world. Therefore, sharp differentiation with American culture becomes necessary to create a clear prototype.

Stereotyping works the same way, as it permits the in-group to see itself as different from a uniform out-group. Typically, stereotypes tend to attribute unfavorable out-group characteristics to the evil, debased, sinful, blasphemous characters within the out-group. Thus, "Muslims act the way they do because they are ignorant, medieval fanatics" is a patently false statement and a clear stereotype held by some non-Muslim people.

Social identities have provided a major evolutionary advantage to us. By increasing our self-esteem, social identities allow us to prevail in the face of hardship. In addition, when our group is threatened, so is our social identity. We are willing to sacrifice for the group to protect our personal self-esteem and to enhance the status, survival, and access to resources for the group. Social identities also reduce our anxiety about an uncertain world. When a social identity has a clear set of beliefs, values, and norms, group members do not have to deal with ambiguity. Their belief systems give them simple answers to complex questions. Since everyone else in the group agrees with those answers, the members reinforce each other and can be more certain that they are right and the out-group is wrong.

The politics of social identity frequently drives conflict. In their quest for power, leaders manipulate personal experiences and exacerbate ethnic, religious, or nationalist differences to mobilize support. Ethnic, national, or religious identities are built on myths that define who is a group member, what it means to be a group member, and, typically, who the group's enemies are. These myths are usually based on truth but are selective or exaggerated in their presentation of history. These mythologies give rise to emotionally laden symbols that politicians can use to gain support and rouse their followers' feelings. Through indoctrination in schools and control over the mass media, political rhetoric inflames past injustices and suffering. This calculated exploitation of social identity binds people into a cohesive group. By exaggerating differences, political leaders help their supporters demonize out-groups to create enemies. People emotionally feel that the other group's gain is automatically their own loss. Emotion-laden status competition also leads groups to view out-groups in all-or-nothing terms and as threatening the existence of their group. Individually, this is interpreted in the brain as a threat to self and triggers a fear reaction.

THE RATTLERS AND THE EAGLES

The experiment called for the selection of twenty-four boys of about twelve years of age from similar, settled, lower-middle-class Protestant backgrounds.[3] The boys were well-adjusted, normal kids in the same school grade. The hypothesis was to see if stereotypes and prototypes, with accompanying conflict, could be artificially created and then de-escalated.

At the camp, the groups were separated. Members in each group were given teamwork exercises designed to create group identity and cohesion. As expected, the two groups formed unique social identities and their own internal status hierarchies. One group named itself "The Rattlers" and the other group called itself "The Eagles."

As each group became distantly aware of the presence of the other group, they identified more closely with their own group. Each group began to defend the camp facilities that they enjoyed, and spontaneously gained, without justification, a perception that that the others might be "abusing" those facilities.

Once the groups were formed and cohesive, the researchers introduced friction between them. In this second phase, the researchers intended to generate intergroup conflict. They announced a series of games and competitions with group and individual prizes for the winners and nothing for the losers.

The Rattlers felt very confident that they would win when they learned of the contests. They spent the day talking about the contests and making improvements on the ball field, which they appropriated as their own to such an extent that they spoke of putting a "Keep Off" sign there. They ended by putting their Rattler flag on the backstop. At this time, several Rattlers made threatening remarks about what they would do if anybody bothered their flag.

The two groups were brought together for the first time in the mess hall. They immediately engaged in name calling, flung insults back and forth, and sang derogatory songs. From this point, the conflict escalated as the groups burned each other's flags and raided each other's cabins.

The contests were discreetly rigged by the researchers so that the Eagles won. Afterward, the Rattlers raided again, stealing any prizes they could lay their hands on. The name calling intensified, and insults to the out-group were expressed in word and deed.

Phase three was intended to de-escalate the conflict over six to seven days. The researchers arranged mixers such as a bean-collecting contest, the showing of a film, and a Fourth of July fireworks display. However, the tensions did not ebb, and several events ended in food fights.

The researchers concluded that contrived situations were not going to de-escalate the conflict, so they introduced challenges that threatened both groups and could not be solved by one group alone.

The camp drinking water came from a reservoir on the mountain north of the camp. The water supply had failed, ostensibly due to vandalism of the system. Both groups were sent out to inspect the pipelines for leaks. When the water tank was discovered to be full and no leaks were found, both groups turned to a faucet that had a sack stuffed into it. The work to unclog the pipe took more than forty-five minutes. When the water flowed, there was common rejoicing. The Rattlers did not object to having the Eagles get ahead of them when they all got a drink, since the Eagles did not have canteens with them and were thirstier.

The next challenge involved a feature-length movie. In the afternoon, the boys were called together, and the staff suggested the possibility of securing either *Treasure Island* or *Kidnapped*. Both groups yelled approval of these films. After some discussion, one Rattler said, "Everyone that wants *Treasure Island* raise their hands." The majority of members in both groups gave enthusiastic approval to *Treasure Island*.

The "problem" was that securing the film would cost $15, and the camp could not pay the whole sum. After much discussion, both groups agreed to pay $3.50 each, and the camp would pay $8.00. While the contribution per person was unequal because some Eagles had gone home, as groups, the Eagles and Rattlers contributed equally.

Other group activities were introduced such that tensions were reduced. At breakfast and lunch the last day of camp, the boys were sitting in mixed groups without apparent group affiliation.

This study turned out to be a classic in the social psychology of social identities, group formation, stereotyping, and conflict. The fact that the researchers could so easily manipulate the boys into conflict through the creation and perpetuation of social identities is sobering. In the international arena, there are no overarching "researchers" manipulating the subjects. Instead, the dynamics of social identity—including ethnicity, familial relations, religion, geography, nationality, tribal affiliation, and larger culture—create powerful group bonds.

SHIFTING SANDS— RECOGNIZING THE COMPLEXITY OF AFGHANISTAN AND PAKISTAN

One of the world's most troubling and complex regions presents a textbook example of the interaction of social identities. The United States has been embroiled in Afghanistan since the 9/11 attacks, with questionable progress and considerable expense. Social identity theory suggests that the current efforts to stabilize Afghanistan as a functional nation-state are doomed to fail.

There are multiple players in Afghanistan. Unsnarling the web these players weave is a complex undertaking and useful to understanding how social identity is crucial in any peacemaking efforts.

THE PASHTUNS

> Their system of ethics, which regards treachery and violence as virtues rather than vices . . . is incomprehensible to a logical mind.
>
> —WINSTON CHURCHILL[4]

Around forty million Pashtuns live in a swath of 150,000 square miles of contiguous territory running from eastern and southern Afghanistan to northwestern Pakistan. This region has been invaded by nomadic Central Asian tribes, the armies of Persian kings, and by Alexander the Great, each in turn attempting to conquer the Pakistan-Indian subcontinent. The invaders met ferocious resistance by the Pashtun, who have lived in the region for thousands of years.

The Pashtun are clan oriented and roughly divide into the hill clans and the flatland clans. These two large tribal groups do not get along. They have in common, however, the *Pashtunwali* code, which governs the social order of Pashtun life. Like the Albanian *kanun*, *Pashtunwali* is an honor code that requires that honor be given, protected, defended, and avenged, with blood if necessary. The *Pashtunwali* is the core of the social identity of the Pashtun and determines social order and responsibilities from birth to death. Understanding the *Pashtunwali* is the key to understanding the Pashtun.

Pashtunwali is literally translated as "the way of the Pashtun." It expresses values about honor (*namuz*), solidarity (*nang*), hospitality, mutual support, shame, and revenge. The defense of honor, even to death, is obligatory for every Pashtun. Like the Albanian *kanun*, revenge is deeply embedded in the *Pashtunwali* as the duty to protect honor. Revenge is particularly applicable to honor around women, wealth, and land (*zar*, *zan*, and *zameen*). Vendettas and feuds are inherent in Pashtun social relations and are a measure of individual and group identity.

Revenge may take time, and as one Pashtun proverb goes, "I

took my revenge after a hundred years, and I only regret that I acted in haste." Generations may pass until the wrong is avenged, but a dishonored family will focus on retribution until honor is restored. The US invasion of Afghanistan, particularly against the Afghan Taliban, has created dishonor among many Pashtuns. On countless occasions, US or Coalition troops have invaded Pashtun homes, stomped through the women's quarters where no men were ever allowed, humiliated the men with searches and seizures, and otherwise incurred huge debts of honor that can only be repaid through blood revenge.

The Pashtun social identity is deeply wrapped in these principles. As with most honor societies, the environmental conditions in Afghanistan are too harsh for an individual to survive, much less prosper. Honor represents a claim on group resources, such as access to women, food, water, herd animals, protection from raiders, and so forth. To lose honor is tantamount to losing one's right to life. When life is hard, with little margin for error, the slightest insult is a very big deal.

The Pashtun are the link between Afghanistan and Pakistan. About fifteen million Pashtuns live in Afghanistan, whereas about twenty-five million live in Pakistan. No recognized or controlled border exists between Pakistan and Afghanistan. Instead, there is a theoretical line called the Durand Line, named after the British civil governor of India, who drew it in 1893. The Pashtuns reject the Durand Line as a legitimate border. Instead, they speak of an area they call Pashtunistan that encompasses ancestral Pashtun lands on both sides of the Durand Line. For all practical purposes, the Durand Line does not exist for Pashtuns, with families, clans, tribes, and business ventures crossing back and forth daily without regard to any international border. Because of this, Pashtun leaders have always controlled large areas of Pakistan: the Pashtun-inhabited North West Frontier Province, (the NWFP) and the Federally Administered Tribal Areas (the FATA). The Pashtun clans, subtribes, and tribes feud and fight like crazy among themselves when left alone. However, when challenged by an outside threat, they band together with sufficient coherency to pose a daunting force.

The likelihood that Pakistan will be able to assimilate the Pashtuns into its vision of an Islamic state is slim to zero. As mentioned in chapter 5, Pakistan is engaged in a serious civil war with the Pashtuns in the Northwest Territories and the Federally Administered Tribal Areas.

THE AFGHAN TALIBAN

During the Soviet invasion of Afghanistan in the 1980s, a diverse group of people came together to defeat the Soviet troops and to remove the pro-Soviet Afghanistan government. Osama bin Laden was one of the scores of Arabs who went to Afghanistan to support the fight and stayed. The Pashtuns, among other ethnic groups, provided warriors to resist the Soviet presence. Pakistan and Iran initially provided training and material support to end the threat. Soon, Saudi Arabia, the United States, China, Egypt, France, and others sent aid to these "freedom fighters," called mujahedeen, through Pakistan.

In the beginning, the Pashtun fought against the Soviet army. They were joined by Islamic fighters from around the globe, and some of the biggest players in terrorism earned their stripes in this war. Along the way, they became heroes to the local Pashtun population. Under the *Pashtunwali*, an honor debt was created that some Pashtun would never forget.

In addition, an important cross-fertilization of social identities occurred as the Arabic fighters fought alongside the Pashtun. The Arabic fighters gained an appreciation of the honor code of the *Pashtunwali* that deeply affected their view of the future of Islam. The values around honor (*namuz*), solidarity (*nang*), hospitality, mutual support, shame, and revenge soaked into these Arabs as a missing piece to make their spiritual and religious experience with the Pashtuns a moment of enlightenment in their lives. In particular the defense of honor, to death, was carried out of Afghanistan with the Arab terrorists wherever they would go afterward.

After the war, many Arab fighters returned home with the ideologies they had formed as a result of their experiences. They spread their new beliefs through small, loosely affiliated cells and kept in contact with Afghanistan war veterans in other countries. Though many left Afghanistan, a significant number of Arabs remained to establish training camps to train future mujahedeen.

In the meantime, with the overthrow of the Soviet-backed Afghanistan government, Afghanistan was reduced to a collection of territories held by competing Pashtun and Tajik warlords. Civil war erupted, and Afghanistan descended again into war and chaos.

At the same time, a band of Ghilzai Pashtuns near Kandahar, led by a rabidly fundamentalist, uneducated mullah named Mohammed Omar, backed by Pakistan, and calling themselves the Taliban, raised the black flag. Their intention was to impose a radical Islamic theology on Afghanistan by crushing the warlords. Under Pakistan intelligence service (ISI) training and guidance, the Taliban was able to unite its loosely aligned regional groups together and form a large militia.

For Pakistan, the Taliban represented what seemed to be a controllable force. Through the Taliban, Pakistan hoped to manage Afghanistan. The ISI, deeply worried about the existential threat presented by India, wanted a weakened Afghanistan at its back door. Funding and arming Omar seemed like a good bet to achieve that goal. In fact, the Taliban was able to defeat the warlords and, in 1996, captured Kabul. Pakistan felt it had secured its interests when the Taliban officially controlled the majority of Afghanistan.

As has been thoroughly reported, the Taliban imposed an extremely repressive Islamic regime on the Afghan people. Women were barred from work and school, and Shiite Muslims of the Hazarra minority were routinely shot or tortured. Men were forced to wear beards. Television, music, and the Internet were banned. Soccer stadiums were filled to witness executions and torture for violating the strict Taliban laws. The Taliban declared its utter hatred for other religions when Mullah Omar destroyed the giant fifth-century Bamiyan Buddhist stone statues carved into a mountain. In short, the Taliban imposed an entirely new social identity on the tribes and people of Afghanistan as it attempted to impose fundamentalist Salafi Islamic teachings over Pashtun tribal customs.

This was the time, in 1996, that the Taliban gave refuge to Osama bin Laden and his associates. Bin Laden was welcomed as a hero from the Soviet conflict, given protection, and allowed to continue his training of what would become the next generation of terrorists. Bin Laden and Mullah Omar, Arab and Pashtun, respected each other and shared a common belief that Western influence grossly degraded their culture and Muslim women and corrupted their children. The West was therefore threatening to their deeply embedded social identities.

THE PAKISTANI TALIBAN

Once the Taliban restored order to most of Afghanistan, the Pashtuns began recoiling against its harsh rule. Sharia law and the *Pashtunwali* code conflicted in many serious ways. The Pashtuns accepted sharia law as interpreted and enforced by the Taliban only as an expediency. However, once peace had been restored, the Taliban was no longer welcome.

Thus, after 9/11, the United States crushed the Afghan Taliban with the initial blessing of the majority of the Pashtun. As a result of the US military offensive, in late 2001, thousands of Taliban and several hundred Arab and Central Asian followers of Osama bin Laden poured into northern Pakistan's tribal areas— including Waziristan. Calling themselves the Pakistan Taliban, fighters of Waziristan's main tribes have instituted a civil war within Pakistan that threatens Pakistanis' existence as a viable state.

THE TAJIKS

The Tajiks are the second-largest ethnic group in Afghanistan and are based in the north. In the post-9/11 days, the outside world heard a lot about something called the Northern Alliance. The Northern Alliance was composed of Tajik warlords and their tribes, whose social identities are very different from the Pashtun.

The Tajik are Dari-speaking people with close social, historical, and cultural ties to Iran. Unlike the Pashtun, the Tajik are not tribal or clan based. Instead, they identify with their city, town, valley, or other geographic region. Most Tajiks in Afghanistan are Sunni Muslim and are bitter rivals of the Pashtun. Their hatred rose as the Pashtun-dominated Taliban oppressed them, and they were only too glad to align with the US forces in 2001 to oust the Taliban from control. Of course, the Pashtuns saw the Tajiks as invaders from the north, which created honor obligations under the *Pashtunwali* to resist them.

Today, the majority of the Afghanistan National Army consists of Tajiks. The Tajiks have no real interest in fighting the Afghan Taliban and therefore are unlikely to respond as a security force of any substance throughout Afghanistan. In addition, the Tajiks do not view Afghan president Hahmid Karzai as their president, since he is a Pashtun ostensibly put into power with the support of foreign powers.

PAKISTAN

As we have seen in chapter 5, the Pakistani army is obsessed with India. Its fear of India requires Pakistan to assure itself of a weakened Afghanistan. The Pakistani military sees the Karzai government as allied to India and thus hostile to Islamabad—which it is. India supported the communist government of Afghanistan and then the Northern Alliance and now supports Karzai. While India is heavily involved in Afghanistan, Pakistan is determined that it will dominate Afghanistan once the foreigners leave.

In the Pakistani military's view, the international community will leave Afghanistan, as they did after the Soviets left, and indeed as President Obama has promised to do. When that happens, Pakistan wants to install a regime in Kabul that will expel the Indian advisers, spies, diplomats, and contractors and provide a friendly area to the rear of Pakistan in the event of another war with India. This is the Pakistani idea of "strategic depth." The most likely candidate for a Pakistan-friendly government is the Pashtun-dominated Afghan Taliban. However, Pakistan is also battling a civil war with the Pakistani Taliban, also composed of Pashtuns. In Pakistan's eyes, the Pakistani Taliban are dangerous rebels, while the Afghan Taliban is the next government of Afghanistan. In fact, the Afghan Taliban leadership remains secure in Pakistan with the cooperation of the Pakistan government. In the meantime, the United States and NATO are fighting the Afghan Taliban and supplying Pakistan with billions of dollars in aid.

The social identities in Afghanistan are mind-boggling. The Pashtun live by a strict honor code. The Taliban consists of the Afghan Taliban and the Pakistan Taliban, with different identities and goals. The Tajiks control the north of Afghanistan. The Pakistanis, or at least their intelligence service, are manipulating everyone to gain control of the Kabul government while other elements of the Pakistan government are fighting a civil war against the Taliban. Mullah Omar is set on regaining control of Afghanistan and reinstalling a grossly oppressive regime. Osama bin Laden remains his friend and benefactor. It is not likely that a traditional diplomatic peace process will be successful in this conflict.

WHAT SHOULD BE THE APPROACH WITH CONFLICTING SOCIAL IDENTITIES?

When the conflict involves competing social identities, mediators must understand the prototypes and stereotypes that are coming to the table. Negotiators are usually selected because they are prototypes of their groups. They hold many of the values and characteristics of the groups they represent and are closely aligned with their leaders. When warring groups come to a peace conference, opposing prototypes are facing each other in the discussions. They do not see each other as prototypes, however. They see themselves as representative of the norm (a cognitive bias) and see their opponent as a stereotype of the enemy. Instead of seeing a complex human being across the table, they see a person they can only characterize by stereotype: evil, violent, dishonest, corrupt, venal, or an infidel. Often, the stereotype is so strong that it creates an emotional reaction, and people commonly resist being in the same room with their stereotypical enemy.

Political solutions alone do not resolve social identity conflicts. This has been the major failing of most peace talks—the mediators have focused on a political solution without considering the underlying conflict dynamics. There are two reasons why political solutions to war do not work. First, the political leaders have developed power based on stereotyping the enemy. When leaders will not serve their people by providing improved standards of living, they manipulate symbols to appeal to popular emotions. The easiest way to do this is to create foreign or domestic "enemies" to blame for the country's problems. In a September 21, 2001, interview with Voice of America, Mullah Omar said, "Almighty God . . . is helping the believers and the Muslims. God says he will never be satisfied with the infidels. In terms of worldly affairs, America is very strong. Even if it were twice as strong or twice that, it could not be strong enough to defeat us. We are confident that no one can harm us if God is with us."[5] Omar's power derives from the jihadist Salafi (radical fundamentalist Islam) hatred of Western culture. Asking him to give up that hatred is like asking him to stop breathing because it is the source of his power.

True peace means dismantling the stereotypes, which means dissipation of the leader's power base. This presents major problems for international mediators. Many leaders feel emasculated when their groups are asked to reintegrate with society. Peace requires that power based on social identity be replaced with power based on legitimate authority, preferably through democracy. If a leader feels threatened by his loss of power, position, and privilege, he will resist peace efforts and renew the social identity conflict. This is exactly what is happening in Afghanistan in mid-2010. As the counterinsurgency is proving ineffective, the United States and the Karzai government are expressing interest in a "negotiated" settlement with the Taliban. Mullah Omar is essentially laughing at the idea, confident in his position of strategic power in Afghanistan and Pakistan. Negotiation would imply a reduction in his current sense of power, so he is not motivated to come to the table.

Even if the political leaders seek peace, when they have unleashed social identity conflicts, the groups are often unwilling to let go of the fight. Radical Islamic fundamentalists, the Salafists, fall into this trap. Salafis are aware that they are the impoverished heirs to a great civilization, which was generating advances in science and literature while Europe was deep in the Dark Ages. To overcome their current feelings of inferiority, Salafis convince themselves that the past glory of Islam demonstrates its superiority over Western civilization. Since they cannot explain away the success of Western materialism, Salafis feel rage and resentment toward the West. The liberal sexual attitude of Western culture adds to the rage. Sexuality and control of women raises issues of male honor. In response, as social identity theory predicts, Salafis have adopted a repressive, almost impossible to follow set of norms against sexual expression of any kind. The Taliban's ridiculously strict rules on sexual display and behavior, to the point of completely eliminating human rights for women, are an extreme example of this type of social identity.

Mediating a reasonable peace agreement in Afghanistan will be one of the most difficult projects on the planet. Any mediator courageous enough to take on peace negotiations in Afghanistan must know how to negotiate within social identities rather than resisting them. First, that means adopting the indigenous Pashtun peace process called the *jirga*. Since the Pashtuns are not highly organized, making peace will require negotiations at the local and tribal levels as well as at the national level. Pashtuns will not accept peace agreements made by the Karzai government with the Taliban. Instead, agreements will have to be made at the regional and local level, reflecting the true state of power in Afghanistan. Did I mention that the Westphalian notion of sovereignty has no meaning in Afghanistan?

Jirgas are somewhat like town hall meetings in the United States, except that they are generally not democratic or participatory. At the village level, elders are selected to the *jirga* to resolve conflicts by consensus. *Loya jirgas* are grand councils convened for larger issues, and members of a *loya jirga* represent villages or regions.

The mediator in Afghanistan will have to consider convening *jirgas* and *loya jirgas* with the assistance of local influential elders. For a model on how to do this, any prospective mediator should read Greg Mortensen's book *Three Cups of Tea*.[6] Mortensen spent twenty years working with tribal leaders of Pakistan and Afghanistan building village schools for girls and is one of the most knowledgeable Westerners on the customs of the people. The purpose of the *jirgas* would be to discuss the terms of disengagement by the foreign invaders, for example, US and NATO forces. Under the *Pashtunwali*, payments will probably be negotiated to end the honor debt respectfully. Negotiators representing the West must be deeply schooled in the customs of Pashtun negotiation and in the principles of the *Pashtunwali*. In effect, the deal should be something along the lines of a *Pash-*

tunwali writ large. "We, the world, will leave you in peace so long as you honor *Pashtunwali* with us. This means no terrorists, no terrorist camps, no poppy cultivation (which is a great dishonor toward the West), and no drug trade. We will, in turn, honor your sovereignty and the right to live under the *Pashtunwali* within Pashtunistan as you desire without interference from the outside." This process may take several years and should become easier as word of the fairness of the *jirgas* spreads.

At the national level, confederating Afghanistan may be the only political solution with a chance of success. Confederation would realign at the internal boundaries of Afghanistan's provinces with the reality of the social identities of the people. Within those boundaries, such as in Pashtunistan, the central government would have a light touch, and self-rule, even if anarchic under tribal traditions, would be accepted. The Tajiks should have self-rule over their traditional northern and western territories. The Pashtuns are in the south and east and should have self-rule over Pashtunistan. The Hazarra have traditionally lived in the central mountainous regions and should have autonomy there.

Afghanistan's current constitution leaves room for confederation, as it seems to limit the powers of the national government to protecting the sovereignty of Afghanistan, securing borders, and providing for the general welfare of the citizens. Thus, the Afghanistan National Assembly could create Pashtunistan as a political and legal reality and embody *Pashtunwali* as the philosophy of self-governance within Pashtunistan.

Jirgas and political confederation do not solve all the conflicts, however. The Taliban will not go quietly, and Pakistan can be expected to block any attempt to create Pashtunistan. At the moment, there does not seem to be any effective way to mediate a settlement with the Taliban. The United States and NATO will therefore have to maintain a significant military presence in Afghanistan to provide security against Mullah Omar and his forces. The west should plan on a twenty-five- to fifty-year commitment to Afghanistan if it truly wants peace in the region.

The true solution, however, will be to mediate peace between Pakistan and India, especially over the status of Kashmir. This conflict is based on its own deep social identities and will require as much skill from the mediator as does Afghanistan.

Social identity conflicts account for much of our world's violence. Geopolitical groups stubbornly resist peaceful resolution because of fear of loss. Traditional diplomacy has not managed social identity conflicts artfully, and more often than not, it has inflamed the conflict. The twenty-first-century international mediator cannot be afraid of evolving norms around sovereignty, central governments, and self-rule. As the world continues to globalize, we will have to learn how to balance compassion for those parts of the world that are catching up with the need for global order and peace. This will require much deeper and broader skills from international mediators and negotiators.

Chapter 7

Fear, Anger, and Decisions

My fellow citizens. At this hour, American and coalition forces are in the early stages of military operations to disarm Iraq, to free its people and to defend the world from grave danger.

On my orders, coalition forces have begun striking selected targets of military importance to undermine Saddam Hussein's ability to wage war. These are opening stages of what will be a broad and concerted campaign.

More than 35 countries are giving crucial support, from the use of naval and air bases to help with intelligence and logistics to deployment of combat units.[1]

With these words, on March 19, 2003, President George W. Bush announced to the world the invasion of Iraq with the stated purpose of overthrowing Saddam Hussein and eliminating the Iraqi potential to manufacture, distribute, and use weapons of mass destruction.

The previous September, at a speech in Cincinnati, Ohio, President Bush gave the world his reasons for the war that he was to commence seven months later:

Tonight I want to take a few minutes to discuss a grave threat to peace, and America's determination to lead the world in confronting that threat.

The threat comes from Iraq. It arises directly from the Iraqi regime's own actions—its history of aggression, and its drive toward an arsenal of terror. Eleven years ago, as a condition for ending the Persian Gulf War, the Iraqi regime was required to destroy its weapons of mass destruction, to cease all development of such weapons, and to stop all support for terrorist groups. The Iraqi regime has violated all of those obligations. It possesses and produces chemical and biological weapons. It is seeking nuclear weapons. It has given shelter and support to terrorism, and practices terror against its own people. The entire world has witnessed Iraq's eleven-year history of defiance, deception, and bad faith.

Iraq could decide on any given day to provide a biological or chemical weapon to a terrorist group or individual terrorists. Alliance with terrorists could allow the Iraqi regime to attack America without leaving any fingerprints.

Some have argued that confronting the threat from Iraq could detract from the war against terror. To the contrary; confronting the threat posed by Iraq is crucial to winning the war on terror. When I spoke to Congress more than a year ago, I said that those who harbor terrorists are as guilty as the terrorists themselves. Saddam Hussein is harboring terrorists and the instruments of terror, the instruments of mass death and destruction. And he cannot be trusted. The risk is simply too great that he will use them, or provide them to a terror network.

Terror cells and outlaw regimes building weapons of mass destruction are different faces of the same evil. Our security requires that we confront both. And the United States military is capable of confronting both.[2]

About 2,600 years earlier, the Corinthians characterized the Corcyreans in somewhat the same way. Corinthian ambassadors in Athens argued:

We must believe that the tyrant city that has been established in Hellas has been established against all alike, with a program of universal empire, part fulfilled, part in contemplation; let us then attack and reduce it, and win future security for ourselves and freedom for the Hellenes who are now enslaved.[3]

What is going on here? Haven't we learned anything in 2,600 years? Are there similarities between the twenty-first-century decision to invade Iraq and the Corinthians' ancient arguments for war against Corcyra and its possible ally Athens?

If we look closely at President Bush's arguments in his Cincinnati speech, we will see his characterization of Saddam Hussein in terms of a threat to US security. Likewise, in ancient Greece, the Corinthians saw a threat of domination from Corcyra. Fundamentally, these threats triggered the primal emotions of anger and fear.

Fear and anger drive violent conflict. They may not always be the emotions that loose the dogs of war, but once people start dying, fear and anger play a dominant role in diplomatic, military, and leadership perspectives. Everyone is familiar with being frightened and being hopping mad. What is not so well known, especially among international negotiators and mediators, is how the emotions of fear and anger distort "rational" decision making.

Anger has three time dimensions. Everyone knows that backward-looking anger is unpleasant. Memories of injustice may trigger strong feelings that we collectively identify as anger. We are angry at ourselves, the situation we are in, and the person who treated us unfairly. Backward-looking anger intensifies our memory, making the situation easier to recall. We learn from this anger to protect ourselves from similar future encounters.

Present anger is the rage of the moment. We are highly reactive as our brain and body prepare for battle. No one thinks clearly in the heat of anger. Crimes of passion are sometimes legally excusable because we know intuitively that our impulse control goes out the window when we are provoked. Most people do not like the feeling of present anger. The hormones that pump into the bloodstream are not pleasure inducing. Instead, we often become hyperalert, ready to lash out at any potential threat. The need to do something, anything is sometimes overwhelming. Angry people shout, throw things, punch walls, hit spouses, and shoot people. None of these behaviors are the signs of rational decision making.

Unlike backward-looking and present anger, forward-looking anger can be very rewarding. We feel a sense of control. We expect to conquer our opponents and obstacles, and we will get what we want. People often find themselves more energized to attack the cause of their offense. Anger is especially exhilarating when we witness the misfortune of people we dislike. Brain imaging studies show that the parts of the brain typically associated with pleasure are activated when we anticipate punishing an offender even if that punishment comes at a personal cost. This explains why the rush and optimism of future anger may lead people to lose sight of their own abilities, their dependence on others, social norms, and other important goals. President Bush's two speeches are examples of how his personal anger and the anger of his advisers propelled him into questionable decisions that cost the United States treasure and blood.

Anger is, however, an important and healthy emotion in the appropriate context. Anger arouses us to action in the face of personal boundary violations and threats. If we are physically attacked, anger fuels us to fight back or defend without quarter. Anger spurs counterterrorism operations, for example. However, anger also creates a feeling of need for vengeance, vindication, and validation. If those needs are not satisfied, our anger can increase and intensify, locking us into a deeper conflict escalation cycle. As we will see, anger also prompts us to take greater risks than are warranted, which can cause us to make catastrophic errors in judgment.

Recognizing that anger can distort the decisions of international leaders, there is also good reason to hold a healthy degree of fear. In our highly globalized world economy, a limited war in urbanized countries would cause financial catastrophe and social anarchy. Modern cities are indefensible against even limited attacks of weapons of mass destruction. Crashing 747s into sky-scrapers would be nothing compared to a dirty, low-yield nuclear bomb, deadly pathogen release, or massive explosion in a busy, rush-hour, downtown city center. Fear causes us to make deci-sions to avoid even small risks. In a fearful state, our brains overestimate the likelihood of harm or loss and tend to make risk-averse decisions even when those decisions are economically and practically unsound.[4] Politicians and bureaucrats are painfully conscious of the price they would pay if a massive urban attack occurred during their watch. Fear of such an attack permeates their decision making and is reflected in overzealous, sometimes ridiculous, homeland security policies.

Understanding anger and fear is important in the context of negotiation and decision making. When anger and fear drive nego-tiations between hostile parties, the outcomes are generally terrible. Furthermore, not recognizing one's own fear and anger, either per-sonal or national, can lead to badly unintended consequences.

In the case of the United States, fear led to the creation of the Department of Homeland Security, restriction of personal freedom, and the torture of captured "enemy combatants," to name a few misguided and expensive policies. Anger also led to the wars in Iraq and Afghanistan and to covert operations around the world.

Had the American people known that there were no weapons of mass destruction in Iraq, and had they known the true cost of the war (now estimated at over $3 trillion from the original Bush administration [Richard Perlman] estimate of $95 billion), would they have supported the invasion? Probably not. Why, then, did the war occur? Unacknowledged, hidden, and unprocessed fear within the Bush administration coupled with the unwillingness of the international community, and in particular, the Arab League, to take fast, strong, affirmative steps to allay that fear.

Why couldn't the Arab League take steps to allay Western fears about Saddam's alleged weapons of mass destruction? Fear. The Arab regimes were fearful of losing prestige among themselves and were quietly desperate to remain in power. Imagine what would have happened if the Arab League members came forward with something like this: "Mr. President, citizens of the United States. We understand and acknowledge your fear of future attack by terrorists and rogue states with weapons of mass destruction. We, too, are fearful. We are fearful of injury, death, and destruction to your land and people. We are fearful for those of our people who will be killed and maimed in your reprisals. While we do not believe that Saddam Hussein has credible weapons of mass destruction, we fear that you will invade and destabilize Iraq. We do not wish that to occur in our region. May we please sit down and talk about our mutual fears and how we, as members of the Arab League, can help allay your fears of future harm?"

Had the Arab League taken a bold step to acknowledge the Bush-Cheney fears driving US policy decisions, perhaps a different conversation would have occurred. Perhaps a different solution would have been tried. Perhaps the Bush administration would have been deterred from invading Iraq.

FEAR

Fear carries a lot of baggage with it. In many societies, to acknowledge fear is to be weak. Many people and many cultures value courage—the ability to overcome fear. In these societies, danger is omnipresent. Whether the danger comes from living in a primitive natural environment or in a war-torn country, fear of death is constant.

Unquestionably, courage in the appropriate circumstances is a good thing. We can admire people who, in the face of emergency or danger, remain cool and collected. Remember US Airways

Flight 1549? Captain Chesley Sullenberger's 2009 power-off landing in the Hudson River six minutes after takeoff resonated around the world. He and his crew were able to act in the face of fear produced by the unthinkable: multiple, catastrophic engine failures in a modern commercial jet. This type of courage is celebrated and held out as honorable. Likewise, the courage of the young suicide bomber facing fear of death is celebrated in some cultures and societies as honorable greatness. The common denominator is fear, and understanding fear is one key to a more sophisticated approach to peace.

FEAR AND THE BRAIN

Each of us is born with an innate fear-response system. Our fear-response system is based primarily in the brain and is composed of brain structures that are phylogenetically very old. The genes for a fear-response system have persisted for hundreds of millions of years of evolution. Fear-response systems can be found in fossils as old as five hundred million years.

In humans, the fear-response system appears to be associated with two small, almond-shaped structures in the brain called the amygdala. The amygdala acts as an early warning system so that we are capable of responding to threats in the environment quickly and without conscious thought. My home in the foothills of the central Sierra Nevada is in rattlesnake country. The rattlesnakes and I pretty much live and let live. Generally, I try not to disturb them out on the land. They get killed if they decide to take up residence near the house. I have dealt with rattlesnakes this way for many years, and it has worked for me. That doesn't mean that I don't have a fear reaction to them, however.

Imagine walking with me on a moonlit summer evening up my dirt road. We can see the stars clearly, and a soft breeze is blowing down from the high country through the lower canyons across us. The smells are of that delicious early summer dry grass and oak savannah so classically Californian. We are chatting and come across a curving shadow on the road not two feet in front of us. I leap back without thought. My heart is pounding, and I am little dizzy from the adrenaline rush. About three-quarters of a second later, as the rest of my brain has time to process the information, I realize that the shadow has been cast by an oak branch off the huge tree to our left, not a rattlesnake. You wonder what got into me. "Better to be safe than sorry," some unconscious part of my brain registers.

Our fear-response system has been finely honed over hundreds of thousands, if not millions of years to make us exquisitely sensitive to physical threats around us. You can imagine that those ancient predecessors who cuddled up to sabertooth kittens were probably washed out of the gene pool rather quickly. Those of our ancestors who reacted to threats and recognized the danger of the cute sabertooth kitty survived to pass on their genes to us. Some of this fear protection is hardwired, but most of it is programmed into us from experience.

In a greatly simplified way, here's how it works: the amygdala receives incoming sensory signals from our five senses. What we see, smell, feel, taste, and hear are pieces of information collected at the periphery of our body and sent to our brain. The information feed is split along two paths. One path sends the information for further complex processing that ultimately results in "knowing" what is out there. The other path sends the unfiltered and unprocessed information to the amygdala.

Based on this raw data, the amygdala makes a snap decision as to whether what has been perceived is good or bad. The judgment process occurs all the time while we are awake. Fortunately, we appear to be spared this judgmental decision-making process while we sleep, although maybe waking up in a cold sweat from a bad dream is a fear reaction. Most importantly, however, the good-bad judgment is made completely outside of our conscious control or awareness. It is a form of preconscious processing, because decisions are automatically being made by us that we do not have a clue that we are making. In fact, it takes 750 milliseconds or three-quarters of a second for us to become consciously aware of what our amygdala has already judged to be good or bad. In brain time, this is a long time. Remember, it took me three-quarters of a second to register that the shadow was caused by an overhanging oak branch. What we experience as conscious awareness lags long behind what other parts of our brain are reacting to. Hence, my leap backward comes long before my slowly dawning awareness that the shadow is not a rattlesnake.

If the amygdala judges something as sufficiently bad, it will send signals out into our brain to arouse us physically to fight, run, or freeze. This is the well-known flight-or-fight reaction to fear. On the other hand, if the amygdala senses that something is good, it will send signals into the brain to approach. Not surprisingly, the only good things, from an amygdala's standpoint, are food and water, sex, and shelter. Everything else is bad, or at best, neutral.

Ever wonder why nut and bolt manufacturers put up posters with scantily clad women next to a machine part? They intuitively know that the male mind will make a preconscious judgment to approach the photo of the woman. Since the bolt is there too, it receives the emotional benefit of the approach. Highly sexist? Yes. Effective from a brain perspective? Yes. Political correctness yields to the judgment of the amygdala every time.

Here's another important fact: The amygdala cannot distinguish between a physical threat and a social threat. We can have the same type of fear reactions in settings where there is no danger of physical threat, and our brain cannot distinguish the situation from facing a sabertoothed cat. A common example is stage fright, where the fear of failure or the fear of performing in front of people causes us to freeze up. There is no physical threat, yet the amygdala perceives the social threat of mistake or failure as if there were a large, very hungry predator stalking us.

Our fear-reaction system is also quite plastic. The amygdala and its connecting systems are capable of learning quickly. This makes sense, because environmental threats can tend to kill. Creating a strong memory about the situation so that in the future we will stay away, run, or avoid the threat is a good thing. If we are highly reactive to threats, we are more likely to survive and pass on our genes.

The strong association between memory and fear creates triggers—cues in our environment that literally fire off a fear reaction. These triggers can be just about anything that we perceive with our senses: words, tone of voice, smells, tastes, sounds—anything, really, that our brains previously associated with a fearful, frightening, or scary situation. At a more subtle level, insults, indignities, and disrespect can trigger a fear reaction if we are particularly sensitive to our sense of self. This is one explanation why face saving and reputational protection is important in many cultures.

Triggers generally happen outside our conscious awareness. Because they occur before we are aware of them, they are called *preconscious* triggers. Remember that our brain takes three-quarters of a second to become consciously aware after we have been triggered. Usually, even then, we are not aware of what the trigger was, only that we are frightened, angry, or anxious.

Negotiation often triggers a preconscious fear reaction. If you know what to look for, you can actually see the pause followed by an emotional outburst. I will never forget mediating a conflict between Sikh businesspeople. Something was said to the matriarch who was a decision maker for one side. It was as if you could see gears turning in her head as she processed what was said and then became reactive and angry. I recall the change in her expression and body language vividly ten years later as my first eloquent example of how negotiation can trigger a fear reaction. In three-quarters of a second she went from being cooperative and collaborative to unyieldingly stubborn. It was amazing to witness, and I have seen the same effect hundreds of times since.

Like just about everything in the brain, what is good in moderation is destructive if it is excessive. When we are exposed to chronic stress, the receptor sites in the amygdala (the neural dendrites) actually grow to make us more sensitive to threats. This makes sense because we may need hair-trigger reactions in a dangerous environment. The result is a higher degree of reactivity and anxiety in anticipating a fear reaction. There is some thinking that post-traumatic stress disorder (PTSD) is based on amygdalic dendritic growth stimulated by intense and prolonged exposure to threats.[5] The growth of hypersensitive neurons in the amygdala may be passed on epigenetically to children so that they are born excessively sensitive to threats. Thus, it seems like anxiety, reactivity, and symptoms of PTSD can be passed on from generation to generation as long as people are living in a trigger-laden environment. Remove the triggers, however, and the traits are no long activated or passed along.

The fear-reaction system is a powerful, sensitive mechanism developed through evolution for its adaptability and survival benefits. Every single human, including international negotiators, heads of state, and foreign ministers, have exactly the same system, modified by personal experience and development. George Bush and Dick Cheney probably had activated amygdalas when they decided to embark on the invasion of Iraq and the overthrow of Saddam Hussein. Iranian president Mahmoud Ahmadinejad seems to show a fear reaction when he speaks out about Iran's sovereign right to develop nuclear power in the face of international criticism. When you start looking for it, you can see subtle signs of the fear reaction in many statements and behaviors of world political leaders and ministers. Behind the blustering, the bombast, and the accusations is a tension and stress that belies the bully image and indicates a fear reaction in operation.

Fortunately, the human amygdala is not always out there running amok. Along with other parts of the brain, the brain's prefrontal cortex is an important inhibitor of the amygdala. One critical role of the prefrontal cortex is to get us to do the hard thing when the amygdala is sending signals to react quickly, decisively, and without reflection.

We have all experienced being insulted or disrespected. If the insult is strong enough, our first impulse is to punch someone in the nose. That is the amygdala acting on the immediate cues and triggers. It is sending signals saying, "Defend aggressively." At the same time, the prefrontal cortex is processing, processing, processing, trying to figure everything out and provide for a more sophisticated choice. Sometimes, the prefrontal cortex is overwhelmed, and we throw the punch, slap the face, or hurl the frying pan. Other times, we pause, really angry and wanting to lash out, but manage to walk out of the room slamming the door. In these moments, our brain is in a huge conflict, and we do not have complete control over our feelings.

The ability to do the hard thing and not lash out in anger is easily subverted. If life experience has made us sensitive to personal insults, our prefrontal cortex will have a difficult time forgiving the offender and moving on. We have all experienced these life situations, yet international negotiators do not always seem to connect the dots that this is how the person across the table is hardwired and "programmed" to be.

What we call self-control in emotional situations is often complicated when our prefrontal cortex must choose between opposite decisions. For example, not lashing out in anger is a case of doing the harder thing when we have to control ourselves. On the other hand, being aggressive may be the harder choice. On a battlefield, for example, a soldier must consciously choose to fight while resisting the amygdala's strong signal to flee. In each situation, the prefrontal cortex has the job of making the call. Remember the experiment with the brownies and apples? If the prefrontal cortex is tired or otherwise occupied with another task, the amygdala wins, and our fear reaction takes over. This is why intense military training is so important—habits have to be developed that will allow a soldier to function without "thinking."

Herein is another fallacy of rationalism as a fundamental assumption of human behavior. The prefrontal cortex allows us to think logically and puzzle through new problems to find solutions. However, that kind of processing takes up a lot of metabolic capacity that is quickly overwhelmed by fear. Our individual fear responses are shaped by our experiences, our families, and our cultures so that we are each uniquely, yet predictably, emotional in situations where clear thinking is called for.

ANGER AND UNDERSTANDING

In a blog post, Betwa Sharma reported on a conversation she witnessed in an Israeli-Palestinian dialogue process in New York City.[6] In the dialogue, two Israelis and a Palestinian gathered in a small church in Manhattan to talk about whether the December 2008 Operation Cast Lead, carried out by the Israeli Defense Forces (IDF), was an aggressive "attack" or an "operation" in Gaza. The choice of words changed the meaning dramatically. Either the military action was an unprovoked violation of human rights or it was a justified and legitimate effort to prevent further violence. The conversation, which is sadly so typical of international conflicts, shows us the effects of anger on our ability to understand each other.

"It is an attack just like when a bomb goes off in a bus. You cannot dehumanize people by calling this an operation," said Eman Rashid, a forty-one-year-old single mother. "I can't sit in a room with a person who calls it an operation because they don't see me as a human being."

An Israeli woman, Naama Nebenzahl, who was studying to be a psychologist, felt "emotionally manipulated" during the conversation. "This level of aggression frightens me," she said, refusing to look Rashid in the eyes. "The operation happened because of what preceded it with Hamas shooting rockets."

Rashid spent several years in Palestine including her senior year at a Quaker High School in East Jerusalem. During this time, she was harassed by Israeli guards when the girls from her school held peaceful protests. Now a primary school teacher,

Rashid recalled that both she and her sister were shot with rubber bullets, but what stood out most in her mind were the swimming pools filled with sparkling blue water.

"You have water for your pools and you don't let us have water to drink," she told the group, tearing up as she speaks. "We're all suspected terrorists. . . . If I had been killed, I would just have been a statistic on your television screen."

Nebenzahl protests that the conversation was turning into a one-sided blame game, but Rashid continues, "I want Naama to understand that I felt subhuman," she said. "You may say you empathize, but you're being defensive and can't hear what I am saying."

*   *   *

In the conversation between Naama and Eman, triggers were firing off outside of their conscious awareness. Naama and Eman experienced the frustration of not being listened to, of being blamed, of being victimized, and of feeling frightened. Let's look at the conversation again, in slow motion.

"It is an attack just like when a bomb goes off in a bus. You cannot dehumanize people by calling this an operation," said Eman Rashid. "I can't sit in a room with a person who calls it an operation because they don't see me as a human being."

Eman's words are challenging. She has been angered by the euphemism "operation" as a characterization of what for her was a violent, aggressive action against Palestinians. Her fear-response system has been triggered, and she is responding emotionally to her own feelings of outrage and indignation. Those feelings have probably cascaded other memories of her perceptions of Israeli abuses of Palestinians, and she is becoming angry. Eman is not doing this intentionally. It is all happening outside of her awareness and conscious control. She is reacting as her amygdala is firing off signals to the rest of the brain to prepare for battle.

Naama Nebenzahl, the Israeli woman, felt "emotionally manipulated" during the conversation. "This level of aggression frightens me," she said. "The operation happened because of what preceded it with Hamas shooting rockets."

The hard thing to do is to look Eman in the eyes, empathically connect with her, and listen patiently without judgment. The easier thing to do is to react preconsciously. That is precisely what Naama did. She felt frightened, even though there was no physical threat. Her amygdala interpreted Eman's behavior as threatening toward her. It overwhelmed Naama's prefrontal cortex, which was probably already overloaded with the stress of anxiety at merely being present for the dialogue. Naama characterized Eman's behavior as "aggressive," and blamed Eman for frightening her. Then she made a counterargument to justify her own fear: "Hamas shot rockets into Israel. We were justified in suppressing Hamas in Gaza through violent military means."

Anger and fear have different effects on decision making. Angry people tend to make more optimistic judgments in choices about themselves than people who feel fear. In effect, fear and anger creates opposing perceptual lenses.

Eman responded, "We're all suspected terrorists. . . . If I had been killed I would just have been a statistic on your television screen." She continued, "I want Naama to understand that I felt subhuman," she said. "You may say you empathize, but you're being defensive and can't hear what I am saying."

Eman experienced revictimization, not at the hands of Naama, but through her personal memories of violence. She, however, targeted the nearest person, Naama, who had no responsibility at all for the aggression. Naama, in the meantime, was shut down emotionally. She justified her withdrawal by asserting that the conversation had reverted to one-sided blaming. Eman correctly felt that Naama was defensive and could not hear what Eman was saying. What Eman did not know was that her personal fear reaction triggered Naama to the degree that Naama could not possibly hear Eman at a deeper, empathic level.

This is not about therapy or singing "Kumbaya." It is about understanding how our brains react to the intense social environment of conflict. Without that understanding, international leaders cannot shift to a more enlightened way of doing business with each other.

Suppose that Eman and Naama were Palestinian and Israeli negotiators discussing a peace proposal between their two countries. Left on their own, their negotiations would most likely end quickly with one side or the other walking out.

What if you were their mediator? What might you do to help Eman and Naama work through their anger in a way that lead to constructive, rather than acrimonious, dialogue?

"It is an attack just like when a bomb goes off in a bus. You cannot dehumanize people by calling this an operation," says Eman. "I cannot sit in a room with a person who calls it an operation because they do not see me as a human being."

"This level of aggression frightens me," responds Naama, refusing to look into Eman's eyes. "The operation happened because of what preceded it with Hamas shooting rockets."

"Let us pause for a moment and think about what has just happened," you say. "Take a slow breath and feel inside yourself. I would like to know what you are feeling. Eman, you are angry and feel disrespected. What else?"

Eman looks at you. "Yes. I am very angry, outraged, in fact. I am angry that I am not being treated as a human."

"And, Naama what feelings are you experiencing?" you ask, turning to the young Israeli woman.

"I am frightened by Eman's aggression. I feel like she is going to attack me. I do not feel safe," says Naama.

"So, Eman. Would you be willing to tell us how you feel when the word *attack* is used as compared to how you feel when the word *operation* is used? And Naama, I would like you to ignore Eman's words. Just focus on what she is feeling and tell us what you think those feelings might be when she is finished."

"When the word *attack* is used, it makes me angry, but at

least the word is honestly describing what happened. The IDF attacked, and innocent Palestinians were killed. It was horrific. When the brutality of the attack is described euphemistically as an "operation," I feel that the horror is being minimized. Human beings who are being ripped apart by automatic weapons are now casualties of an 'operation.' They are no longer humans, no longer suffering beings. That insensitivity to the Palestinian plight enrages me," says Eman.

"Naama, tell us the feeling Eman was experiencing as she spoke."

Naama looks at you. "She was mad. She felt outraged. She felt disrespected. She felt dehumanized."

"Eman, did she get it right?"

"Pretty good. I am just so angry that this attitude persists!"

"Naama, what feelings did Eman experience? And this time, tell them to Naama rather than to me."

Naama for the first time looks at Eman and says, "You felt angry and frustrated."

"Yes, that is it," Eman said with visible relief.

"Naama, how do you feel now?"

Naama pauses as if to check herself. "I no longer feel fearful. I feel safe."

"And Eman, how do you feel now?"

Eman pauses, then says, "I feel good. I feel as if I had been listened to and heard. I am not so angry. I would like to hear why she used the word *operation* instead of *attack*."

"Would you be willing to ignore her words and simply listen for her feelings?"

"Yes, I think I can do that," Eman responds.

You look at Naama. "We are at war with Hamas, not the Palestinian people. Hamas shells us with rockets. It is a violent terrorist group. As such, we respond with the IDF in as limited a way as possible to avoid Palestinian injury. We do not 'attack' Gaza. We engage in a very precise military operation designed to kill terrorists. An 'attack' would be a broad assault on Gaza. Our

IDF operation was precise and limited. Furthermore, it was responding to provocation by Hamas. If anyone attacked, it was Hamas attacking the settlements."

"Eman, what were Naama's feelings?"

"Angry, frustrated, unhappy, disrespected," says Eman.

"So let us talk about . . . ," you say, and the discussions move forward.

Your intervention as the mediator helped the parties reflect on their own feelings and the feelings of their adversary. The simple human touch of listening for feelings while ignoring the words can have a profound effect on relieving anger and fear in important conversations. This type of intervention is completely missing from international negotiation.

ANGER AND ITS AFTERMATH IN NEGOTIATIONS

On the morning of April 28, 2009, the US Air Force conducted a low flyover of downtown New York City using Air Force One for a photo op. Local and state law enforcement officials had been forewarned of the event but were asked to keep it quiet so as to not frighten the public. The opposite occurred, with people in Manhattan wondering if they were being subjected to another terrorist attack as the distinctively marked 747 circled low and slow over the Upper New York Bay near the Statue of Liberty. The news media instantly picked up the story and, within minutes, the White House was besieged with calls.[7]

A White House administrator had authorized the flyover and afterward lost his job. President Obama was reportedly furious at the incident, according to White House press secretary Robert Gibbs.[8]

Let us suppose that later that afternoon, President Obama was scheduled to meet with the senior executives of General Motors, Chrysler, and Ford to negotiate whether and on what terms the federal government might be willing to bail out the

American automotive industry. This meeting did not occur, but let's assume that it did. What would we expect President Obama's stance to be toward the auto executives?

We would probably expect him to be respectful, to listen, to be deliberate, to attempt some problem solving, and to try to find a solution that worked fairly for the automotive industry, the American people, and the federal government. President Obama, if asked before the meeting, might even say something like this. However, our expectations and his best intentions would be far off the mark.

First, the president would still be deeply influenced by his fury over the morning flyover incident. Anger persists in our unconscious until the events causing the anger are resolved. Thus, we can unconsciously retain anger for days, weeks, or even months and not be aware of it in our day-to-day lives. Science clearly points to a dramatic carry-over effect of intense emotional experiences.[9] Because the flyover occurred that morning, we can be certain that President Obama was unconsciously still very angry about the flyover because it had not yet been resolved to his emotional satisfaction.

Second, even though the flyover was completely and totally unrelated to the hypothetical auto industry bail-out negotiation that afternoon, the president's fury would make a big difference in his decision-making process. The evidence clearly shows that when we are angry, we tend to make much riskier choices, take more and bigger gambles, and feel more self-assurance and self-control than is objectively the case. It's those dang cognitive biases again.

Incidental anger, unrelated to the problem or issue being negotiated, has the same effect as direct anger. One study showed that incidental anger created through movies, readings, and memories of anger-inducing events affected employees' judgments of their coworkers and acquaintances.[10] Angry participants were mistrustful even though the coworkers and acquaintances had no role in evoking the anger. The mere experience of anger can automatically activate prejudice and stereotyping.

The upshot is that President Obama would still be affected by his morning anger when negotiating with the auto executives. He would be a less prudent, deliberate, thoughtful negotiator. He would tend toward snap judgments and be overly optimistic about the future. He might be influenced by vindictiveness or vengeance. Most importantly, he would not be consciously aware of any of these influences on his decision making or his behaviors. Anger is an insidious and powerful unconscious influence on negotiators of all types.

FROM CLIMATE TREATY NEGOTIATIONS TO DAVOS: ANGER AND FEAR REIGN SUPREME

Carbon is an interesting element. It is the basis of life on our planet; it is the basis of energy; and it is the basis of many deep and emotional conflicts between nations. When carbon oxidizes (fire being the earliest carbon-oxidizing technology), heat is produced. Our ancestors fifty thousand or so years ago figured out that rapidly oxidizing carbon breaks down animal proteins and renders fat for a tasty haunch of wooly mammoth, or rabbit, if they had a bad week. Technological evolution and development took it from there.

Carbon, in the form of oil, coal, and natural gas, has created many world conflicts that continue to this day. The climate-change negotiations are a great illustration of how fear reactions led to impasse at the December 2009 COP15 global-warming treaty conference in Copenhagen.

The conflicts on global warming go like this: Carbon energy is cheap and remains readily available on the planet. Some countries, such as the United States, Canada, Australia, and the European Union, developed economies based on carbon better and earlier than others. These countries, as the early adopters, are generally the industrialized, developed countries of the world. When carbon is oxidized, a bunch of gases are produced, including CO, NO, and CO_2, the so-called greenhouse gases. They trap heat generated on the planet. As a result, the energy in the atmosphere changes (mostly by increasing), which changes the weather and the atmospheric temperatures. The effect is analogous to what happens in a greenhouse as the sun pours heat through the many windows and is not allowed to escape; hence, the term *greenhouse gas*. The shorthand name for the effects caused by these trapped gases is called *climate change* or *global warming*.

Depending on who you believe, listen to, or disregard, this is something that could be, will be, or will not be catastrophic. There is significant conflict around the mere existence of global warming. However, as we will see, the conflict is not about greenhouse gases; it's really about fear.

The politics are straightforward and simple. Those countries that have made buckets of money on cheap energy are not too interested in cutting back. To them, cutting back (carbon emission limits, cap and trade, etc.) means less energy or more costly energy, and therefore fewer jobs, less wealth, and less continued economic growth.

Countries such as China, Brazil, and India are developing industries based on cheap and plentiful coal and oil. Telling them to cut back is telling them to slow or stop industrial development, job creation, wealth creation, economic power, and, based on all of that, geopolitical power. In other words, they feel they are being told to be satisfied with second-class economic and political status in relation to the industrialized countries.

They reject this idea as insulting, disrespectful, elitist, and unfair. To make their case, they recount stories of oppression during imperialism and colonization. The stories, although old news, have truth to them, as industrialization developed in the Western hemisphere. Thus, the sense of injustice expressed by the emerging countries has some moral support in history.

Then there is everyone else. These are the countries that are, by the definitions of the developed countries, woefully undeveloped. They may remain undeveloped for many reasons, yet they aspire to the wealth of the developed countries. Many of these countries have huge forests. Trees absorb CO_2 and are therefore valuable in maintaining a balanced planetary atmosphere. Trees are also commercially valuable or cover land that could be converted to growing food. Some countries therefore face pressure to preserve and sustain their forests against pressure to harvest the forests and clear the land.

Other countries have significant populations in low-lying coastal areas that will be flooded if sea levels rise due to melting ice caps or severe storms caused by global warming. These countries fear physical extinction from rising oceans.

The effect of the greenhouse gases emitted by the industrialized and the emerging economies is, according to most scientists, overloading the planet with CO_2. This may or may not, depending on whom you believe, melt ice shelves, extinguish species, create droughts, precipitate floods, inundate islands and coastal regions, displace cities, stop employment, or kill tens, if not hundreds of millions of people. The issue is highly controversial, and the rhetoric is emotional.

These three groups—the industrialized countries, the emerging economies, and the nonindustrial countries—have to figure out how to coexist in a world where carbon energy is still cheap and plentiful and where there is great concern over whether and how carbon oxidation affects climate change.

Everyone pretty much agrees that COP15, the December 2009 international conference to negotiate a final deal on carbon emissions and climate change, did not work out as expected.

After fourteen days of discussions, the international negotiators were unable to agree on a draft treaty. Heads of state flew into Copenhagen on the evening of the fourteenth day, only to learn that no progress had been made. On Thursday, a group of fourteen heads of state met to negotiate something so the conference participants would not come away empty-handed. A short paper with no great substance was finally negotiated. The heads of state flew away, and the conference delegates, representing all the nations participating, were asked to endorse the paper. Here's what happened as captured by a video recording.[11]

The president of the conference introduced the paper. The Venezuelan representative pounded on his table loudly to get attention. He was ignored by the president, who recognized the Tuvalu representative.

After giving a brief critique of the paper, the Tuvalu representative said, "I regret to inform you, Tuvalu cannot accept that document."

The representative from Venezuela started a loud pounding on the table, shouting, "It is with indignation that we are speaking. This document is not acceptable!"

The president ignored the disruption and recognized the Bolivian representative, who said, "We have learned about this document through the media, not through you. Now we are given 60 minutes to accept something already agreed upon by other states. We are seeing actions in a dictatorial way. This is unacceptable and anti-democratic. We say to the people of the world: They shall judge upon it. The rights of our people are not being respected. We are not going to decide about so many lives in only 60 minutes. This is a group of a small number of countries."

A number of people applauded this statement, then the Cuban representative was recognized.

"Four hours ago, Obama announced an agreement which is non-existent. He is behaving like an emperor. We have seen the version being discussed by secretive groups in the last hours and days. Cuba will not accept your draft declaration. At this conference, there is no consensus on this document. I associate my voice to Tuvalu, Venezuela, and Bolivia. The target of 2 degrees is unacceptable."

The Costa Rica representative said, "For the reasons that we have heard, this document cannot be considered. . . . This can only be an INF doc; it's just for information. [I have an] additional question."

The president said, "The next speaker is Sudan."

Ambassador Lumumba of Sudan said, "The document . . . is one of the most disturbing events in the history of the climate change treaty process. This document threatens the existence of the African continent. It is murderous; it condemns Africa. It asks Africa to sign a suicide pact. Total absence of morality. This is like the 6 million Jews who died in Europe [referring to the Holocaust]. There is no African minister or president who has a mandate to destroy Africa. Two degrees is a certain death. It's immoral to even think that this document was issued by a UN or UN-related body. The promise of $100 billion will not bribe us to destroy the continent. As such, we do ask you to withdraw the paper and delete it from the conference system."

The representative from the Maldives said, "Sudan suddenly gets the right to speak again. I did not finish. I want to put on record you, president, have been biased and violated all rules of transparency."

At that statement, Michael Zammit Cutajar, a former United Nations official leading the working group on a new treaty, left the room, frustrated with the process.

The Maldives representative continued, "We have a real danger of the talks going the same way as the WTO talks. Science suggests we have a window of seven years! In the course of the last days, I have sat together with 25 countries. I have seen huge differences of opinion because large emitters do not [accept their responsibility for global warming]. [At] over 1.5 degrees, many islands would vanish. We tried very hard to get 1.5 degrees in the text. This was [blocked] by large emitting countries. [The] president suggested forming a group of states. This document is acceptable. It is not what we were looking for. I will be the first to be unsatisfied with this document, but it is a starting point. This document allows us to continue talks and come to a legally binding [treaty]. I ask you all; please do not delete this document."

The Egyptian representative said, "We should end this conference as soon as possible. For Egypt to accept this document, we want the names of the countries supporting it to be inserted so that we can see who has drafted this document and who is morally bound by it."

The Spanish representative said, "We totally agree with the words of the president of the Maldives. Free expression should prevail here. What was said by Sudan was not true. It dishonors an important project."

The Canadian representative said, "It is legitimate to express one's views, but to compare this with the Holocaust is offensive to our delegation. It is offensive, and these remarks should be withdrawn."

The Australian representative added, "We are absolutely astonished that this document is criticized by the parties who sat at the table. We have the greatest sadness for the people who really need the help."

Ethiopia, on behalf of African Union said, "The document in front of us is a compromise document, but as the president of Maldives has said, postponing is not an option."

France said, "To request by Egypt, my country supported the inclusion of 1.5 degrees because the [science supported it]. Only one big country [China] opposed it. What we heard yesterday, [indicated that] we were facing failure. This text may be imperfect, but we can obviously improve this draft."

Sweden, on behalf of the European Union, said, "We strongly support Maldives. The reference to the Holocaust is unbelievable."

The president regained a little control over the session and said, "Okay, then US."

The US representative said, "No, let the UK go first, it was their turn."

The United Kingdom representative said, "I think this institution faces a moment of profound crisis. We have a choice of two roads. Down one road, the proposed document is by no means perfect. We have many problems with it, but it will make the lives of people better. $30 billion fast start, $100 billion in a long-term plan. So it does very important things. Down the other road, the one of Ambassador Lumumba with the disgusting comparison with Holocaust would mean wrecking this process."

Many delegates stood up, and there was a long applause.

The president of the conference asked, "Is there anyone who will oppose this? [Counts:] 1, 2, 3, 4 oppose it. Hmm, does this mean we cannot adopt it? How are the rules? I am not familiar with UN rules. Do we need consensus?" And on that note, the most important climate treaty conference to date came to an end.

If we consider this plenary session through the lens of emotions, we can see reactivity as part of the explanation for the general collapse of meaningful discussion. Venezuela started off disruptively by pounding the table. Tuvalu expressed a feeling of disrespect. Bolivia asserted that it is being dictated to in an unacceptable and undemocratic way by a small group of powerful countries. Cuba accused President Obama of being an emperor. Sudan compared the document to the Holocaust, which later made international headlines. Finally, the president of the conference, apparently not familiar with the procedural rules, ended the plenary. No doubt many of the representatives left Copenhagen frustrated because of the organizers' inability to manage the emotions of the attending countries.

Here's another example of the emotionality of anger and fear between international leaders occurring at the 2010 Davos World Economic Forum:[12]

During a lengthy debate about the December 2008 Israeli offensive into Palestinian territories, Recep Erdoğan, prime minister of Turkey, told Shimon Peres that the Israeli air strikes and invasion of the Palestinian territory were "very wrong" and said "many people have been killed." Peres responded angrily, and a shouting match ensued.

Erdoğan tried to rebut Shimon Peres and asked the moderator, *Washington Post* columnist David Ignatius, to let him speak once more.

"Only a minute," Ignatius said.

"I remember two former prime ministers in your country who

said they felt very happy when they were able to enter Palestine on tanks," Erdoğan said. "I find it very sad that people applaud what you said. There have been many people killed. And I think that it is very wrong and it is not humanitarian."

"We can't start the debate again. We just don't have time," said Ignatius.

"Please let me finish," said Erdoğan.

"We really do need to get people to dinner," Ignatius replied

"Thank you very much. Thank you very much. Thank you very much. I don't think I will come back to Davos after this," Erdoğan replied.

The confrontation stunned the audience.

"I have known Shimon Peres for many years, and I also know Erdoğan," the former Norwegian prime minister, Kjell Magne Bondevik, said to a reporter. "I have never seen Shimon Peres so passionate as he was today. I think he felt Israel was being attacked by so many in the international community. He felt isolated. I was very sad that Erdoğan left. This was an expression of how difficult this situation is."

Amr Moussa, the former Egyptian foreign minister who heads the Arab League, said Erdoğan's action was understandable. "Mr. Erdoğan said what he wanted to say and then he left," he added. "That's all. He was right." Of Israel he said, "They don't listen."

Indeed, no one seems to listen as the habitual anger and fear of international leaders deeply affects the decisions that shape the world and make peace so elusive. Perhaps if they allowed highly skilled mediators to assist them in their conversations, they might feel listened to and heard. After all, there is no real difference between Naama and Eman, and Erdoğan and Peres.

Chapter 8

Kofi Annan and the Kenyan Crisis of 2007–2008

The Kenyan scenario provokes debate. If democracy is to solve Africa's problems, many historical, socio-political, cultural, and economic woes must be dealt with. If they remain untackled, electoral democracy will remain a fantasy. Historical wrongs, societal injustices, and poor governance must be corrected, otherwise deep wounds cannot heal.

—MILDRED NGESA,
JOURNALIST FOR THE *DAILY NATION*, NAIROBI, KENYA[1]

THE BACKGROUND STORY

The players in this story are Mwai Kibaki, Raila Odinga, and Kofi Annan, former secretary-general of the United Nations and the mediator in this conflict.

Mwai Kibaki was elected president of Kenya in 2002, succeeding Daniel arap Moi, who controlled Kenya for twenty-four years. Moi was a Kalenjin tribal member and consummate power politician who had worked the Kenyan ethnopolitical conflicts to his advantage for a quarter century. His game was to keep the Kikuyu, a powerful tribe, under control, and pit the minority tribal elements against each other to neutralize them. Obviously, his tribe, the Kalenjin, came out on top.

Odinga was a Luo, another powerful and rival tribal group. When Kibaki ran for president in 2002, Odinga supported him, even though Kibaki, like Moi, was a Kikuyu.

Kibaki and Odinga opposed Moi's anointed successor, Uhuru, the son of Jomo Kenyatta, the first "president" of Kenya. Uhuru was not the brightest button in the drawer and was apparently considered controllable by Moi. Uhuru was, like Kibaki, a Kikuyu, so that in the 2002 election, two Kikuyus were facing off. One represented the past; the other represented the hope of a democratic future.

Kibaki was elected in December 2002 with 62 percent of the vote, and everyone, including the international community, felt that democracy had triumphed.

Kibaki brought economic growth to Kenya. However, the new wealth benefited the old elites with no trickle-down to the majority of the people. The rich got richer, and the poor stayed in poverty. Under Kibaki, social inequality grew, and corruption reached new heights.

According to an editorial in the Nairobi newspaper *Daily Nation*, "Kenya practices a brutal, inhuman brand of capitalism that encourages a fierce competition for survival, wealth, and power. Those who can't compete successfully are allowed to live like animals in slums."[2] The facts seem to bear this out. A person born in the western Nyanza Province, the bedrock of Odinga's support, could expect to die sixteen years younger than a fellow citizen in Central Province, Kibaki's home. Child immunization rates in Nyanza were less than half those in Central.

While almost every child in the Central Province attended primary school, only one in three did in the North Eastern Province. More than nine out of every ten women in North Eastern Province have no education at all. In Central Province, less than

3 percent of the women lack education. In the Central Province, there is one doctor for 20,000 people, while in the North Eastern Province; there is one doctor for 120,000.[3] Kibaki's people benefitted, while everyone else lived in poverty and without basic education or health care.

There was nothing new here. The issue was not so much about ethnic conflicts as about equal economic, social, and educational opportunities. The Kenyan elite have basically excluded the masses from the middle class, keeping for themselves the country's wealth, power, position, and privilege. It is the same story repeated in many parts of Africa.

As a result of decades of illegal and forcible land acquisition, the country's political class, wealthy families, and their associates all acquired vast tracts of land. The family of Kenya's first president, Jomo Kenyatta, collectively owns about 500,000 acres. The family of the former president Daniel arap Moi owns a vast swath of fertile land in the Rift Valley. The president Mwai Kibaki owns hundreds of thousands of acres. Prime Minister Raila Odinga, who campaigned on promises to more equitably distribute resources and tackle corruption, has been implicated in a questionable land deal in the Rift Valley. All these families stand to lose if serious reforms are undertaken. Today, about half of Kenya's arable land is in the hands of an elite 20 percent of Kenya's population, while most Kenyans scrape a living off one acre or less.[4]

Until constitutional reforms in 2010, the president had all the power. Elections were winner-take-all affairs, and opposition groups had no power in the parliament. Low-level violence during elections was a political sport by the elites for decades. During elections, each side tried to intimidate voters with death and injury meted out by hired thugs. The Mungiki gang, a weird cross between pre-Christian Kikuyu paganism and an extortionist gang, followed this tradition and for years hired out its thugs to political candidates during campaigns. In 2002, however, the Mungiki chose the wrong horse and lost considerable political clout. After the election, it made up for its lost power by intensifying its grip on the slums. The Mungiki's power consolidation challenged Kibaki's ability to maintain social order within Kenya's urban areas.[5]

The Kenyans became frustrated with the situation, especially as their hopes for reform dimmed with each passing scandal. Raila Odinga, who supported Kibaki in 2002, became the opposition candidate of the Orange Democratic Movement (ODM). He capitalized on the popular frustration by exploiting ethnic, political, social, and economic issues. He claimed that the Kikuyu had grabbed everything, and all the other tribes had lost wealth, opportunity, and power. He stated that Kibaki had betrayed the 2002 promise for change by allowing corruption, crime, and violence to get out of control. Finally, he asked how the Kenyan economic "miracle" had benefited the ordinary people of Kenya.[6] By the beginning of December 2007, Odinga and his party enjoyed a huge lead in opinion polls and seemed ready to sweep Kibaki and his cronies out of power.

THE DECEMBER 2007 ELECTION

The December 2007 elections selected the parliament as well as the president. The parliamentary campaign was robust as 2,548 candidates from 108 parties competed for 210 seats. In the presidential election, three candidates were competing: the incumbent Mwai Kibaki, Raila Odinga, and Kalonzo Musyoka. Musyoka knew he had no chance of winning, but was positioning himself as a strategic postelection ally to the winner.

When the votes were counted, the problems began. Odinga's ODM party had won 92 seats in the parliament; Kibaki's PNU party had won 34 seats; Musyoka's party had won 16 seats, and Uhuru's Kanu party had won 11 seats. It looked like the ODM party was the big winner.

In the presidential election, however, the results became

immediately suspicious. The Kenyan Electoral Commission declared that Kibaki had 4,584,721 votes to Odinga's 4,352,993. The margin, about 2.5 percent, was problematic considering that the same voters had voted for Odinga's ODM party on the same ballot. There was evidence of vote rigging in the field on both sides of the political divide and even greater irregularities in the vote-counting process in Nairobi.[7]

After announcing a victory for Kibaki, the electoral commissioner said that he was under pressure to announce the vote and could not be certain that Kibaki was in fact the winner. It appeared that Kibaki's people had manipulated the ballot count to give him the presidency.

The results were explosive. When the Electoral Commission, under Kibaki's control, declared him the winner on December 30, 2007, the people in the Nairobi slums and in the western province exploded with violent protest. The slum dwellers were fed up with their social inequality, and the westerners were angry with the continued Kikuyu land oppression.

Violence was initially directed primarily against Kikuyu in mixed areas, including the Rift Valley and Western Province, and was followed by reprisal killings against non-Kikuyus primarily in the Rift Valley towns of Naivasha and Nakuru. There was an alarming incidence of rape in Nairobi's slum areas. The Kenyan police force proved ineffective, and worse, there was widespread documentation of excessive use of force, murder, sexual abuse, and looting by the police.

Hundreds of thousands of Kikuyus fled the Rift Valley, while Kikuyu militias retaliated by chasing Luos, Luyahs, and Kalenjins from areas considered Kikuyu territory. At the end of the violence, 650,000 people were displaced from their homes and more than 1,133 were violently killed.

To fuel these fires, it also looks like some of the violence was planned and organized by an elite group of Kenyans. A year and a half after the violence and the mediation, which is described below, Kofi Annan handed over to the International Criminal

Court a list of top suspects. Powerful individuals on both sides of the political divide were suspected to be on the list, and the political elite were divided on whether to create a special tribunal within Kenya to investigate and prosecute those on the list, or to let the International Criminal Court lead the effort.

THE MEDIATION

Clearly, a crisis had erupted in Kenya. As reports of the organized violence started to trickle out, the media began to use the word *genocide*, bringing back harsh memories of Rwanda. The regional and international community became distressed at the idea of a destabilized Kenya enmeshed in civil war. US assistant secretary of state for African affairs Jendayi Frazer traveled to Nairobi, followed by secretary of state Condoleezza Rice, to push the two sides to an accommodation. President Kikwete of Tanzania and President Kufuor of Ghana intervened on behalf of the African Union. Desmond Tutu and Cyril Ramaphosa of South Africa offered their offices. In addition, foreign heads of state rushed to Nairobi to offer assistance. These included former Presidents Chissano of Mozambique, Masire of Botswana, Kaunda of Zambia, and Mkapa of Tanzania, all members of the Africa Leaders Forum. It looked like everyone and their uncle wanted to mediate this one.

Ultimately, former UN secretary-general Kofi Annan was asked to chair a Panel of Eminent Personalities sponsored by the African Union. The panel was composed of himself; Graca Machel-Mandela, former First Lady of Mozambique; and Benjamin Mkapa. Together, they mediated the dispute between the Kibaki and Odinga factions over forty-one days in January and February 2008. Martin Griffiths, the executive director of the Centre for Humanitarian Dialogue, interviewed Mr. Annan on May 9, 2008. The following are some of Annan's recollections of the mediation from that interview.[8]

Mr. Annan explained how he was selected as mediator:

I happened to be in Accra, and the President of Ghana, Kufuor, was then Chairman of the African Union; he called me and said, "You know what has happened. We'll need your advice and help." So I spoke to him on and off, and then he decided to go to Kenya. . . . He spent two or three days there, he saw the President [Kibaki], he saw Odinga—he had attempted to bring them together. It didn't work. So he called me and said, "It is not going well; I will have to return, but we will have to find some way of assisting them, and I'm pleading with you to assist me, and I may also ask Ben Mkapa and Graca to join you as a panel of eminent personalities." So I spoke to both Graca and Ben Mkapa who had himself been in Nairobi when President Kufuor got there, as part of the group of former heads of states who are members of the African Forum.

I had a mandate which was quite unusual, and very short—almost one line—which is sometimes good. I also felt, as it was an African Union mandate, we were going to need strong support from the international community, and I felt I had to organize it before I got in: get them to understand how I was going to approach the problem, what sort of support I needed from them, and how we should coordinate. Because I know that sometimes, when these things happen, lots of people rush in and sometimes different mediators come in and it leads to confusion. So I wanted to get it right from the beginning—that we should speak with one voice, and that I'm going in to do my best and there should be [just] one mediating process. They all agreed and said, "We fully support what you are going to do."

I had some general ideas of what I would want to see, but it crystallized as I went along.

One of the ideas I had was to address the early signals that you can't ignore—that there was an ethnic element, which you really need to be concerned about because that can really push things in the wrong way, and you can get it hopelessly wrong. So there was a need for prompt action to try and stem that.

Of course, Mr. Annan was correct about stopping the violence, but he erred in believing the violence was based in ethnic differences. Fundamentally, Mr. Annan formed a working hypothesis without analyzing what was really going on.

Ethnicity, in terms of tribal membership or affiliation, was not the issue. As John Githongo, formerly the Kenyan official in charge of uncovering and rooting out corruption in the government, said at the time:

> Ethnicity is a mobile and nebulous concept. It means different things at different times, and sometimes matters more than at others. Today, ethnicity in Kenya means politicized kinship more than it does anything else; a kind of overpowering identity informed by grievance, a sense of being wronged, of being under siege.[9]

Mr. Annan apparently did not fully appreciate that the underlying conflict dynamics related to economic and social inequality, corruption, and land reform. Instead, he saw the violence in terms of ethnic tribal group against tribal group. That was not how the Kenyans saw it, and Mr. Annan probably should have asked more questions about the structural problems. As a result, he too narrowly defined the scope of the mediation and consequently failed to have Kibaki and Odinga focus on the broader problems in Kenya.

> One of my first acts on the second day of my arrival was to get the two leaders together in public for them to shake hands, and send a message to the people—to those groups that you think are going to kill each other: "Here are the leaders shaking hands, so hold your horses." So that was one thing I felt was very important.
>
> The other thing that I had wanted to do was see how we deal with the question of the elections. I had come to an early conclusion that a rerun would be a bad decision, and bad decisions get more people killed. Enough had been killed already, and in that environment any kind of election was going to be acrimonious and was going to get people killed. So I felt that

we needed to find a way of dealing with the disagreement over the election by looking forward, and not trying to rerun, repeat or something that would not give you the result you want, but may also get people killed.

And when looking at the election results, it was clear to me that there was no way that either party could run the government effectively without the other. So some type of partnership/coalition was going to be necessary.

I was concerned that, given the niche of the conflict, if one doesn't intervene quickly, it could get out of hand, and the protagonists were so intransigent. From our conversations with them, there appeared to be a certain lack of urgency about tackling the issues.

Since there was such tension between the two of them, I thought it would be wrong of me to bring the two together to negotiate—to shake hands fine, but to get them into straightforward negotiations given the tensions may in fact complicate matters and blow up everything, and if I had a group of three each and we sat talking and they fed [the Principals] what was going on, it would help diffuse the situation, giving them a sense that they are involved but not immediately confronting each other. . . .

They knew each other so well; they had too much history, which we knew.

Annan made a fundamental strategic decision not to work with Kibaki and Odinga together. His instinct was right in one sense: when people are in an escalated conflict, they cannot profitably negotiate with each other. However, the primary work of a mediator is to de-escalate the conflict between the principals so that they can work together to solve problems. Especially when there is to be an ongoing relationship between people in a deep conflict, the mediator has an obligation to help them learn how to work together collaboratively rather than contentiously.

In most conflicts, people cannot stand to be in the same room with each other—they are angry, mistrustful, vengeful, anxious, and frustrated. The very idea of sitting across from one's hated enemy is repugnant. It doesn't matter whether the fight is over a neighbor's barking dog, a divorcing husband and wife, a sexually abused victim confronting a church hierarchy, or political competitors facing off after a contested national election—people in conflict experience deep, complex, and intense emotions. We also know from experience with thousands of complex and difficult mediations that the best outcomes occur when the parties are persuaded to work out their differences together.

This is where the power of the mediator comes forth. An experienced, knowledgeable mediator understands and accepts the hot emotions in the room. The mediation process has to confront those emotions and give them space to be heard. Otherwise, while agreements might be made, the underlying conflict will persist. Thus, the mediation process has to create emotional safety, slow the conversation down, and invite the people to talk about what is really bugging them.

For example, in this case, Mr. Annan might have done the following:

"Gentlemen, the history between you is well known. However, you can help me help you by telling me more about how you personally have experienced the last three weeks since the election results were announced. What have you felt? What thoughts have gone through your head? How have you experienced the violence in your country?"

These questions would undoubtedly take Messrs. Kibaki and Odinga by surprise. They see their conflict has a battle over political power and control of the government. However, underneath that perspective are deeper layers of injustice, betrayal, anger, desire, fear, and hope that, if allowed to surface, could dramatically change the course of the conversations.

"Well," you might be thinking, "That is just unrealistic. To expect national political candidates—one of whom probably rigged the outcome, the other of whom probably organized violent gangs to terrorize the countryside and create outside political pressure—to talk about how they have experienced things is a waste of time."

The truth is that this objection is raised in all difficult mediations—no one wants to confront the emotions and feelings in the room, even though those same emotions are driving behaviors and decisions that affect tens of millions of people.

Unfortunately, the standard response is all too often to separate people because their feelings "may complicate things." In fact, the emotions are what complicate things and so must be addressed early on. Think of it this way: if people were not tense and emotional, they could probably negotiate out their differences without a mediator. It's the emotions that get in the way of productive conversations. The mediator's job, first and foremost, is to help the parties deal with those emotions, and that can only happen when they are together in the same room. This takes skill, experience, wisdom, and courage on the part of the mediator.

TRUST AND OXYTOCIN

Paul Zak describes himself as a neuroeconomist. His research interest at the Claremont Colleges near Los Angeles where he is a professor is decision making and the brain. In particular, he became interested in how trust in decision making arises. While he did not have mediators or peace processes in mind, his work has given many mediators pause to think about how they conduct their mediations.

"I wondered if oxytocin, which is both a hormone and a neurotransmitter, had any relationship with trust," Paul said. "We knew that previous studies of animals like prairie voles suggested that oxytocin in the brain encouraged long-term mating in pairs of adults and nurturing behaviors by mothers toward their offspring. In the prairie vole studies, it turned out that one species of these little rodents had high levels of oxytocin and were monogamous. Another closely related species had naturally low levels of oxytocin and were pretty licentious little critters. Monogamy was not their thing. It turns out that oxytocin was the mediating factor in the prairie vole's sexual behaviors and pair bonding."[10]

Paul and his colleagues therefore designed an experiment to see whether elevated levels of oxytocin had any effect on the trust one person placed on another.[11] They created an investment game in which the subject had to decide how much money to give to a trustee who would invest it in a high-risk deal. In other words, how much trust would the subject place in a person he had never met before? The study was conducted with fifty-eight college men who were each paid $64 to participate in the experiment. They were paired up, and one man in each pair was randomly selected to be an investor. The other man was the trustee.

Each investor was given twelve tokens valued at thirty-two cents each and redeemable for cash at the end of the experiment. The investor had to decide how many tokens to give to the trustee to invest for him. Both the investor and the trustee knew that the experimenters would quadruple the investment. So, for every token entrusted to the trustee by the investor, the trustee got four tokens from the researchers. The trustee then had to decide how much of the gain to return to the investor. He could keep it all, give some back, or give it all back to the investor. The investor knew that the trustee could make any of these choices and had to trust him to "do the right thing."

The control group of investors inhaled a nasal spray with no oxytocin—just a plain saline solution. The study group of investors inhaled a nasal spray spiked with oxytocin.

The investors who inhaled the oxytocin were far more trusting. About half of them gave all their tokens to their trustees, and most of the rest invested a majority of their tokens. In contrast, only one-fifth of the non-oxytocin investors invested all their tokens, and a third parted with a majority of their tokens.

"Oxytocin specifically affects an individual's willingness to accept social risks arising through interpersonal interactions," Zak and his colleagues concluded in *Nature*.[12]

At a high-level conference for experienced mediators at UCLA in the fall of 2009, Zak was asked about the application of these findings to mediation, decision making, and peacemaking.

"Oxytocin naturally elevates when people shake hands, work together in the same room, eat meals together, and otherwise socialize," he said. "While no studies have looked at trust in mediation, it would seem to be a good practice to keep people together when possible."[13]

Swiss neuroscientists, pursuing a slightly different line of study around oxytocin, found that central nervous system oxytocin reduces stress responses in conflict. In their study,[14] forty-seven couples took the oxytocin or the saline nasal spray. They were instructed to have a conflict conversation, which was videotaped. Each conversation was coded for verbal and nonverbal behavior (e.g., eye contact, nonverbal positive behavior, and self-disclosure). Cortisol, which rises in stressful situations, was repeatedly measured during the experiment through saliva sampling.

Oxytocin significantly increased positive communication during the couple conflict discussion and significantly reduced salivary cortisol levels after the conflict, compared with the couples inhaling the saline placebo. So oxytocin not only raises trust, it helps people communicate more positively with one another. Both trust and positive communication are obviously highly valued commodities in mediation.

The studies suggest that oxytocin fosters the trust needed for friendship, love, families, economic transactions, and political networks. Building trust is modulated in part by the levels of oxytocin people have within their bodies. Whatever a mediator can do to elevate oxytocin levels naturally will therefore increase the chances that the parties will trust each other.

When Mr. Annan decided not to work with Kibaki and Odinga together, he might have lost an opportunity to let oxytocin do some heavy lifting for him. By separating them, they obviously could not work together to build the trust that would later become essential for an effective power-sharing agreement.

Instead, Mr. Annan asked them to each nominate three sur-
rogates to represent them. Eventually, four representatives per
side were selected. This process, representative negotiation,
always poses challenges in mediation. First, the representatives
are generally not the decision makers. They therefore have limited authority to bind their side to a decision. Second, they are
not accountable to the process. They can be used by the absent
decision maker to delay, stall, prevaricate, obfuscate, and otherwise engage in nonproductive behaviors without accountability.
With representatives, the principal can always have plausible
deniability. Third, there is always too much chance of confusion
around messages when representatives have to report second-
hand their experiences to their principal, and then report back
the principal's reactions to the mediation conference. As will be
seen, Mr. Annan reached an impasse with the representatives and
was finally compelled to force Kibaki and Odinga to meet
together. He probably could have saved weeks of process had he
insisted on direct meetings at the beginning.

Mr. Annan goes on in his interview:

> When [representatives] first came together I could see there was
> some tension within the group, so when we were setting up the
> agenda, it became clear to me that if I could give them some-
> thing they could agree on in the early stages and build confi-
> dence, it would help the process. I was very grateful that they
> agreed on the agenda very quickly, because it could have taken
> a long time, but they agreed that this was urgent. I said, "You
> are going to make history, you are going to save your nation."
> And so we moved on.
>
> They were very clever—very smart people. I think some
> may have realized because in a way I was very open. I put all
> the items on the table. I did not say, "Let's discard this." I put
> all the items on the table and let them run, and . . . took them
> through what each option means. For example, if you are going
> to do a rerun, it's almost like organizing full elections. And they
> knew the situation on the ground; "Given the environment, do

you think we can have a rerun? . . . Counting 11 million votes and sending people to all the constituencies—it's another election, and it's going to get people killed. Is that what you want? Re-tallying gives you bits and pieces of paper, but it doesn't give you anything else. The so-called forensic audit doesn't really make sense. If this is the case, we don't want to sweep the election issue under the carpet. We have to find some way of dealing with it." And . . . I thought the independent review would be the way.

And I also thought it would give people the sense that the issue of their concern—over which some had been killed—had not been brushed under the table. Because usually when these things happen, we focus on the needs of political leaders. So I pushed Kibaki to set up a compensation fund for victims, which we discussed here too, and he has done that. So, as we went forward, I wanted them to agree and to put aside all the issues that had been really tearing them apart, but they had to get down that path.

I felt that the only way to go was a political option, but given the arguments they were bringing from their Principals, I thought if I put it down to them they will shoot it down. So I had to take them through all the issues, a bit like the electoral issue, and let them come to the conclusion that they had no option but to share power.

Mr. Annan's strategy was generally sound here, although he might have jumped to problem solving too early instead of spending more time eliciting the perspectives of the representatives on how they felt about the unfolding events. Many less skilled mediators overlook the power of storytelling. Every person has stories to tell, and every human is attracted to the stories of others. Skilled mediators help the parties draw out their stories for all to hear. Storytelling, although simple, is very subtle. Stories don't seem to have much place in the high-stakes games of international conflict, yet the human beings in those conflicts respond exactly the same way to stories as everyone else. At a minimum, exchanging stories provides a foundation for future understanding.

Mr. Griffiths, who was conducting the interview, asked, "I remember one of the difficulties you had as the chair and moderator of the talks was that they kept on returning to history, telling you how much they won, the details of the election, that facts needed to be restated. Did you find yourself after two-and-a-half weeks down there—you had been sick beforehand—did you get cross? Did you find your patience wearing thin?"

Mr. Annan responded, "There were moments when I got cross and irritated. There were moments I would say, 'Gosh, why are they doing this? This is serious, people are dying, and they are going through these silly games.' So, yes."

This exchange tells us much. First, the representatives seemed to continue to go back to their histories and restating things over and over again. This is a common situation in mediation, and, to an experienced mediator, is an indicator of process problems. Technically, when people repeat themselves and cannot seem to let go of their stories, they are said to be *blocking*. Blocking generally occurs because people are not feeling heard. In other words, an empathic connection has not been sufficiently created between the parties or with the mediator.

There are several responses to blocking. I have found that the best solution is to stop, listen, and "mine the emotional data field" of the speaker. So, the conversation might look something like this:

"Kibaki and his people stole the election. We know that Odinga won fairly. Kibaki is a liar, cheat, scoundrel, and should be thrown out on his ear."

"So you are angry, frustrated, and feeling betrayed."

"Kibaki is a crook. He and his cronies have stolen from the people. He has allowed gangs to terrorize the cities. His police brutalize his opponents."

"Yes. You are angry, betrayed, anxious, and fearful."

"Not fearful. We are not afraid of him!"

"Yes. Not fearful of harm, but fearful that he might steal the presidency."

"Yes, yes."

The mediator may not even address the substance of the statements. Instead, the focus is on the emotions expressed within the statements. When this is done properly, the blocking automatically stops and the conversation can move forward.

Another method for dealing with blocking is to ask the speaker about feelings.

"Kibaki and his people stole the election. We know that Odinga won fairly. Kibaki is a liar, cheat, scoundrel, and should be thrown out on his ear."

"Yes. So when you think about Kibaki stealing the elections, how does that make you feel?"

"What? What do you mean how I feel! Are you my therapist?"

"I am not sure how you are feeling about Kibaki stealing the election, so I am just asking you what you feel so that I don't make any wrong assumptions."

"Oh. Well, I am mad and really angry."

The result is somewhat the same. The emotions and feelings are put out on the table. Usually, that is enough to stop the blocking and allow the process to move forward.

So when Mr. Annan heard the representatives repeating themselves like a looping sound bite (what in predigital days was called a broken record), he had several ways of dealing with the blocking. He would have saved himself a lot of frustration and personal annoyance.

The conversation between Mr. Griffith and Mr. Annan continued:

We had agreed on all the other items and we got stuck on the governance issue [power sharing]. So at the end of a morning meeting I said, "Look—the lawyers are going to sit together, there are four of you here, and you are going to consider this and come to us with options. Set a table for four for them. They will sit together and eat alone and they will come back to us." So they all headed to one table, and they discussed it, and then they sent Mutula and Ruto to work further on this, and they came with some options they thought were workable. And I said, "Let's continue this on Friday," and Martha said, "No, we have to go now, on Thursday afternoon, to consult with our leaders."

[Griffiths asks if they did go on the Thursday.] Yes, and they left on Thursday to go and consult their leader. It was a long weekend and they came on Monday with hardly any ideas or guidance. So I was beginning to get irritated with them.

The problem of representative mediation had come home to roost. The representatives took options back to Kibaki and Odinga with instructions from Mr. Annan to come back with ideas on which options would work. Not surprisingly, the process went backward.

As Mr. Annan observed, "I had sent them there [on the retreat] so they could relax, breathe free air without people calling them from the ministries and all that. Each time they said 'We need to consult,' I expected them to come back with some wise positions, but they came empty-handed."

This is a common situation in mediation. If the mediator allows people to go off to discuss matters with nonparticipating decision makers, more often than not, the parties revert backward. That's what seemed to happen here. Mr. Annan did a very wise thing at that moment. He went to visit Kibaki:

I went to see him and they brought the whole cabinet there. I said, "Mr. President, some of your people think the panel is biased. We are not biased, but the others do their homework. They put forward their ideas and proposals. Your side produces nothing. They keep repeating the same argument. And I suspect they feel that they don't have to produce anything because you are the President, and they claim you won fair and square. So if this is the position, it is a problem."

Mr. Annan was clearly putting responsibility where it belonged—on Kibaki and his people, not on the process or the mediator. Nevertheless, impasse was looming.

Mr. Griffiths asked, "Then we come to the moment when you suspended the talks. Now, that happened on a Tuesday. You had this difficulty from the government side." Annan responded:

They had had the weekend, they had been consulting, and instead of removing brackets, they were adding brackets. I said, "Look, this is getting nowhere, so I've decided I'm suspending talks." And apparently, when I announced that, there was gloom around the country even though I said I had suspended it to be able to move faster and to act in a different way. I had done my duty and believed the leaders should do theirs.

On February 28, 2008, Mr. Annan asked for a meeting with Kibaki and Odinga alone to finalize the agreement on Agenda Item 3. Mr. Annan allowed only five participants to attend: President Kibaki and Raila Odinga, former Tanzanian president Mkapa (member of the panel), Tanzanian president Kikwete (chair of the African Union), and himself. President Kikwete was asked to attend because the Tanzanian model of governance combined strong roles for the prime minister and the president, providing a good comparison to what was being proposed in Kenya.

At the meeting the following day, Mr. Annan said,

The only way to save this nation is cooperation and coalition. The two of you have the responsibility to work together, to heal, unite, and reconcile this nation, and I know you had the chance to talk to your fellow President and neighbor—head of your Union—and you can live with a Prime Minister. I know your people say you can't, but I think we must also agree and understand the rationale behind the coalition, so I would want you all to read this paper.

He handed out the one-text agreement that had been the focus of discussions.

In that meeting, Mr. Annan recalled,

> Kibaki read it very carefully—he must have read it twice. And then I said, "I also want you to go through the text of the Act. There are a lot of brackets, which your people couldn't remove; it doesn't make sense to me, and I think we can remove them here—between the five of us."
>
> So we got to work! We went through paragraph by para- graph—some we dropped, some we didn't. And then we got to the constitution issue.

After five hours of discussion, the parties finally reached agreement. Kibaki would assume the presidency, and Odinga would assume a new post, prime minister, and would be account- able only to parliament, not to the president. The political crisis was over, but not the conflict.

Kofi Annan quit the mediation in March 2008, leaving the most contentious issues, including land reform, to be mediated by Nigerian former foreign minister Oluyemi Adeniji. Media reports indicate that Adenjii completed whatever work he did in June 2008. Unlike Annan's work, there was very little media or acad- emic coverage of Adeniji's mediation efforts, so there is no way to evaluate his efforts.

THREE YEARS LATER

After the political crisis was over, the Kenya National Dialogue and Reconciliation (KNDR) monitoring project began. South Consulting was retained under a grant from the Foundation Open Society Institute to monitor the progress of the KNDR. South Consulting has been issuing annual and quarterly reports since 2009.

The report for the first quarter of 2010 was a sobering wake-up call to the fact that few of the conflicts that caused the violence in 2007 and 2008 have been adequately addressed.[15] Furthermore, the personal relationships between the Kibaki and Odinga factions seem to have deteriorated to the extent that decision making around reforms is paralyzed.

For instance, the cabinet did not meet between early February and mid-March 2010, delaying decisions on several issues. Even when the cabinet has met, conflict between the principals has made governance almost impossible. Because Kibaki and Odinga refuse to work with each other, their partisan interests have prevented promotion of the greater interests of the nation. Despite the agreement mediated by Annan, Kibaki and Odinga continue to argue over who has what power and whether or not power should be or is shared equally.

As a result of these continuing conflicts, the image of "two-governments-in-one" persists. Divisions along ethnic and political lines are based on the unending suspicion and mistrust that characterized relations before the postelection violence.

There is no structured consultation between the two principals, and they refuse to recognize that power sharing is a reality. They have continuous disagreements on the meaning of power sharing, which in turn has increased incoherence. On the whole, the problem of power sharing continues to poison relations between the two partners. Worse, the personal conflict between Kibaki and Odinga has deepened patronage politics. Ministers now appoint their friends and political allies to senior positions on the basis of patronage rather than merit and without following due process. Some are making appointments on the basis of ethnicity or nepotism.

New alliances are forming in the power vacuum created by Kibaki and Odinga's failure to share power responsibly. Some of the new alliances are aimed at blocking important policies if they threaten to undermine the individual interests of key leaders. Some have emerged to block ICC prosecutions and undermine any efforts to bring leaders to account. The government's failure to address high-level corruption reflects the influence of individual political interests over national interests. Some politicians feel they can disregard orders without any consequences.

The report lists dozens of other shortcomings, failures, and problems that were supposed to be addressed, but are being ignored or subverted by elements within the government. It seems that the mediated agreement solved a short-term political crisis, but created much worse long-term conflicts.

What are the lessons to be learned about effective international mediation from the Kenya experience?

First, crisis provides opportunity. In this case, the argument can be made that Mr. Annan missed the opportunity to help Kibaki and Odinga openly discuss the structural issues that drove the conflict. Focusing on a political solution did not help the parties confront the underlying social and economic inequalities within Kenya. Instead, as is so often the case, posturing around the political issues allowed for easy avoidance of the much more serious and difficult issues. Once everyone breathed a sigh of relief on February 28, 2008, the momentum to follow through on discussions about other issues evaporated. The fact that Professor Oluyemi Adeniji apparently made no progress on these issues as the follow-on mediator supports the idea that when the pressure was off, it was back to business as usual.

Second, mediation provides an amazing opportunity to learn how to talk with your enemy. If that lesson is learned well through a professionally conducted mediation, the parties may develop a newfound capacity to work through the inevitable difficult problems they will face in the future. In the Kenya mediation, it appears that Mr. Annan spent little or no time coaching, educating, and teaching the parties how to work through their differences. There are no reported discussions about how the parties would confront future policy differences or conflicts. Fundamental to any good mediation is the understanding that peace is hard work, that future conflicts are inevitable, and that the parties must develop a plan for how they wish to deal with conflicts as they arise. That practice is strangely absent from most international mediations and is certainly absent in this mediation.

In addition, Kibaki and Odinga worked face-to-face for only five hours at the end of the process. Here are the two most powerful leaders of Kenya, locked in a power struggle, facing enormous structural problems that may affect their personal wealth and status, who are negotiating a power-sharing arrangement that will require intense interpersonal cooperation, communication, and leadership to be successful. They obviously lacked those skills before the mediation. Did Mr. Annan and his panel of Eminent Personalities truly believe that once an agreement had been signed that these two men would suddenly gain the capacity or motivation to work with each other?

The mediator's moral imperative goes beyond superficial political agreements. In this case, that imperative was to help these men forge a working partnership, gain the skills to talk and negotiate with each other, and give them the ability to call for help when they got into trouble with each other. This did not happen, and the breakdown described in the South Consulting report is a predictable result of that failure. Unfortunately, the people of Kenya have continued to suffer because of this failure.

Too often, international mediators believe that because a "deal" has been signed, the conflict and problem is solved. Experienced and skilled mediators know otherwise. Deep, intractable conflicts may take years of mediation and may require dedicated perseverance to the process of peace after the flashbulbs and media lights have gone on to the next crisis du jour. If Kibaki and Odinga can't solve conflicts, the mediator should be there to help, getting the parties to the table yet again, and again, and again—forcing them to confront and decide issues they would rather not face. That is the obligation and sacred trust imposed on the mediator if he wants to truly call himself a peacemaker.

Chapter 9

Mediating Justice and Accountability

Accountability of perpetrators, including their accomplices, for grave human rights violations is one of the central elements of any effective remedy for victims of human rights violations and a key factor in ensuring a fair and equitable justice system, and ultimately, reconciliation and stability within the state.
—UN COMMISSION FOR HUMAN RIGHTS,
RESOLUTION 2003/72:25[1]

On Monday, July 12, 2010, the International Criminal Court added charges of genocide to the list of crimes Sudanese leader Omar al-Bashir had been accused of committing.[2] Before the ruling, al-Bashir had been charged with seven counts of war crimes and crimes against humanity for his role in orchestrating an extermination campaign against the African tribes of the Fur, Masaalit, and Zaghawa living in Sudan's western region of Darfur. Human rights groups hailed the decision, saying that it sent a strong rejection of impunity to Sudanese leaders.

A spokesman for the US National Security Council, Mike

Hammer, said, "The United States strongly supports international efforts to bring those responsible for genocide and war crimes in Darfur to justice and believes that there cannot be a lasting peace in Darfur without accountability."[3] Two days later, however, Scott Gration, the US special envoy to Sudan, expressed concerns about how the new indictment would affect his efforts to secure the cooperation of al-Bashir in bringing peace to Sudan. He said, "The decision by the ICC to accuse Sudanese president Omer al-Bashir of genocide will make my mission more difficult and challenging especially if we realize that resolving the crisis in Darfur and South, issues of oil and combating terrorism at a 100%, we need Bashir. Also the issues of citizenship and referendum, the North holds a lot of influence so this is really tough. How will I carry out my duties in this environment?"[4]

General Gration's question frames the problem perfectly for international mediators. On the one hand, the international community wants to hold war crimes criminals accountable through an international retributive justice system, yet on the other hand, the cooperation of those criminals is often necessary to secure peace. How can these two apparently inconsistent goals be managed in an international peace process? There is no magic bullet that solves this problem. What is required for peace and accountability is a deeper understanding of justice. The conflict between peace and accountability is really a conflict around the different meanings of justice. Understanding justice is therefore critical to reconciling peace with accountability.

JUSTICE INDEFINABLE

"OK, give me a definition of *justice*," I said.

The law students taking my Peacemaking for Lawyers course stared back at me as law students do. I could see the confusion and alarm in their eyes. They suddenly realized that in three or four years of law school, no professor had ever asked them to think about the meaning of justice. It was just, sort of, ummm, assumed that everyone knew what justice was.

"C'mon. You guys are seniors. You are sitting for the California Bar Exam in less than six months. Surely, you can give me a definition of *justice*?" I pestered them.

Uncomfortable silence.

"OK. What is the difference between, say, social justice and retributive justice? Or retributive justice and restorative justice? Or retributive justice and distributive justice? How do the classical theories of justice relate to retributive justice? And what the heck *is* social justice?" I fired off.

The confusion was now complete. These concepts of justice were obviously foreign to very bright, hardworking law students nearing the end of a rigorous graduate education. And, I had made my point. Justice has a lot of different meanings.

Confusion about these meanings also creates tension in international peacemaking. Many mediators avoid talking about justice and accountability for fear that parties who probably have engaged in gross human rights abuses will not want to negotiate as long as they face criminal liability. Uganda presents such a case.

THE PROBLEM OF JUSTICE IN UGANDA

The conflict in northern Uganda began when President Yoweri Museveni took power by force in 1986. In response, the rebel Lord's Resistance Army (LRA), headed by Joseph Kony, rebelled. Kony's rebels have been notoriously vicious. They have routinely cut off the noses, lips, and ears of civilians to terrorize the population into silence. They have engaged in wholesale murder of villagers, mostly from their own Acholi people. They have kidnapped girls to raise as AIDS-free sex slaves. They have forcibly recruited boys to become child soldiers. By anyone's definition, the LRA is bad.

In reprisal, Ugandan soldiers committed numerous human rights violations including killing, torturing, and raping the Acholi people because they were suspected of protecting the LRA. The Ugandan government forcibly moved many Acholis into squalid displacement camps, arguing that the move was needed to protect the population from the LRA. In actuality, the forced relocation was punishment for supporting the LRA.

In 2000, as a way to break the violent stalemate, the Ugandan parliament passed a blanket amnesty for LRA rebels who renounced violence and surrendered to the government.

"The act was passed in a deliberate effort to try and find a peaceful way of ending the conflicts and rebellions the country has had," Justice Peter Onega, chairman of the Amnesty Commission, wrote in his paper, "The Amnesty Process: Opportunities and Challenges." "Battered into a position of submission, aggravated by the fact that many of the rebels inflicting atrocities on them were their own children forced into rebellion, elders and religious leaders from the [worst affected] Acholi region began to advocate for amnesty," Onega explained.[5]

Although many people benefited from the amnesty, it failed to end the violence. Consequently, in December 2003, President Museveni asked the newly operational International Criminal Court (ICC) to investigate the LRA.[6]

In July 2005, the court issued arrest warrants for the top five LRA leaders—Joseph Kony, Vincent Otti, Okot Odhiambo, Raska Lukwiya, and Dominic Ongwen, charging them with widespread systematic murder, sexual enslavement, rape, and war crimes.[7]

The announcement was met with a great deal of criticism. The Refugee Law Project, for example, believed that the ICC investigation would motivate the LRA to continue its violence and would "obliterate" any opportunity for a negotiated peace.

Before the indictments were issued, Acholi leaders said that the issuing of "international arrest warrants would practically close once and for all the path to peaceful negotiation as a means to end this long war, crushing whatever little progress has been made during these years."[8] The Roman Catholic archbishop in northern Uganda, John Baptist Odama, saw the ICC's decision to issue indictments against the LRA leadership as "the last nail in the coffin" for efforts to achieve dialogue.[9]

According to Barney Afako, the lead legal adviser to Riek Machar, the South Sudanese mediator in the Juba talks between the Ugandan government and the LRA, "From the outset, the ICC and the Rome Statute were planted firmly at the heart of the talks. Although other parties adjusted their positions, the LRA, with the most to lose, remained implacably opposed to ICC trials. Against this clear stance, the only issue left to discuss was what form national justice processes needed to take."[10]

Afako went on, "For the LRA, the prospect of its leaders being paraded before an international court represented a particularly acute form of political humiliation. Behind the ICC's intervention, LRA leaders saw only the hand of the Ugandan government. Pointing to the charges made exclusively against members of the LRA, its leaders detected collusion between the ICC and the government's political agenda."[11] The ICC arrest warrants were clearly at the center of the discussions and created a major sticking point. If the peace agreement failed to address the issue of individual justice for the LRA leaders, the agreement would be rejected by the international community. If the LRA leaders were not somehow shielded from prosecution by the ICC, however, disarming them was unlikely.

The solution was to create several ways to try criminal cases. Depending on the severity of the case, the matter would be handled through a special division of the High Court of Uganda or through a traditional tribal justice process. The more severe cases would go to the High Court, while the lesser offenses would be handled through the tribal justice process. High Court cases were to be brought against those "alleged to have committed serious crimes during the conflict," with prosecutions focusing on those "alleged to have planned or carried out widespread, systematic, or serious attacks directed against civilians, or who are alleged to have committed grave breaches of the Geneva Conventions."[12] The intent of this agreement was to deprive the ICC of jurisdiction, since the ICC could not act if a national court was able to hear a case. Despite this, impasse was not avoided. At the end of the talks, the LRA refused to sign a final peace agreement until the ICC warrants were withdrawn. The government of Uganda responded that it would not do so until a final peace agreement was signed.

In looking back at the Juba talks, Afako commented, "Juba showed that the dilemmas posed by the tensions between justice and peacemaking are real and are sharply accentuated when an international court or tribunal intervenes in a situation. Mediators cannot wish away the legal and political complexity of these circumstances, nor can they be ambivalent about the merits of dialogue. They must be prepared to take a firm lead, prioritizing a careful search for a workable settlement."[13]

International mediators, in particular, must have a firm grasp of the many meanings of justice. Without that understanding, they will flail around in the negotiations without giving structure and guidance to conversations about justice and accountability. Let's get into these meanings and see how they inform us about peace.

CLASSICAL THEORIES OF JUSTICE

There are three classical theories of justice. They are called the *positive law* theory, the *social good* theory, and the *natural rights* theory of justice. Each theory describes justice differently, and understanding these differences is important to any negotiation about justice. Much of the argument between impunity and accountability is really an argument about which theory of justice should be applied to the conflict.

The *positive law* theory of justice makes three statements. First, it says that justice is objective and measurable. Second, because the law takes precedence over justice, justice cannot measure law. That is, no law can be unjust. Finally, the law provides the whole measure of justice so that justice is nothing more than conformity to law. A person who obeys the law is just, and a decision that conforms to law is a just decision, regardless of the outcome.

This theory of justice leads to a controversial conclusion. Because each society defines its own laws, justice is relative. Thus, a democratic society has "democratic justice," an oligarchic society has "oligarchic justice," and a totalitarian society has "totalitarian justice." Positive law is not concerned with "goodness" or "rightness" except insofar as it is a means to social order. An oppressive law is "just" because it is "the law."

While human rights and social justice advocates sharply criticize this view, they often miss that positive law theory is concerned with order, not with fairness. Under this theory of justice, society measures justice by obedience to the law.

When people talk about bringing human rights abusers to justice or talk about judicial tribunals or international criminal courts, they are typically speaking about positive law justice. As we saw in the previous chapter, in a morally perverted, but logical sense, human rights offenders will invoke positive law as justification for their behaviors—"What I did was just because I was following orders," or "I was following the law."

The *social good* theory of justice says that laws are just according to how well they promote the social good. Some conduct may be outside the law but still may be just because it is socially good. For example, a parent may be just or unjust to children in matters where the law leaves the parent free to act without interference.

The social good theory of justice allows for amnesty of gross human rights abuses if amnesty ends war, and the society deems peace the highest good. Even though amnesty would violate the positive law and natural rights theories of justice, under social good theory if amnesty benefited the most people, society should consider amnesty the most just action. Thus, letting war criminals go free would be a just result, even though victims may experience personal injustice.

The third classical theory of justice, *natural rights*, asserts that people possess rights as individuals before they form a political society. These natural rights exist because humans are conscious of their existence and are able to communicate their consciousness to one another. Thus, justice must answer not only to the needs of law and society but also to the needs of people. Natural rights proponents frequently declare a number of specific rights. For example, the American Declaration of Independence asserts that "all men . . . are endowed by their Creator with certain inalienable rights, that among these are life, liberty, and the pursuit of happiness." The French Declaration of the Rights of Man and of the Citizen claims "natural, inprescriptible, and inalienable rights." Some natural rights authors, like John Locke and Thomas Jefferson, have claimed that natural rights are self-evident. Thus, the task of the law is merely to secure their observance. All natural rights proponents agree that justice is broader than law, and questions of justice can arise independent of any question of law.

The concept of human rights is a natural rights theory of justice. Its proponents argue that human rights justice trumps positive law and social good so that it dictates vindication of the human right to exist in safety and security over peace through amnesty. However, these same proponents use positive law theory to compel obedience to the law.

In the Juba talks, justice was never fully expressed and discussed. What was underneath the conversation was the unresolved conflict between positive law, social good, and natural rights justice. The human rights abuses, based on natural rights, found expression in positive law, international criminal statutes, and the ICC, arguing that the highest social good comes from prosecuting war crimes offenders. The desire for peace, based on social good, found expression in positive law, the peace agreements, and arguing that natural rights would be reestablished by peace. If this seems complicated, it is. Yet sophisticated mediators should understand this complexity and be able to frame the issues such that people's underlying beliefs around justice are brought to the surface of the conversation.

RETRIBUTIVE JUSTICE

Justice based on punishment, which goes back to the biblical concept of *lex talionis* or an "eye for an eye," is called *retributive* justice. "You hurt me, so I am going hurt you." Proponents of retributive justice have offered many justifications for it, including deterrence, definition of clear social values, public vengeance, rehabilitation, protection of freedom, legitimizing the authority of the state, and incapacitating dangerous people. When people talk about holding criminals accountable, they are talking about retributive justice.

Fundamentally, retributive justice is about revenge, and the passionate desire for "justice" is about returning the harm to the offender. Retribution looks to the past to determine what was done, who was the offender, and who was harmed. The remedy applied by retributive justice is punishment in the present and the future. By its very nature, retributive justice is not healing. Furthermore, accountability under retributive justice is measured by verdicts of guilt and by punishment. Criminals are said to be held accountable when they are imprisoned for their crimes. Usually, criminals are not compelled to make things right with their victims or the communities affected by their offenses.

However, retribution as a basis for accountability raises some interesting complexities.

Imagine that you have been punched by your older brother. In retaliation, you punch him back. You think you are using the same force, but in fact, you punch him harder. He responds in kind, and now you are in a fight. Mom intercedes, and you claim, "But he hit me first!" Your brother argues back, "But he hit me harder!"

In every human society, "He hit me first" is the primary rationale for war and violence. Both civil and religious laws have long prohibited violence, unless it is a response to violence, in which case it is perfectly fine as a form of self-defense.

Hitting someone who has not hit you is wrong, but hitting back is OK. The English language even has special words such as *retaliation*, *retribution*, and *revenge* that remind us that the second punch is different than the first punch. In other words, retributive justice is served when there is an even-numberedness to the punches. If the war crimes criminal punched first with human rights abuses, the International Criminal Court, for example, evens things up by punching second. There is symmetry to this type of offense and punishment that feels right and feels just.

This is also why parties in intractable conflicts have offered the even-numberedness of their punches as justification for their continued violence. Thus, the Israeli Defense Force justifies the Gaza blockade on the basis that the Gaza Palestinians continue to attack Israel.

The problem with the principle of even-numberedness is that people miscount their own punches. While retribution is great in theory, it is poor in practice.

In a 1987 study conducted by William Swann and his colleagues at the University of Texas, pairs of college men played the roles of world leaders trying to decide whether to initiate a nuclear strike.[14] The first fellow was asked to make an opening statement; the second was asked to respond. Then the first young man was asked to respond to the second, and so on. At the end of the conversation, the men were shown several of the statements that had been made. On a sheet of paper, they were asked to write down what statements had been made just before and just after.

When shown one of their own statements, the men easily remembered what had led them to say it. But when they were shown one of their partner's statements, they remembered only how they had responded to it. In other words, they remembered what caused them to make their own statements, and they remembered how they responded to their partner's statements. They did not remember what the partner said that provoked their statement.

What this means is that our reasons for punching will always be more meaningful to us than the punches themselves, but that the reasons for the other's guys punches will be meaningless to us—only the other guy's punches will mean anything.

Examples aren't hard to come by. Shiites seek revenge on Sunnis for the revenge Sunnis sought on Shiites; Kurds retaliate against the Turks who retaliated against them; and everyone in the Middle East claims they are simply defending themselves. In each conflict, people on one side say that they are only responding to provocation and dismiss the other side's identical claim as a gratuitous and obvious lie. But research suggests that these claims reflect genuinely different perceptions of the same conversation. In fact, we forget that we might have been the cause of the other guy's punch.

If the first principle of legitimate punching is that punches must be even-numbered, the second principle is that an even-numbered punch may be no more forceful than the odd-numbered punch that preceded it. Legitimate retribution is meant to restore balance, and thus an eye for an eye is fair, but an eye for an insult is not. It is OK to hit back, just not too hard. The problem is, we can't do that. We routinely hit back harder than we were punched, even when we are trying return the punch with precisely equal force.

In a study conducted by Sukhwinder Shergill and his colleagues at University College London, pairs of volunteers were hooked up to a mechanical device that allowed each of them to squeeze their partner's fingers.[15]

The researcher began by squeezing the first person's finger. The first volunteer was then asked to squeeze with the same amount of pressure on his partner's finger. The partner was then asked to squeeze back exactly the same. And so on. The pair took turns squeezing each other's fingers while the researchers measured the actual amount of pressure they applied.

You would think this would be easy, and you would be wrong. Although the pairs tried to reciprocate with equal force, they typically squeezed 40 percent harder than they had just experienced. Each time one person was squeezed, he squeezed back harder, which led the partner to squeeze even harder. What began as a game of soft touches quickly escalated to hard, crushing squeezes, even though both partners were doing their level best to respond in kind.

Each person was convinced that he was responding with equal force and that, for some reason, the other guy was escalating. Neither realized that the escalation was the natural by-product of a neurological quirk that causes the pain we receive to seem more painful than the pain we produce, so we usually give more pain than we have received.

It gets worse.

The need for vengeance appears to be hardwired into at least male brains. In 2006, researchers at University College London, curious about vengeance in the brain, scanned the brains of men and women while they watched "guilty" or "innocent" actors receiving a mild electric shock.[16]

When "innocent" actors received this stimulation, both men and women showed empathy activation in pain-related areas of the brain. When a "guilty" actor received a shock, women showed empathy, but men did not. In the men's brains, the punishment of the "offender" caused a surge in the reward areas of their brains. In other words, seeing the guilty person punished felt good.

"[Men] expressed more desire for revenge and seemed to feel satisfaction when unfair people were given what they perceived as deserved physical punishment," said Dr. Tania Singer, who led the study.[17]

"This type of behavior has probably been crucial in the evolution of society as the majority of people in a group are motivated to punish those who cheat on the rest. This altruistic behavior means that people tend to protect each other against being exploited by society's free-loaders, and evolution has probably seeded this sense of justice and moral duty into our brains. This investigation would seem to indicate there is a predominant role for men in maintaining justice and issuing punishment," Singer concluded.[18]

What this tells us is that retribution is not a rational meting out of just deserts; it is an emotional reaction to an offense that stimulates the reward centers of the brain. As a result, retribution more often than not escalates conflicts. The conflicts quickly become intractable because the parties can see only their reasons for acting, not the other person's reasons, and because vengeance, at least in men, is physically satisfying—it just feels good to thump the bad guy.

Nevertheless, criminal justice systems around the world are based on the idea of retribution, and retribution becomes a cause in and of itself, not because it helps the victim. In fact, the victim's voice is often lost in the retributive process.

RETRIBUTIVE JUSTICE WRIT LARGE— THE INTERNATIONAL CRIMINAL COURT

On July 17, 1998, after five intense weeks of negotiations during the Rome Diplomatic Conference, representatives of 120 states from all regions and legal traditions agreed on a treaty creating the International Criminal Court (ICC) in The Hague. The ICC is the world's first permanent court mandated to accuse and try the perpetrators of the worst crimes known to humankind—war crimes, crimes against humanity, and genocide—when national courts are unable to do so.

The treaty, known as the Rome Statute, became effective on July 1, 2002, following ratification by the required sixty states.[19] The United States is not a signatory to the treaty. In March 2003, the first eighteen judges of the court's bench were sworn in, and the chief prosecutor, Luis Moreno-Ocampo, took office in June 2003.

Since then, the prosecutor has opened investigations in the Democratic Republic of Congo (DRC), northern Uganda, the Darfur region of Sudan, the Central African Republic (CAR), and Kenya. These investigations, all of which have been conducted in situations of instability or ongoing conflict, have led to criminal charges against at least twelve alleged perpetrators "bearing the greatest responsibility" for crimes against humanity.[20]

The Rome Statute blends European and Anglo-American law traditions to create a unique relationship between the pretrial judicial division and the prosecutor. While the Rome Statute stops short of creating an investigative judge in the tradition of European civil law, it gives the judges powers and functions that would be out of place in an Anglo-American common law legal system.

The Office of the Prosecutor is the driving engine of the court. The court's ability to dispense retributive justice is largely shaped by the prosecutor's decisions about what cases to investigate and what cases to bring to trial. For victims, the prosecutor's selection strategy provides the earliest and most visible measure of how the court will address the suffering they have endured. The prosecutor's selection of alleged perpetrators and charges also has practical implications for victims: it determines which victims will be eligible to have their voices heard as participants in proceedings. Unlike any other court in the world, under the right circumstances, victims have the right to counsel and to participate in the trial.

The prosecutor's office has made a number of strong policy statements in two significant areas that directly affect the execution of its judicial mandate. The first area involves the prosecutor's interpretation of the "interests of justice" pursuant to article 53 of the Rome Statute.[21] Under article 53, the prosecutor may decline a case if he decides that investigation or prosecution would not be in the "interests of justice." This discretion is subject to pretrial judicial review, which means that aggrieved parties can appeal the prosecutor's decision to not take a case or to not try a case.

The phrase "interests of justice" is intentionally ambiguous to give the prosecutor wide latitude in deciding how to allocate his resources. Included within the phrase is the interplay between peace processes and criminal prosecution of war criminals. The Office of the Prosecutor had initially suggested that it might consider peace and stability as one of the factors underlying a decision not to act. As we saw in Uganda, many people argued that the prosecutor should decline the prosecution of the Lord's Resistance Army leaders because it would not be in the "interests of justice." However, the prosecutor has decided that it will not consider the broader concerns of international peace and security in the independent pursuit of his mandate to bring war criminals to trial.[22]

The prosecutor has additionally decided that parties to a peace negotiation cannot compromise the issue of criminal accountability.[23] In other words, if the ICC hands down indictments to parties engaged in peace negotiations, those indictments cannot be bargained away as part of a peace agreement.

The effect of this policy adds a new wrinkle to peace negotiations with war crimes offenders. Since the ICC does not have the power to prosecute if the state has the ability to do so, the parties in peace negotiations will now have to consider how to create and implement national and local criminal accountability mechanisms that will satisfy the ICC. Even then, war criminals will be subject to some accountability process or will otherwise face the ICC. Bargaining away criminal complicity for crimes against humanity is no longer on the table.

However, this policy does open up the possibility of broader, more restorative methods of accountability, and this leads to a consideration of restorative justice.

RESTORATIVE JUSTICE

In the mid-1970s, Mark Yantzi, a young Mennonite probation officer in Kitchener, Ontario, was sitting in court watching three young men being arraigned on vandalism charges. They had gone through a quiet neighborhood breaking windows, defacing doors, and generally raising hell. They were caught and were now beginning their journey through the Canadian juvenile criminal justice system.

That evening at a men's group meeting, Yantzi told the story of being in court. He wondered aloud what would happen if the three offenders made amends to the homeowners by paying for the damage they had caused and apologizing for their behavior. The rest of the group thought Mark should take a run at trying something like that with the kids. So, Mark made an appointment to see the judge assigned to the case. As Mark describes the conversation, the judge looked at this young probation officer and said something to the effect of "Well, the law doesn't say I can do this . . . but it doesn't say I can't either. If the young men are willing, give it a try and report back here in a month."[24]

Mark and a more experienced colleague, Dave Wirth, met the boys, who agreed to try to make things right. That Saturday, with Mark and Dave standing behind them, they marched up to each house, knocked on the door, introduced themselves as the kids that had caused all the damage, asked how much money was needed to fix things up, apologized, and promised to pay it back. Mark and Dave took notes of each conversation and the amounts needed. The kids went out and got jobs, earned the money in three weeks, and marched up the street again. This time they had checks in their hands for every homeowner.

At the next court appearance, Mark and Dave reported on the work. In addition, many of the homeowners showed up to speak of their appreciation for what the boys had done. After listening to the stories, the judge dismissed the charges. The kids all went on to college and grew to have successful careers as adults. The modern restorative justice movement had begun.[25]

Today, restorative justice is a movement and a philosophy that looks at crime and violence as injuries to the victim, the community, and even to the offender. Restorative justice is not about retribution and punishment; it is about victim needs and offender accountability directly to the victim and to the community.

The academic literature describes restorative justice in terms of participants, purposes, and processes, emphasizing the roles of the victim, offender, and the community. Restorative justice processes include victim-offender reconciliation, victim-offender mediation, negotiated restitution, community justice conferencing, family justice conferencing, and reintegrative shaming, among others.

In essence, restorative justice is a way of responding to crime that makes things as right as possible for all affected. We say that restorative justice has occurred when the victim, offender, and community have recognized the conflict or harm, and the offender has taken responsibility, the damage (physical and relational) has been repaired as much as possible, and where future accountability plans and agreements are created that will prevent the same thing from happening again.

Restorative justice contrasts with retributive justice in that it empowers victims and offenders to talk about the offense and its aftermath, to negotiate the best way to make things as right as possible, and to discuss how to prevent future offenses. In contrast, retributive justice often leaves the victim out of the process, and accountability is measured by punishment, not by healing.

While not explicitly referring to restorative justice, there have been international peace processes that allude to it. In the Juba talks, traditional or tribal justice was considered as one approach for less severe offenses. The mediator and the parties did not develop what the tribal process would look or feel like to the victims. However, many indigenous peace processes have elements of restorative justice embedded within them.

DISTRIBUTIVE JUSTICE

There is yet another concept of justice unrelated to the classical theories or the retributive-restorative models. This is called *distributive* justice because it involves the question of how to divide fixed resources.

Imagine we are in a clan one hundred thousand years ago. I go out one day and slay a woolly mammoth all by myself. I drag the carcass back to our encampment one hunk at a time. Around the fire that night, I get the first choice of wooly mammoth haunch. No one protests because I was the guy who brought home the bacon, so to speak.

This illustrates the first leg of the three-legged stool called distributive justice. It is about *equity*. Equity says that I should receive in proportion to what I contribute. If I contribute a lot, I should get a lot. If I do not contribute much, I should not get as much as the guy who contributed more.

Once I have my mammoth steak, all the adults take their shares of the sizzling meat. We are all equal members of the clan and are entitled to equal shares of the meat. This illustrates the second leg of the distributive justice stool, *equality*. Because we are equal members of the clan, we share equally. Being an equal member entitles me to an equal share of the group resources regardless of my contribution.

There is still some woolly mammoth meat cooking on the fire. Several of the adults cut off pieces and feed the children, the few who are sick, and the elders. This is the third leg of the stool, *need*. In every group, there are members who cannot provide for themselves but who nevertheless have a claim on group resources. The young, the sick, and the elderly have a claim on the meat because of their need. Without the meat, they would starve. Because of their age or health, they cannot fend for themselves.

Distributive justice is therefore the delicate balance of equity, equality, and need. We each perceive that balance subjectively. Massive wars have been fought over perceived imbalances in equity, equality, and need. Yet distributive justice is rarely discussed in international mediation or negotiation.

When someone claims unfairness around wealth, resources, or economic development, distributive justice is in play. If elite Kenyans manage to gather 90 percent of the country's economic wealth for their own benefit, a distributive justice problem exists. In countless mediations, I have seen distributive justice imbalances drive the conflict. People get angry when they are not receiving what they think is their fair share. I have found that explaining the concept of distributive justice helps people access where they feel imbalance. Breaking the concept into equity, equality, and need allows for deeper penetration of the conflict. Any agreement that addresses distributive justice issues explicitly is more likely to be honored than one that is silent.

TRUTH COMMISSIONS AND RECONCILIATION

Transitional justice has evolved as another way of striking a balance between the need for vengeance, retribution, and accountability and the need for peace going forward, and it has had mixed success. The primary form of transitional justice is the truth commission.

Truth commissions developed in the last quarter of the twentieth century as a means of dealing with mass human rights abuses after civil war or insurrections within a country. The fundamental purpose of a truth commission has been to establish an accurate record of a country's past human rights abuses. The theory is that by creating an honest account of past abuses, history will not repeat itself nor be lost or rewritten. Governments have created truth commissions at a point of political transition to demonstrate or underscore a break with a past record of human rights abuses, to promote national reconciliation, and to gain political legitimacy.

Truth commissions face the same conceptual problem as

international mediations—how to choose the appropriate form of justice and how to reconcile that justice with the need for peace. Satisfying any theory of justice does not lead automatically to reconciliation, and reconciliation may be contradictory to some theories of justice. Therefore, a fundamental issue facing creation and operation of a truth commission is how it chooses to define justice. To date, there is little evidence that in forming truth commissions, the framers have considered the inherent complexities of justice. Instead, they seem to have used the term *justice* without clearly defining its meaning. This is one reason why truth commissions have had unsatisfactory results for their people: the expectations of justice were never established and communicated.

Justice raises a number of questions for mediators negotiating a truth commission process between parties. Some of them are:

- What values of justice should a truth commission serve?
- Does a truth commission process fulfill the classical theories of justice?
- How should a truth commission measure the "quality" of justice?
- Does the truth commission process provide a subjectively favorable experience of justice?
- When is a truth commission process appropriate?
- When is a retributive process such as the International Criminal Court appropriate?

Truth commissions cannot meet all definitions of justice. If truth commissions strive to serve positive law theory, they are relegated to seeking obedience to law, without regard to outcome fairness. If truth commissions strive for social good, the sponsors must define what is good for the most people. Generally, this will mean that an oppressed minority may experience injustice. Should a truth commission tolerate a poor outcome for one party that, in the larger context, is good for society? If truth commissions strive to elaborate justice based on natural rights, how are conflicting rights reconciled? If one side's natural rights must be subordinated to the other side's rights, has justice been met?

These answers cannot be answered in the abstract. Each conflict presents its own challenges and measures of justice. Thus, no objective measure of justice is possible or desirable. Experienced mediators should realize the ephemeral and subjective nature of justice and open a space to talk about what justice means to the society and its government.

RECONCILIATION

In so many conflicts, the violence has been between people who have lived together in the same region. The end of war requires former enemies to learn to live together in peace. This is a difficult challenge and requires some thought about reconciliation.

Reconciliation is a complex and complicated concept. There is no clear definition of reconciliation. It seems to be defined by circumstances, practices, sacrifice, and inner change. It is defined more by the nature of the environment than by any strict definition. In that sense, reconciliation can be compared to water. It lacks any shape until placed within an environment that contains it, and then it reflects the shape of the container.

Reconciliation is also defined by practice. Human relationships create reconciliation and at the same time, the reconciliation process challenges relationships. Reconciliation allows for judgment and removes the reason for that judgment. Reconciliation requires both parties to participate in and give to the process. Reconciliation is a mutual process, while forgiveness is unilateral.

Reconciliation also includes the idea of sacrifice. Whether at the individual, community, or national level, reconciliation requires moving beyond concrete positions of right and wrong. People must sacrifice an old identity and create a new identity and story to support it. This identity sacrifice is what makes reconciliation difficult to achieve.

Finally, reconciliation includes inner change within an individual. This form of reconciliation comes from letting go of negative affects and harmful thoughts, which can be very challenging.

There are four forms of reconciliation. The first is "individual to individual" reconciliation, typified by victim-offender reconciliation. In this process, the offender offers an apology, and the victim acknowledges the apology. The power of this personal reconciliation depends on the sincerity of the offender. If the offender's apology is based on true vulnerability, it is more likely to be accepted. Skilled restorative justice mediators spend a lot of time explaining apology to offenders in hopes of witnessing the openness of sincere regret and remorse.

The victim may or may not engage in forgiveness. Nevertheless, the acknowledgment of the wrong and acceptance of the acknowledgment allows people to move forward with their lives in peace. This process is what many think of as reconciliation.

The second form of reconciliation is "individual to many." This may occur when a national leader apologizes to a group targeted in attacks or singled out for mistreatment by authorities in power. Usually, the individual asking for reconciliation is a spokesperson or representative of a group guilty of wrongs. This form of reconciliation moves reconciliation from a personal, and perhaps intensely private, arena into a public arena. Sometimes, the spokesperson provides symbolic compensation for the wrongs, although compensation is not typical.

The third form of reconciliation is "many to individual." An example of this form might be a tribunal or court apologizing as a whole for the wrongs done against an individual. This type of reconciliation requires that the more powerful party give up its claim of a superior moral position and abdicate its power in favor of the victim. Again, individual compensation is not typical, and if provided, it may only be symbolic.

The last form of reconciliation is "many to many." This form of reconciliation occurs when rival groups engage in a mutual reconciliation process. For example, in Voinjama, Liberia, two tribal groups reconciled after a brutal civil war by conducting a Feast for the Dead together. Large bowls of food were prepared, and members of each tribe sat together around a bowl. According to tradition, before any person could eat from the bowl, he or she had to release all feelings and thoughts of enmity or hatred. To eat without a clear, forgiving mind cursed the children for three generations. In this form of reconciliation, demands or offers of compensation are unusual and may be insulting or disrespectful to either group.

Reconciliation forces people to talk about difficult subjects when it does not appear that there is an opening for dialogue. Reconciliation exposes the silence around injustices and brutalities held in the thoughts of the people. As conversation is created through the process of reconciliation, the potential for storytelling opens up. In this space, people can fully reveal their opinions and emotions, experiences and beliefs, while allowing the other to hear their side of the story. This creates a place for healing and understanding. All is laid out on the table, both sides tell their side of the event, and the truth that they feel is revealed. Unlike retributive law, which looks backward to find justice in the present, reconciliation looks backward to create possibilities for a peaceful future.

The nature of reconciliation makes it difficult to say how long a reconciliation process might take. Reconciliation may be measured by how a population views itself in response to the process, the things that it places value in, and its understanding of past events. Reconciliation is therefore a process and not an event, and must be thought of in terms of decades and perhaps generations.

Reconciliation can be assessed by how a society deals with its past. If the past is still an issue of discussion and argument, then reconciliation may not be complete. Does a society hold one or multiple versions of the past? A reconciled country has a more unified understanding of the past. If there are disagreements in what happened to cause the conflict, the conflict can arise again. Similarly, are the relationships between former opponents based on the past or the present? Reconciliation is about building relationships in the present for the future—relationships that relive the past are vulnerable to resurfacing old antagonisms. Reconciliation has occurred when there is one truth of the past for all involved.

COWS AND RECONCILIATION

In postgenocide Rwanda, reconciliation seemed like an impossible task. After all, the Hutus and the Tutsis had literally been at each other's throats for generations. After the genocide in 1994, most people were of the view that peace building and reconciliation efforts should be practical and beneficial to the society, and not theoretical or ideological.

Christine Makahumure lost everything in the horrible genocidal war that ravaged Rwanda in 1994. When her family tried to flee the fighting, they were caught in a cross fire, and Christine watched in horror as her husband and son were shot down before her eyes.

For years afterward, Christine, her daughter Catherine, and her parents lived a life of barest subsistence. The family would shut themselves indoors from sunset to late morning the following day, due to lack of money, activity, or friends. They never dared to hope for anything more in life. Then they heard about an organization that was giving out cows, Heifer International.

In partnership with the Rwandan government and the United States Agency for International Development, Heifer International started the Cows of Peace project in Rwanda's Byumba province. This project started in 2001 to help impoverished people acquire improved breeds of cows and to teach them zero-grazing technology.

One of the groups supported by this project was the Giramata Association, which means "May you have milk" in the Byumba municipality. The association was made up of thirty-one members, nineteen of whom were women. Most of the women were either widows of genocide victims or wives of imprisoned men suspected of having committed genocide.

Christine became a member of the Giramata Association and was eventually elected as its president. Her pregnant cow arrived, whom she named Umugeni Mwiza, meaning "the best bride," and delivered its calf two weeks later. Immediately the village homestead became a hub of activity with a stream of excited visitors, inquisitive schoolchildren, and high-ranking officials. The cow's name signified the presence of a benevolent mother, to whom many come for solace.

Christine said in an interview with representatives from the Rwandan National Unity and Reconciliation Commission:

> I was the first beneficiary of the project in our association. After receiving the cow, I realized that one neighboring family was in abject poverty. Their children were sick and malnourished and the whole family was living in a makeshift structure. I started giving them 4 liters of milk on a daily basis free of charge but I found it to be costly and uneconomical. My cow produced a calf which could not be passed on so I decided to sell it off and build a zero-grazing structure for the family to get it ready for the next acquisition of heifers. Subsequently, the family acquired a cow, and, as of today, it has built an iron-roofed house and can afford paying school fees for the children who look healthy. I can sleep peacefully because I know that these people have something to eat, drink milk and can sell some to be able to buy items they could not afford before.[26]

Cows have brought people in from isolation. People once suspicious of each other now come together to share ideas. Since every community member is a potential beneficiary, each person feels responsible for the security of the cow. Neighbors meet in the evening to talk and keep company in the home where the cow is kept. Culturally, this is a place for sharing and building trust and solidarity and is one of the purest forms of peace building and reconciliation.

The cows have also enhanced the status of women in their communities. Before the Cows of Peace program, women were thought to be unable to manage cows. Even though cows were a valuable asset in Rwandan traditional culture, managing them had been traditionally a job for men. With the introduction of new laws that gave women an equal right to own property, they can now own cows.

"Women have proved to manage these cows better than men because we have noticed that those cows look healthier and are more productive than those managed by men," reported the local veterinary assistant.[27]

Traditionally, cows played a role in the resolution of conflicts. In postgenocide Rwanda, these cows are now used as instruments to promote peace and reconciliation among communities. They are fostering such a strong sense of mutual support that some members of Giramata Association have begun to feed prisoners in the provincial prison of Byumba with milk and food.

"We have volunteered to take milk to prisoners as a way of preparing them to change positively before they are released from prison," Christine Makahumure stated.[28]

This may seem mundane to a person from the developed world until we understand that milk is a precious food item in the Rwandan culture. The gift of milk to prisoners is a sign that peace and reconciliation is taking hold in Byumba.

Any nation recovering from evil, war, and violence faces the challenging task of balancing the various ideas of justice, reconciliation, and truth in a process that must fulfill potentially conflicting expectations. After human rights abuses, the desire for oppressors receiving their just deserts is strong. Validation, vindication, and vengeance are powerful forces, and channeling those forces toward reconciliation takes courage. Mediators play a pivotal role in asking questions, provoking thought, and guiding the parties to solutions that will work for them.

When thinking about reconciliation, mediators must be careful not to set expectations too high. Deep personal reconciliation is not likely to happen between antagonists without investing in a community-based restorative justice project such as the Cows of Peace project. So far, the move toward deeper reconciliation practices has not been attempted. If future peace processes remain focused on narrative truths through testimony and depositions, reconciliation at the individual and community level is more likely to occur over a time measured in years and decades. Likewise, if a society is interested in a healing process, significant resources must be devoted to therapeutic counseling at an individual and community level. Even then, the potential cultural resistance to seeking help for problems such as post-traumatic stress disorder may prove to be a significant challenge.

Ultimately, mediators have the responsibility to help parties consider the value of truth in relationships to the varying needs for justice and reconciliation. When the complex issues of justice, reconciliation, and truth are not raised by the mediator, peace will remain elusive.

Chapter 10

Making Peace Illegal

"Blessed are the peacemakers!*"
*Not valid in all jurisdictions, some restrictions may apply. See Congress for details.

—ANONYMOUS BLOG POSTING

I magine that you and your team are called to mediate a violent regional conflict. One of the parties that must be at the table has been identified by the US secretary of state as a foreign terrorist organization. You and your team begin meeting with the parties separately, including representatives of the terrorist organization, engaging in dialogue, coaching on process, and facilitating an eventual joint problem-solving conference. At the conference some months later, you work with all the parties by facilitating collaborative problem solving, identifying and discussing deep injustices, and, along the way, coaching parties, de-escalating them, re-engaging their moral compasses, listening, asking questions, and creating a strong, safe container for the work. Months go by, and finally the parties are able to find a way to stop the violence. They agree to continue their work nonviolently. A small miracle of peace has occurred in large part because of you and your team's efforts.

At the end of the engagement, you return to JFK International Airport. As you enter the terminal, you are met by a team of FBI agents who proceed to arrest you, handcuff you, make you do the perp walk in front of the national media, and book you into federal prison. You have been charged with multiple violations of the Patriot Act and face fifteen years in prison for each charge.

All you did was bring peace to a land torn by years of violence.

One has to question the commitment of countries like the United States to peace when they make peacemaking work with the most violent groups on the planet illegal. As Justice Department lawyer Douglas Letter stated in oral arguments to the Ninth Circuit Court of Appeals, "Congress wants these organizations to be radioactive."[1] But that lawyer and his political masters have failed to ask and answer the question, "If terrorists are 'radioactive,' how can we ever find peace with them?"

THE PATRIOT ACT

The US government claims it has an interest in cutting off support to any terrorist organization because support of any kind may benefit the organization.

"Hezbollah builds bombs. Hezbollah also builds homes. What Congress decided was when you help Hezbollah build homes, you are also helping Hezbollah build bombs," argued Elena Kagan before the US Supreme Court.[2]

Federal law makes it a crime to provide material support to any organization designated as a terrorist group by the secretary of state. But the definition of "material support" includes not just providing weapons, money, or bomb-making skills; it includes providing any sort of expert advice, training, or personnel— including advice on how to resolve disputes peaceably or training on how to make human rights claims before the United Nations. Interestingly, the law permits religious training without exception. So you can teach revolution by jihad and bomb making, as long as you do it within the boundaries of religious training, but you cannot teach peacemaking if it is secular.

No person within the United States or subject to its jurisdiction may "knowingly" provide "material support or resources" to a designated foreign terrorist organization. Material support or resources includes anything you can imagine. It includes training, expert advice or assistance, facilities, and transportation. If, as a mediator or peacemaker, you were to arrange for a conference room (a facility), provide for a bus ride (transportation), teach negotiation or other peaceable means of conflict resolution (training), or be a mediator, facilitator, or go-between (assistance), you have, according to the US attorney general, committed a serious federal felony.

Juan Zarate, who served as President George W. Bush's deputy national security adviser for counterterrorism, has said:

> If you're training them on how to make their case before a U.N. tribunal, what you're doing is giving them the skills, the ability to legitimate their cause to advocate their position, and from a U.S. government standpoint, that's dangerous.
>
> Part of the issue here is that we are dealing with multiple terrorist organizations around the world that are complex organizations. In many respects, they are not just militant organizations, they have charitable wings, they have political arms, and so the application of the statute runs into complications because there may be cases in which it appears legitimate to deal with these organizations from a political or humanitarian standpoint.
>
> It's hard to put your arms around it sometimes because it may appear to be a distinction without a difference. But I think in terms of the law, it's actually a very important distinction, one in which the U.S. government is saying, "This group, these groups listed by the secretary of state, are off limits to U.S. citizens."[3]

The problem this poses to peacemaking in the world is not esoteric. Peacemaking, conflict resolution, human rights advocacy, and the provision of aid to civilians requires direct engagement with people who resort to or support violence, including terrorists. For example, mediators must negotiate with armed rebels and governments. Each side must be provided with strategic advice and expertise on identifying injustices and interests and how to satisfy them. Peacemaking often requires direct persuasion and lobbying of armed factions to choose nonviolent means to achieve their ends. Human rights advocacy requires peacemakers to persuade offenders to stop their abusive practices, to explain moral and legal obligations under human rights and humanitarian law, and to teach compliance with those obligations.

Major institutions for peace could easily be indicted for their peacemaking work. For example, the Carter Center mediates conflicts, helps implement peace agreements, strengthens rule of law, and facilitates dialogue between warring factions. It offers mediation and facilitation services for peacemaking in Africa, the Middle East, Latin America, and Asia. It has worked with, among others, the PLO, Fatah, Hamas, Hezbollah, the SPLN in Sudan, the Lord's Resistance Army in Uganda, and the Maoists in Nepal. This work requires meeting with all sides to a conflict, including violent people designated as foreign terrorist organizations. You can't do peacemaking from a university campus—you have to be in the thick of the conflict engaging with the parties moment to moment.

The Patriot Act calls all of this work into question. It makes peacemaking and humanitarian efforts with the most violent people in the world illegal. The very thing that the US government professes to want the most, peace, has been made illegal. Former president Jimmy Carter, a Nobel Peace Prize Laureate, could be indicted and convicted by the government he once led, for his personal peacemaking efforts.

THE FREEDOM RIDERS

In the spring of 1961, a civil rights group, Congress for Racial Equality (CORE), decided to test President John F. Kennedy's commitment to end segregation in the South. The president had talked about civil rights but was afraid that an aggressive policy of desegregation would alienate Southern Democrats. Since he had won the presidency by a narrow margin against Richard Nixon, his political concern was real.

The civil rights leaders were not satisfied and decided to push the young president to act on his promise of broader civil rights enforcement. They planned a Journey of Reconciliation, dubbed the "Freedom Ride," modeled after a similar effort fifteen years before. Blacks and whites would ride buses headed for the Deep South. The white people were to sit in the back while the blacks sat in the front. At rest stops, the whites would go into blacks-only areas and vice versa.

At that time, despite federal laws and court decisions, the white majority of the Deep South continued to practice segregation based on skin color. Different water fountains, restrooms, restaurants, public areas, and bus seats in the back and front were specified for the black-skinned people and the white-skinned people. An entire social order was created around this "separate, but equal" concept, except that the separation was not so equal. Take restrooms. In a modern 1960s bus terminal, the white-skinned people's restrooms were spacious, clean, and well lit. The restrooms for black-skinned people were around the back. They were small, old, filthy, vermin and insect infested, unsanitary, and many times not working. The indignities went well beyond public restrooms, of course. Black-skinned people were expected to remain at the bottom of the socioeconomic food chain and be satisfied with their lot in life.

In the months preceding the Freedom Rides, the US government had reluctantly liberalized regulations covering interstate travel, including bans on segregated services. The Freedom Riders wanted to test the resolve of the federal government and the patience of the local white Southerners. The plan was to load public buses with blacks and whites, travel throughout the South, and flagrantly, but peacefully, use the white-only services or reverse social roles so that the white Freedom Riders used the black people's facilities.

In an interview with journalist Juan Williams, CORE director James Farmer said, "This was not civil disobedience, really, because we [were] merely doing what the Supreme Court said we had a right to do." Still, they expected resistance.

"We felt we could count on the racists of the South to create a crisis so that the federal government would be compelled to enforce the law," said Farmer. "When we began the ride, I think all of us were prepared for as much violence as could be thrown at us. We were prepared for the possibility of death."[4]

The Freedom Riders encountered the resistance and violence they expected. As the various buses made their way south through Mississippi and Alabama, the Ku Klux Klan turned out in force. Freedom Riders, both black and white, were violently beaten, arrested, and imprisoned. Criminal cases were filed, and counterinjunctions sought as the nation became caught up in the brutality of this new activist phase of the civil rights movement.

The national media immediately picked up on the story, seeing the obvious drama in the conflict between civil and con-stitutional rights and an established Southern social order that oppressed non-white-skinned people in violation of those rights. The editors of *Life* magazine, one of the most popular and widely read national magazines of the time, chose the Freedom Riders as the "Story of the Week" on June 2, 1960, and ran ten pages of photographs telling the story. Later in the week, *U.S. News & World Report, Nation, Newsweek*, and *New Republic* ran major stories on the Freedom Riders. It was one of the first major media events of the modern, post–World War II age.

That same week, on June 2, 1961, a Republican federal dis-trict judge in Montgomery, Alabama, issued a two-sided injunc-tion that prohibited violation of civil rights and enforcement of segregation laws and told the Freedom Riders to behave them-selves by not engaging in civil disobedience. At 11:30 a.m. that morning, eight Freedom Riders left the Montgomery Trailways

Bus Terminal on a bus going to Jackson. As was the plan, the white riders used the black-only restrooms and the black riders used the white-only restrooms and segregated areas. Although a lot of people were standing around and watching, the event was peaceful and uneventful. Among the eight was a young civil rights activist named Ralph Fertig.[5]

The bus stopped near Selma, Alabama, and Sheriff Jim Clark climbed onboard. He took one look at Fertig and arrested him on the spot. The charge was "bothering a white woman." Fertig himself was white and from Chicago. He was hauled off the bus, and it was sent on its way with the seven remaining Freedom Riders. Ralph was not so lucky.

He was handcuffed and roughed up, then thrown into the back of a sheriff's cruiser for a short trip to the Selma jail where a welcoming party was waiting for him. In the general containment cell, Clark had rounded up a bunch of low-life thugs and malcontents, most of whom were members of the Ku Klux Klan.

When Ralph was thrown into the cell with the crowd of rowdies, the sheriff made sure to yell out that Ralph was a "nigger-loving civil rights Yankee Jew." That was all it took. The crowd jumped on Ralph and began issuing a severe beating. He was slugged, kicked, and pummeled until he collapsed to the floor. The men kept kicking him on the floor until the sheriff's men, who were watching outside, decided enough was enough.

They entered the cell. The men inside stepped aside quickly and respectfully, having done their duty as they saw it. Ralph was carried out and dumped on a street in Selma. Every one of his ribs was broken, and he was a mass of bruises and contusions. A couple of civil rights lawyers heard that Ralph was on the street, arranged to pick him up, and got him emergency care. He was transported back to Chicago, another wounded veteran of the war for freedom and justice for all.

THE HUMANITARIAN LAW PROJECT

In later years, Ralph became a lawyer. His sense of justice had not abated, which led him to the Humanitarian Law Project, a non-profit organization dedicated to helping oppressed minorities around the world seek redress for human rights violations through peaceful, nonviolent means. Ralph, as an active member and leader in the Humanitarian Law Project, was approached by a contingent of Kurds. The Kurds claimed that, as a minority group in Turkey, their human rights were being systematically violated by the Turkish armed forces. Ralph became interested in the plight of the Kurds and traveled to that part of the world to investigate the claims.

The Kurds are a tribal group with their ancestral home in northern Iraq, Syria, Iran, and Turkey. In Turkey, the Kurds have been a brutally oppressed minority trying to assert the right of self-determination. Ralph felt that there was something he should do to try to work with that. So he started meeting with Kurds. He talked with them about nonviolent ways to work through the difficulties they were having. He began teaching them how to petition to the United Nations for assistance and how to petition the US government, particularly the State Department, for assistance. He taught them nonviolent ways of dealing with conflict and oppression. He did not ask if any Kurds belonged to any terrorist organization. He did not want to know; he was just interested in helping what he felt were an oppressed people gain a voice.

In 2005, the Patriot Act was amended by the Congress to prohibit anyone from training or providing any kind of benefit at any cost to any organization that had been designated as a foreign terrorist organization by the secretary of state. Within the Kurdish people is an organization called the PKK, which has been designated by the secretary of state as a Kurdish terrorist organization. However, Ralph was not working with the PKK; he was working with Kurds generally. Being a lawyer, he understood that he was subjected to criminal risk if he continued to work with the Kurds, so he filed a lawsuit in federal court claiming that the Patriot Act was a violation of his First Amendment right to free speech. Peacemaking, he argued, is a form of protected speech under the First Amendment.

Amazingly enough, Congress changed the law, which mooted the case. Ralph had to refile after the amendment, and the case has proceeded. His case was ultimately heard by the US Supreme Court in February 2010 and decided in June 2010.

"I've always been involved in the civil rights movement. As our country and society have gone increasingly global, it's clear that the oppression of people in other lands impacts our ability to sustain freedom in the United States," said Ralph when I interviewed him on my radio show in May 2010.

I remember when I first talked to Martin Luther King about joining the Freedom Rides—I'd known him before and worked for him Chicago—"Wouldn't my coming south be resented? Wouldn't I be seen as an outsider?" And he reminded me, as I knew he would, that no man is free anywhere until we are all free everywhere. That's particularly true today when you look at an economy that is dependent upon the work of people overseas, the consumption of resources from other lands, and the exploitation of labor.

Some people from the Kurdish community came to me and said that they had been denied very fundamental rights in a part of the Middle East that is now Turkey and was at one time the Ottoman Empire. After World War I, the empire was divided up into many nations that did not exist before then, such as Iran, Iraq, Syria, and Turkey. In those countries, they divided up a territory that had been intact for six thousand years called Kurdistan.

The Kurds in Turkey were not allowed to speak their own language, not allowed to name their kids with Kurdish names, and not allowed to honor Kurdish traditions. They were told, "We are all Turks."

Some resistance grew to that position, and Kurdish villages were wiped out—ten thousand villages in all. Literally millions of Kurds were dislocated and moved out the area of southern Turkey known as Anatolia. Many Kurds went into a diaspora, some in America, many in Western Europe where they worked in factories, mines, and mills.

"So Ralph, as I understand it, as the Turkish oppression began, some Kurds started going into a diaspora with some coming to the United States. You were contacted at some point in time?" I asked.
"That's correct," he said.

I was asked to look into the situation where the Kurdish people were starting to fight back. The Turkish government sent armed forces into Kurdish villages. The military ordered the Kurdish people to report any activity of people speaking in the Kurdish language. People were arrested, sent to prison, and tortured for speaking the Kurdish language.

Some young men ran off into the hills to resist this. The Turks said they were terrorists and should not be given recognition as a national liberation struggle as provided for under the UN protocols.

So I went to Kurdistan, studied the situation, and prepared a report for the United Nations. I determined that the resistance was not terrorism because the resistance was not going after third-party innocent civilians.

"Tell us more about the kind of work you were doing with the Kurds."

I showed them how they could go before the United Nations and present their claims about human rights violations; to appear before the Council of Europe, and meet with members of Congress, several of whom have tried to condition support to the Turkish armed forces based upon their engaging in less violent activities toward the Kurds. It has paid off. There is now some recognition of the rights of the Kurds. For the first time in decades, Kurds are allowed to speak Kurdish. There is even some Kurdish-language radio a couple of hours a week. This is due in part by the Turkish interest in becoming a part of the European Community. So some of my work had led to a lessening of the punitive attitude toward the Kurds.

Over the years, I became involved in the Kurdistan liberation struggles. This included my work with some people in the organized resistance group known as the PKK. Well, in the 1990s, the US secretary of state, Condoleezza Rice, designated the PKK as a foreign terrorist organization. I believe this was basically a political decision because the United States very much needed to use Turkish airbases for the US Air Force and to place ground troops in Turkey as a staging area for the Middle East.

"What happened next?" I asked.

When Congress passed the US Patriot Act and made it a crime punishable by fifteen years in prison for anybody that provides material support to groups named as terrorists by the secretary of state, there was a problem. What was meant by "material support"? I went into federal court in Los Angeles and asked for a definition to see if my peacemaking activities would be exempted. What I was doing was not supporting military activities but trying to promote peace. Teaching people from the Kurdish community to speak to the United Nations, to petition for the violation of fundamental human rights, and so on to try to build peaceful alternatives.

So I was engaged in peacemaking activities, but was that covered in the words "material support"? I received a temporary restraining order so the government could not prosecute me for the work I was doing. But the federal government wasn't happy with that. It appealed to the Ninth Circuit Court of Appeals. We went back and forth over the years as Congress, little by little, changed the law. Finally, it ended up before US Supreme Court.

"If I were to assemble a team to mediate the issues and injustices between the Kurds and the Turkish government, I could be convicted and sent to prison for many, many years?" I asked.

"Well it really strikes at the most fundamental liberty we have in America, and that is freedom of speech. We protect people's right to say just about anything. It could be vicious, it could be racist, it could be pornographic, or even libelous. People have a right to say what they want. But we have no free speech rights when it comes to speaking on behalf of an oppressed minority and that minority is irritating an ally of the United States."

"I think it goes beyond that. As I read the briefs and listened to the arguments, what the government is saying is that any act that in any way supports, whether it is direct or indirect, a terrorist group is illegal. I think we can all agree that supplying hand grenades and training people how to build bombs is illegal and should be illegal," I said.

"It is illegal in the United States too," Ralph agreed.

"I do not think First Amendment protections extend any kind of activity like that. But the government position strikes me as being ludicrous. If I were to go to the PKK and teach them how to mediate and how to negotiate and how to be peacemakers and how do active listening and all the stuff . . . ," I commented.

"That's exactly what I have been doing," Ralph said.

"It is illegal to do that. I am sorry. I just cannot understand how the government can take that position," I said.

"We think the law as written is overly broad. There is a standard in the law called 'strict scrutiny.' Strict scrutiny requires that where there is a fundamental liberty involved, like speech, and the government claims a compelling state interest in prohibiting that speech, the courts have always said, 'Well, you have to tailor the law to prohibit the governmental interest from invading the fundamental interest.' The government cannot say that any form of training or any form of service to that group results in a conviction and fifteen years in prison. You have to say that training that contributes to a military capability, training that leads to the use of violence, should be illegal. And it should be illegal. But to say that any training, including peace training, is illegal should be unconstitutional. The law must be specific," Ralph said.

"Think about the mindset that got the government into this mess," I said. "How do we go about convincing people that engaging people who disagree with us, even terrorists engaged in the most vile, vicious, heinous acts of violence, that engaging them at some peaceful level might be more productive? How do we engage people who are so fearful that they want to make the very people we need to talk with, in the words of the government, radioactive?"

"Well, I think that history can point the way. For years, the IRA engaged in terrorist activities, although because of its political activities in the United States it was never named as a terrorist group despite the fact that it engaged in terrorist actions. Yet we had a US senator intervene and mediate between the parties and arrive at a peaceful solution."

"Yes. That was George Mitchell's work."

"Exactly. The African National Congress was once designated by the US State Department as a terrorist organization until it took a majority in the South African parliament, and its leader, Nelson Mandela, brought peace to that country. There are always back channels such as between Hamas, Hezbollah, and the Israelis. You have to negotiate with your enemies. You don't have to negotiate with your friends. You have to try to work things out with your enemies. Isolating them and making it impossible for people to approach them with peaceful alternatives just worsens the situation."

"Obviously, you can't tolerate their violence, but at the same time you have to extend an olive branch and say, 'Look, is there anything to talk about?' How do we convince our government to do that sort of thing?"

"Well, we need a more enlightened leadership in our government and our country. We have to have a broader popular understanding," Ralph said. "On two different occasions in the past two years the Kurds unilaterally went to nonviolence. They went for years without engaging in any violence. But the Turkish armed forces did not expect that and went ahead and summarily executed Kurdish leaders, threw them in prison, and tortured them. They left a bloody trail and got away with it so long as they had the support of the United States."

"Let's assume the court overturns the Ninth Circuit, dissolves the injunction, and leaves the law as it is. What are your plans? What are you going to do?"

"My plan is to go to Europe or to the Middle East and offer my help to try and make peace for the Kurds with the Turkish armed forces. The government will have to decide whether or not it wishes to charge me with violating the law, and we will have a criminal case we will have to defend."

"It won't be the first time you've had that problem, will it?"

Ralph laughed, "That's correct."

"This is not a matter that is intimidating to you at all. It is a matter of conscience."

"It is a fundamental matter of conscience."

THE SUPREME COURT

February 23, 2010, the United States Supreme Court Building, Washington, DC.

"We'll hear argument first this morning in *Holder v. Humanitarian Law Project* and the cross-petition," said Chief Justice John Roberts.[6]

Mr. Chief Justice, and may it please the Court. This as-applied challenge asks whether the government can make it a crime for Ralph Fertig and the Humanitarian Law Project to speak in association with the Kurdistan Workers Party. Specifically, they seek to advocate for legal reform in Congress and the UN, to write and distribute articles supportive of Kurdish rights, to inform the Kurds of their international human rights and remedies, and to advise them on peaceful conflict resolution. It is undisputed that the Kurdistan Workers Party engages in a wide range of lawful activities and that plaintiffs seek to support only lawful ends. The government has a concededly compelling interest in combating terrorism, yet it has not tried to defend these prohibitions under strict scrutiny. Instead, it rests its entire case on the proposition that criminalizing plaintiffs' speech is a regulation of conduct, not speech, and therefore can be upheld under O'Brien.

Thus began the oral arguments in Ralph's case against the US government before the US Supreme Court. Ralph was represented by constitutional law professor David D. Cole. The conservative justices quickly became focused on whether Ralph's peacemaking work was pure speech or conduct.

Justice Anthony Kennedy asked Professor Cole if the government could prevent someone from giving tsunami aid to a terrorist organization. Professor Cole answered that giving money was different than training people in legal advocacy or peacemaking skills. The government could prohibit tsunami aid in the form of money but should not be able to prohibit someone from training terrorists in how to apply for and receive that aid. "I think the test is whether the speech has been provided with specific intent or knowledge that it will further unlawful terrorist ends of the group," said Professor Cole.

"Could the government stop you from meeting anywhere with the terrorists?" asked Justice Sonia Sotomayor.

"From meeting? No, I don't think so," answered Professor Cole.

Justice Antonin Scalia had a problem distinguishing between pure speech, which is protected, and some forms of conduct, which are not.

"Well, it hasn't criminalized speech. It has criminalized providing aid and assistance to these organizations. Most of that aid and assistance that is prohibited is not in the form of speech, but it happens to include speech as well," said Justice Scalia. "I think that's quite different from a law that is directed explicitly at speech." From Justice Scalia's perspective, it appeared that peacemaking training could be prohibited.

Professor Cole framed the question more precisely in answering a question from Justice Samuel Alito: "The question simply is whether training in what international human rights consist of, in how to advocate for international human rights, and how to advocate politically in Congress and other bodies. That's the speech that's at issue here."

Professor Cole distinguished different types of speech. "I think it depends upon the form of speech. There may be some forms of training that are so closely connected to the—to the end that Congress seeks to—legitimately seeks to proscribe, like training in bomb making or training in military exercises," he explained.

Scalia jumped in and asked why Congress could not outlaw the mere existence of terrorist organizations by making aid of any kind illegal. He said, "The theory of the legislation is that when you aid any of their enterprises you're aiding the organization. Hamas, for example, gained support among—among the Palestinians by activities that are perfectly lawful, perhaps running hospitals, all sorts of things."

"Right," answered Mr. Cole.

"But that is what fosters the terrorist organization and enables the terrorist activities. Why isn't that a reasonable connection? Any assistance you provide to these organizations cannot be separated from assistance to their terrorist activities," asked Justice Scalia.

Professor Cole pointed out that in a case involving membership in the Communist Party, the Court faced the same question. In the *Scales* case, Congress had found that the Communist Party was a vast international conspiracy controlled by the Soviet Union and intent on violent overthrow of the US government through terrorism. Congress therefore outlawed membership in the Communist Party. The Court found that the broad scope of the statute violated the First Amendment even though the government had a strong interest in stopping assistance to the Communist Party. That raised a question from Justice Kennedy.

"Then you say 'Nor does it involve speech advocating or teaching criminal or violent activity.' But it does involve speech, let's say *arguendo*, that is tantamount to material support. Suppose the speech is tantamount to material support in that it legitimizes, encourages, or strengthens the organization?" asked Justice Kennedy.

Professor Cole said that there were a host of Court decisions striking down the Communist Party statutes, saying that the government had to distinguish between aid that was intended to further lawful activity, such as mediating and conflict resolution training, and aid that furthered illegal activity, such as teaching people how to build improvised explosive devises.

Then Justice Scalia made an astounding statement that either reflected a gross ignorance of history or an intentional disingenuousness. "I think it's very unrealistic to compare these terrorist organizations with the Communist Party. Those cases involved philosophy. The Communist Party was—was—was more than a—than an organization that—that had some unlawful ends. It was also a philosophy of—of—of extreme socialism. And—and many people subscribed to that philosophy. I don't think that Hamas or any of these terrorist organizations represent such a philosophical organization."

"Your Honor, Congress's findings were not that this was a philosophical debating society, but that it was an international criminal conspiracy directed by our enemy to overthrow us through terrorism," answered Professor Cole.

"That may be, but people joined it for philosophical reasons. They joined it for philosophical reasons. These terrorist organizations have very practical objectives. And the only reason for joining them or assisting them is to assist those practical objectives," said Justice Scalia.

Somehow Scalia forgot about the thirty years of fear of the Red Scare and the mass anxiety that existed during the Cold War. He ignored the overwhelming belief that the Communist Party was actively plotting the overthrow of the US government and that the stated goal of communism was, in the memorable words of Nikita Khrushchev on November 18, 1956, "to bury you!" He apparently forgot about Khrushchev's intransigence and the fear evoked from his infamous shoe-pounding incident at the United Nations on October 12, 1960. Congress reacted to all of this by making any association with the Communist Party illegal, and the Court responded by making the laws unconstitutional because they violated First Amendment rights.

In many ways, the terrorist threats of today are far less dangerous to the stability of the United States than the threat of communism was fifty years ago. When Scalia dismissed this powerful historical difference, he indicated his willingness to uphold the Patriot Act no matter what its effect on the ability to create peace processes with terrorists.

When Professor Cole pointed out that Ralph's activities were not in any way, shape, or form betraying the United States, Scalia asked, "What about—what about aiding organizations that are acting criminally, killing innocent civilians, with regard to one of our allies? And we're seeking to gain the assistance of these allies against those terrorists who aim their terrorism at us, and yet we are supposed to allow our citizens to assist the terrorist organizations that are directing their violence against them? Why isn't that a sufficiently serious reason for the government to do what it's done here?"

Professor Cole explained that there is simply no realistic connection between advocating peace or teaching nonviolent ways to end disputes and killing Americans.

"When—but the way you define the speech that you want protected is speech that is advocating some lawful activity," said Justice Sotomayor. "So what's unlawful about teaching people medicine and how to cure people from infection?"

"If that were what they were doing, Your Honor, then it would be protected by the First Amendment," answered Mr. Cole.

"So you're not advocating a difference in this case between training that could reasonably be used in terrorist activities, because teaching people how to care for the ill could be used to teach people how to care for the wounded?" clarified Justice Sotomayor.

"Right," answered Professor Cole.

Eventually, solicitor general, now associate justice, Elena Kagan had her turn on behalf of the government.

"With your permission, Mr. Chief Justice. This may take some time," began Solicitor General Kagan.

(Laughter.)

"I'm sure it will on the other side, too.

> The material support statute is a vital weapon in this nation's continuing struggle against international terrorism. The statute prohibits, in terms that ordinary people can understand, the provision of material resources, material resources of all kinds, to foreign groups that engage in terrorist acts that threaten the security of the United States or its citizens.
>
> The statute does not prohibit in any way petitioners' independent advocacy. Petitioners can say or write whatever they wish about the PKK or the LTTE, and all their activities both legal and illegal.
>
> The statute does not prohibit the petitioners from petitioning peacefully. What the statute does is to prohibit petitioners from giving support to foreign terrorist organizations in their ability to petition international organizations. And that's a very different thing. . . . Petitioners can do whatever independent advocacy they wish. What petitioners cannot do is to provide support to a foreign terrorist organization.

"You recognized in your brief that they could meet with members of these terrorist organizations. They could meet and communicate with them, but they can't communicate advice on how to pursue their goals through lawful means?" asked Justice Ruth Bader Ginsburg.

"Justice Ginsburg, you're exactly right that, in addition to engaging in independent advocacy, petitioners can meet with members of the foreign terrorist organizations, can join the foreign terrorist organizations, that membership is not prohibited by the statute. What the statute does prohibit is active support of all kinds," said Ms. Kagan.

"Under the government's view, attending a peace conference with known terrorist organizations is permissible. However, providing mediation services in a conflict involving a known terrorist organization is prohibited. So you can chat, have lunch, and talk about the weather with terrorists, but the moment you start facilitating peace, you go to prison."

"Can they advocate to the association?" asked Justice Kennedy.

"Absolutely. If Judge Fertig or the other petitioners wanted to say to these organizations, 'You should change your ways,'" said Ms. Kagan.

"Can you say to an organization, 'Look, you guys really should lay down your arms'?" restated Ms. Kagan.

"And here's how to do it. And here's how to go to the UN, and here's how to apply for aid, and here's how to file an amicus brief," said Justice Kennedy.

"Well, now you can't, because when you tell people here's how to apply for aid and here's how to represent yourself within international organizations or within the US Congress, you've given them an extremely valuable skill that they can use for all kinds of purposes, legal or illegal," said Ms. Kagan.

"So you can—you can communicate, but the communications are censored. That's—you said you can meet with—you can be a member, you can attend meetings, you can discuss things, but there are only—there's a certain point at which the discussion must stop, right?" asked Justice Ginsburg.

"The discussion must stop when you—when you go over the line into giving valuable advice, training, support to these organizations," said Ms. Kagan.

"So, according to the government, over cucumber sandwiches at the peace conference, you can tell Abdul, "Look man, you guys should really try working out your conflicts nonviolently.""

"How would we do that?"

"Oops, sorry. Patriot Act. Can't tell you how to do it. Here, have another sandwich." This ludicrous conversation is exactly how the government sees the application of the Patriot Act.

THE DECISION—PEACEMAKING IS ILLEGAL

On June 21, 2010, the Supreme Court ruled against Ralph, stating that peacemaking is illegal under the Patriot Act. Writing for the six members of the majority, Chief Justice John Roberts said:

> Most of the activities in which [Fertig] seeks to engage readily fall within the scope of the terms "training" and "expert advice or assistance." [Fertig] wants to "train members of [the] PKK on how to use humanitarian and international law to peacefully resolve disputes," and "teach PKK and MEMBERS how to petition various representative bodies such as the United Nations for relief." (Citation omitted). A person of ordinary intelligence would understand that instruction on resolving disputes through international law falls within the statute's definition of "training" because it imparts a "specific skill," not "general knowledge." [Fertig's] activities also fall comfortably within the scope of "expert advice or assistance": a reasonable person would recognize that teaching the PKK how to petition for humanitarian relief but for the United Nations involves advice derived from . . . "specialized knowledge."[7]

Turning to the First Amendment challenge, Judge Roberts characterized the issue as whether the government may prohibit material support to the PKK in the form of speech. Roberts determined that peacemaking activities provide illegal material support to terrorist organizations:

> Material support meant to "promot[e] peaceable, lawful conduct," can further terrorism by foreign groups in multiple ways.

> "Material support" is a valuable resource by definition. Such support frees up other resources within the organization that may be put to violent ends. It also importantly helps lend legitimacy to foreign terrorist groups—legitimacy that makes it easier for those which persist, to recruit members, and to raise funds—all of which facilitate more terrorist attacks.[8]

In other words, despite the fact that peacemaking activities may ultimately stop violent activity, the fact that those activities may assist terrorist organizations makes them properly illegal. According to Chief Justice Roberts, the government held a legitimate interest in preventing terrorism by prohibiting material support in the form of training, expert advice, personnel, and services to foreign terrorist groups, even if that support was in the form of peacemaking and nonviolence.

Justice Stephen Breyer wrote for the three dissenters. Essentially, the dissent disagreed with the majority conclusion that material support is fungible regardless of its composition. *Fungibility* is a legal term meaning that one thing can be substituted for another, such as one bushel of wheat for another bushel of wheat. Wheat is said to be fungible because we really do not care which bushel of wheat we get, as long as we get a bushel of wheat. Thus, the dissent argued that the government did not show that peacemaking activities were the same as more sinister activities such as making bombs. Justice Breyer pointed out that the mere fact that peacemaking activities might legitimize a terrorist organization was not sufficient grounds for limiting free-speech rights. All speech has the potential for legitimizing activity, and if legitimization becomes the basis upon which speech is determined to be constitutional or not, there is no natural stopping place for regulating speech. The danger of the majority decision, said Justice Breyer, was that it adopted a rule of law that would automatically forbid the teaching of any subject in a case where national security interests conflict with the First Amendment.

MAKING PEACE ILLEGAL

This is the first time the US Supreme Court has permitted the government to criminalize advocacy for lawful, nonviolent activity and is therefore a dangerous constitutional precedent. Beyond the constitutional implications, the *Humanitarian Law Project* decision moves the United States away from peace and toward more war. According to the United States Supreme Court, Congress has the power to make dialogue in conflict zones a criminal act. Peacemakers convicted under the statute are felons, just like drug dealers, arms dealers, and murderers. This is a misguided, incredibly stupid policy that undermines efforts to provide nonviolent solutions to violent groups. The government of the United States of America is clearly not promoting peace and cannot credibly contend that it is a peace-seeking nation. The decision and the policy underlying it are, in a word, shameful.

Where the seeds of peace could be planted by American peacemakers, the ground will remain fallow or open to the noxious weeds of oppression and terrorism. Where there could be light, there will continue to be darkness, as the most powerful country in the world turns its back on peace.

The isolationism sought by those sponsoring the legislation and supporting the decision are cutting off people from the possibility of seeing nonviolence as another way toward resolution of grievances. Many people in conflict zones without local facilitation depend on outsiders for an opportunity to try nonviolent solutions or to humanize their supposed enemies. American peacemakers, with their access to resources and money to support them, are barred from working in the most intense conflict zones with the people who need to hear the alternatives to violence the most.

The decision in *Holder v. Humanitarian Law Project* sends a message from America to the world. The message is that dialogue is dangerous to the United States, and that it will resort to economic deprivation or even preemptive war only to achieve "peace." It ignores that the violent interventions against "terrorists" in the years since September 11, 2001, have been costly and ineffective at best and immoral at worst. It rejects dialogue, mediation, and nonviolence as legitimate and moral means of working with terrorists.

David D. Cole told the *New York Times*: "This decision basically says the First Amendment allows making peacemaking and human rights advocacy a crime."[9] Not only is making peace illegal a constitutional problem, it is a national security problem. Human rights and peacemaking organizations, already strained by the economic collapse in 2008, will now find their work legally indefensible. By the time someone in Washington wakes up, the peacemakers will be dead or in jail. No wonder peace is so elusive in this world.

Chapter 11

Evil, War, and Violence

A LESSON IN GENOCIDE

"**M**aster, tell us how to use genocide as a means to protect my power, prestige, and privilege," asked the Student.

"Ah, genocide. It is indeed a way to protect power, prestige, and privilege, but it is a dangerous path for a leader to take. However, charismatic leaders like you may wish to embark on genocide when the timing is propitious," mused the Master. "I will tell you what I know, and what I have observed."

"Thank you, Master," said the Student.

"I suppose the place to start is in considering how the decision to engage in genocide arises. It is not a chance matter. Genocide results from the deliberate choice of a leader to foster hatred and fear to keep himself in power. Observe my use of the masculine; women have not been implicated as leaders of genocide in modern history. This is a man's invention and device. Most often, women are innocent victims of genocide. So I will refer to leaders in the masculine unless I otherwise note," said the Master.

"What are the conditions I must consider if contemplating genocide?" the Student asked.

"Since genocide is a last-resort strategy, you must be convinced that you will lose your power, position, and privilege either at the bargaining table, on the battlefield, or in future political struggles without it," explained the Master. "For example, in Rwanda, the Hutu leaders faced loss of power, position, and privilege with the Tutsi-based Rwanda Patriotic Front. Something had to be done, and genocide was deliberately selected as the strategy," said the Master.

"But what about the mediation efforts?" asked the Student.

"Notably, the negotiations in Arusha were not moderated by skilled mediators who truly understood the complexities of the conflict. As the peace negotiations progressed, the Hutus were losing support, and internal factional fighting was weakening its military and political strength. As is fortunately often the case, the mediators excluded the hardliners in the talks for fear that the hardliners would obstruct progress. Exclusion is always a good predictor for failure of peace negotiations," observed the Master. "But we are offtrack here.

"You are assisted in your choice of genocide when groups have fought each other over land, jobs, resources, justice, equality, respect for ethnic identity, power, governance, and so forth. If one faction has politically dominated the other, so much the better. If gross injustices have occurred, that is good. The outrage and resentment, when not acknowledged or reconciled through true peacemaking efforts, will provide the deep reservoir of emotional energy needed to ignite and sustain the genocide," said the Master.

"Yes, I see that," said the Student. "Again, in Rwanda, the Belgians treated the Tutsis as superior to the Hutus for many years, then flipped and favored the Hutus. And the British favored the Irish Protestants over the Irish Catholics."

"Exactly. Hatred can only grow where there are festering injustices caused by gross imbalances in power and resources," said the Master. "What you must do is transform the injustice into self-righteous hatred and then into massive killings."

"How do I go about this transformation?" asked the Student.

"You must first develop a charismatic leader hungry for power and ruthless in demeanor," said the Master. "Genocide only occurs in the presence of strong leadership."

"And in the absence of leadership in the international community," observed the Student.

"Indeed. More on that topic in a moment," said the Master. "Surround this leader with elites interested in protecting their power, position, and privilege at any cost. They will provide the support network and complex logistics necessary for the extermination."

"What about the existing government bureaucracy? What is to be done with it?" asked the Student.

"Co-opt the existing civilian and political hierarchies into supporting and encouraging the extermination," said the Master. "Bureaucrats are not generally agile, independent thinkers and prefer clear instructions from authority over making important decisions in morally ambiguous situations. Do not let the bureaucracy think—lead it to action! How else was Hitler able to mobilize Teutonic efficiency in designing, building, and operating the ovens and gas chambers of Auschwitz?

"You will twist the natural tendencies of these hierarchies to serve their leaders. Genocide will become another campaign that calls on citizens and officials alike to contribute extra efforts for the public good. The urgency and importance of the objective will justify departing from usual bureaucratic practice," said the Master. "Allow ambitious men to bypass the law. Trust me; some will do so with all of the zeal you could hope for."

"So you are saying that the government bureaucracy will be helpful in genocide?" asked the Student.

"Yes," said the Master. "Most importantly, enlisting the bureaucracy to promote rapid and effective execution of the killing campaign will also complicate the task of assessing responsibility for crimes. All who seek accountability for the genocide must take care to ensure that officials of lesser rank, but greater power, not escape blame for crimes that are wrongly imputed to their superiors alone. The vast number of people involved will overwhelm the international judicial system, making prosecution of all but a tiny few impossible."

"There is safety in numbers, then?" asked the Student.

"Of course," said the Master. "We will talk of precautions against being tried for war crimes and crimes against humanity in a moment.

"Remember the importance of euphemisms. We shall call the people to be exterminated the 'targets' so as to disconnect our feelings from them as humans. This is a subtle and important technique," continued the Master.

"How does the campaign begin?" asked the Student.

"Begin by portraying the targets as collaborators of the enemy or the opposition. Spend time developing stereotypes and labels for the targets. Let this evolve into a media campaign of fear and hatred of the targets. Invoke patriotism, sacred values, the Mother Land, and ethnic purity as being threatened by the targets. Bring up old memories and histories of oppression, abuse, and a history of domination by the targets. Exaggerate and lie as necessary and stifle all dissent through control and manipulation of the media," answered the Master.

"So I should pass laws that require the target to carry special identification cards and imprison those who do not to set an example," said the Student.

"Excellent, you understand the point," said the Master. "Recognize that shattering the cords of connection between ethnic groups may be difficult. They often share a common history, a single language, and many identical ideas and cultural practices. They have lived next to one another and seen many cross-marriages. They have worked together, gotten drunk together, prayed together, and gone to school with each other. All of this must be erased through distortion, deception, and manipulation."

"What about the actual 'work' itself? How should it begin?" asked the Student.

"Ah, good euphemism. Very good. The 'work' as you say

should begin with small massacres in outlying areas to test the waters. See who dares to protect the targets and exterminate them or label them as sympathizers of the targets," said the Master.

"What about international attention?" asked the Student.

"Generally, in this early stage, there will be some media reports that get out. You cannot stop them. However, what appear to be small, random outbreaks of violence will not be picked up by the mainstream media, especially in the developed countries. There is simply too much competing news," said the Master. "Besides, in the extremely unlikely event that international concern rises to the level of possible intervention, you can always back off and wait for a more advantageous time."

"Well, I plan to take over all media—radio, television, newspapers—with force if necessary. My European public relations firm has prepared broadcasts of hate ahead of time for release during the extermination," said the Student.

"Very good. Controlling the media and the message is critical to your success. Even the jamming of your radio and television stations could be devastating to your efforts," said the Master. "However, the international community has failed to take even that elementary step in preventing genocide. I see no indication that it will act differently in the future."

"What about the logistical planning?" asked the Student.

"Mass extermination requires weapons—many weapons. Keep the weapons as simple as possible—machetes worked well in Rwanda. You will save money in the long run," said the Master. "There are discount arms dealers from whom you can purchase large quantities of cheap rifles and ammunition. Again, the international community has little interest in shutting these suppliers down, and these arms dealers profit greatly off of the occasional genocide. They will be happy to work with you."

"How will I convince the military and police to do the 'work'?" asked the Student.

"You will do best to recruit a militia from the hordes of disaffected, unemployed young men in your country. They will relish the excitement of violence. Keep them separate and secret from the organized military and the police authorities. Find former soldiers to train and lead this militia. Remember the Pashtun in Afghanistan was able to raise a substantial militia on the promise of US$5 per-day wages. To a poor man with no hope of advancement, this is good money."

"The Janjaweed of Sudan comes to mind as well. What other logistics should I consider?" asked the Student.

"Recruit local political partisans in each region, city, and village. Have them recruit and begin to compile names of the targets, where they work, and where they live. Pay attention to women and children as they must be exterminated as well. Make up lists and assign those lists to death squads. Check off the master lists as the death squads report their 'work' up the chain of command," advised the Master. "Genocide is a complex exercise in organizational management. Your effort will collapse without adequate planning and infrastructure to support it."

"There may be resistance to killing the women and children. How should I manage that?" asked the Student.

"Instruct your militia to rape as many women as possible, in front of husbands, brothers, and fathers, if possible. Kill the children without mercy, calling them the evil spawn of the target. Have your commanders watch for the occasional militiaman with some moral courage to resist or question. When spotted, execute him publicly as an example," said the Master.

"What will set off the mass executions?" asked the Student.

"Create or stage a triggering event. The assassination of the head of state or a revered public figure is always a good choice. Blame the targets for the assassination and begin the violence. Describe it as 'self-defense,'" said the Master.

"More euphemisms," smiled the Student.

"Yes, more euphemisms. You are asking people to do things that are not natural to them in a peaceful state. Directing their attention away from the reality of what is happening is important," said the Master. "Genocides are extremely fragile creatures and can usually be prevented or at least stopped in the early stages with minimal expenditures of resources by the international community. Fortunately, genocide provokes a self-protective instinct in international political leaders, causing them to avoid action until it is too late."

"What are the most efficient ways to carry out the executions?" asked the Student.

"Most successful genocides are organized in phases. In Phase 1, death squads go into homes and kill the families. This sets up a sense of terror in the communities.

"In Phase 2, send out directives for the targets to congregate in 'safe areas.' They will be thankful that the government is trying to protect them. Once you have driven the targets from their homes into meeting areas, mass extermination can be efficient. Have large trenches prepared to accept the corpses," said the Master.

"The Khmer Rouge created killing fields this way," observed the Student.

"Yes. They were very efficient," said the Master.

He went on, "Once the killing begins, encourage the reluctant with strong authority. Command the extermination. Remember the experiments of the American social psychologist Stanley Milgram and take those lessons to heart. People will give up their own moral decision making in the face of strong authoritarian commands and the absence of moral counterweights."

"How should the government respond to the concerns that genocide is occurring?" asked the Student.

"Create an aura of legitimacy. The government should give its officials and citizens the cover of 'legitimate' orders to hide from themselves and others the evil they were doing. In all ways, couch the extermination in terms of the legitimate day-to-day activities of the people. Presume an order of normalcy in the time of extermination," said the Master.

"And the international community? At some point, there will be a hue and cry, will there not?" asked the Student.

The Master smiled and said, "Do not worry about the international community. The Europeans and North Americans will find it in their best interests to look the other way. The Asians will see an opportunity for trade and profit if you are successful and thus will remain uninvolved. The greatest factor in the success of genocide is the apathy and lethargy of the international community. No genocide could have occurred without it."

"But what about the United Nations?" asked the Student.

"The UN will remain toothless and clawless. The UN secretary-general has no power, the UN security forces have no resources, and the Security Council requires a unanimous consent to take any action. At the least, some member of the Security Council will see a benefit from the chaos of the extermination—either because it discomfits the more powerful nations or because it presents lucrative future trade and profit. The NGOs will protest, but they have no power to stop you. The political will, leadership, and resources to stop the extermination will not materialize," declared the Master.

"This sounds too good to be true," mused the Student.

"It almost is. While the international community will not intervene in the actual extermination, be aware of the aftermath," warned the Master.

"Are you talking about war crimes tribunals?" asked the Student.

"Yes. After the extermination, the major international powers will atone for their inaction by aggressive investigation, arrest, and prosecution of the leaders of the genocide. They will be lucky to catch a few, but they will find prosecution of most of the leadership impractical. The International Criminal Court is underfunded, understaffed, and underpowered to create anything other than an illusion of justice. Foist a few unimportant junior leaders as the ringleaders and let them be prosecuted to satisfy the international community," advised the Master.

"Thank you, Master. This has been most enlightening."

"You are quite welcome."

THE NATURE OF EVIL

Why is it that otherwise normal people might act in evil ways? The best answer seems to be a combination of personal disposition, "Who I am," and situation, "What I face." The dispositional school includes researchers like Lawrence Kohlberg.[1] Kohlberg has developed a cognitive-developmental approach to moral decision making. In his model, moral decision making grows in maturity from a primitive level to a mature level through five stages. The situational school includes the well-known researchers Stanley Milgram and Philip Zimbardo. Their respective obedience and prison experiments demonstrate how "ordinary" people can be easily induced into evil acts because of the situation they are in. In Milgram's obedience experiments, subjects were introduced to a "student" who was the researcher's secret accomplice. The student was shown to be wearing cuffs as if in an electric chair, behind a screen separating him from the subject. The subjects were told that they would "help" the student learn a set of tasks. If the student made a mistake, the subject was to administer an electric shock via a dial and button. The dial controlled the intensity of the shock, and the button administered the shock. An authority figure sat next to the subjects and instructed them on how much of an electrical shock to administer. In nearly all cases in which the administrator directed the subject to administer full power, with the student behind the screen screaming in apparent agony, the subject complied.[2]

In Zimbardo's famous Stanford Prison Experiment, college students screened as perfectly normal were randomly selected to be inmates or guards in a mock prison setup in the basement of the Stanford University Psychology Building. Within forty-eight hours, the student guards had dehumanized the student inmates and were subjecting them to cruel and degrading treatment. Zimbardo shut down the experiment early when one of the student inmates had a psychological breakdown.[3] Both of these classic experiments appeared to demonstrate that good people put into bad situations will lose their moral compass and do evil acts, especially under the guise of obedience to authority.

MORAL MATURITY AND DECISION MAKING

Kohlberg's model of moral decision making says that we grow in our ability to make moral decisions.[4] He establishes six stages of moral development as shown in this table:

Stage	What Is Considered to Be Right
Level 1: Preconventional	
Stage 1: Obedience and punishment orientation	Obedience to authority for its own sake. Sticking to rules to avoid punishment.
Stage 2: Instrumental purpose and exchange	Following rules only when it is in one's immediate interest. Right is an equal exchange, getting a good deal
Level 2: Conventional	
Stage 3: Interpersonal accord, conformity, mutual expectations	Stereotypical "good" behavior. Living up to what is expected by peers and people close to you.
Stage 4: Social accord and system maintenance	Fulfilling duties and obligations of the social system.

Upholding laws and rules except in extreme cases where they conflict with social duties.

Level 3: Principled

Stage 5: Social contract and individual rights	Upholding rules because they are the social contract if they are consistent with values such as fairness and rights and the greater good (not because of the majority opinion).
Stage 6: Universal ethical principles	Following ethical principles of justice and rights.

Acting in accord with principles when laws violate principles[5]

Stage 1 individuals make moral decisions simply to avoid punishment. "If I don't share my toy, Mom will yell at me," or "If I disobey orders, I will be tortured." A level 1 person can be expected to consider questions like "What's in it for me?" At stage 1, a person might ask, "Can I get away with it?" or "Will I get caught or punished?"

At stage 2, moral decisions are judged in terms of "You scratch my back, I'll scratch yours." At stage 2, the moral calculation is "How will I benefit or what will I get in return if I do this?"

As a person matures in level 2, he is less self-centered and has internalized the shared moral rules of his group. His moral decision making is based on how well he lives up to the expectations of others, fulfilling duties and obligations, and following rules. A level 2 person looks to others for moral guidance when deciding what to do. He might think to himself, "If everyone else is doing it, it must be OK."

At stage 3, what's right is thought to be that which pleases or helps others. "I will share my toy with my brother because Mom will approve of me." A stage 3 person would likely ask, "What would my peers do?" or "What would my trusted supervisor advise?"

At stage 4, the moral perspective broadens to consider society. Moral decision makers are concerned about following rules that promote the common good. A stage 4 person recognizes that rules exist for good reason, and she follows them because the social system works better when people cooperate. At stage 4, the considerations would be broader, such as "What do the rules or laws prescribe?" Kohlberg's research placed most American adults at level 4.

A level 3 principled individual has developed the capacity to make moral decisions autonomously. This person looks to higher ethical principles such as justice and human rights. At stage 5, moral decisions are still based on rules and laws, but stage 5 decision makers are willing to question the law and to consider it for socially useful purposes. A stage 5 individual would take into account moral laws above society's laws, such as considering what decision would create the greatest societal good.

Kohlberg found that most people are at level 2. This means they are highly susceptible to external influences on their judgment about what is ethically right and their subsequent action. Moral decisions about what's ethically right are largely based on what others think, say, and do. These individuals are not autonomous decision makers who strictly follow an internal moral compass. They look up and around to see what their superiors and their peers are doing and saying, and they use these cues as a guide to action. Therefore most people are likely to do what's expected of them as a result of reward systems, role expectations, authority figure demands, and group norms.

Higher-stage moral decision making is more independent. The principled thinker looks to justice and rights-based principles to guide ethical decision making. Research has demonstrated that these people are also more likely to behave consistently with their principle-based decisions—they're more likely to carry through and do what they think is right. More principled individuals also have been found to be less likely to cheat, more likely to resist pressure from authority figures, more likely to help someone in need, and more likely to blow the whistle on misconduct. Autonomous decision making based on principles of justice and rights is the exception rather than the rule.

MORAL DISENGAGEMENT

So how is it that the average level 2 person can become evil? The answer seems to be found in Albert Bandura's idea around moral disengagement.[6] As we grow up, we internalize standards of moral conduct. As adults, we judge our behavior against these standards. If we consider behaving unethically, we anticipate the pain of feeling guilty or shameful and stop ourselves. Psychologists call this *self-influence*, and our moral conduct is motivated by it.

Normal people cannot act malevolently until they have justified the morality of their actions to themselves. Thus, evil must be internally portrayed as serving a higher moral purpose. Without this justification, evil people could not preserve their self-esteem while inflicting atrocities on others. This is why appeals against violence usually fall on deaf ears. War criminals sanctify their violent actions but condemn the violence of their enemies as barbarous evil. Each side feels morally superior to the other.

Research has found that people deactivate their self-control system through eight moral disengagement mechanisms. These moral disengagement mechanisms allow individuals to engage in evil behavior without feeling guilty or shameful. The eight mechanisms fall into three categories: *recharacterization*, *distortion*, and *dehumanization*.[7]

Recharacterizing evil acts can be done through euphemisms, moral justifications, and advantageous comparison. Euphemistic language makes evil conduct respectable and reduces personal responsibility. Research studies show that people behave much more cruelly when their violent actions are verbally sanitized than when the violence is called out for what it is.

Euphemism occurs by replacing descriptive, emotional words with neutral words that deaden the emotional centers of our brains. Soldiers "waste" people rather than kill them. Bombing missions are described as "serving the target" in the likeness of a public utility. The attacks become "surgical strikes," arousing images of hospitals and doctors. The innocent people killed by bombs are converted to "collateral damage." Special Forces soldiers are called "operators," as if they were operating a machine instead of killing people. "Ethnic cleansing" describes the horrors of genocide in a clinically cold manner. People are not fired. Instead, they are given a "career alternative enhancement," which sounds an awful lot like a promotion. Acid rain has been called "atmospheric deposition of anthropogenically derived substances."

Politicians are despised for spinning unpleasant or painful facts into euphemisms that are patent attempts at deflecting strong emotional reactions, notably disapproval. In a *New York Times* interview, Anthony Lake, national security adviser in the Clinton administration, said that during the Rwandan crisis his administration refused to use the term *genocide*.[8]

"It was based on the belief that if you used the word, then you're required to take action. They didn't go the sophistry route—using the word and finding a way to weasel out of it. Now in Sudan, we've used it and we're wriggling out of its meaning. Which is more unattractive? I don't know," he said.[9] Euphemisms make immoral decisions easier to live with.

Moral disengagement may also be justified through exonerating comparisons. Evil is morally justified based on what is thought to be socially good. Former Bosnian Serb leader Radovan Karadzic illustrated this in his opening statement at his war crimes trial in March 2010. Karadzic strongly defended his actions, calling the Serb cause in the 1992–1995 Bosnian war "just and holy," arguing that Bosnian Serbs were not to blame for the war and accusing Bosnian Muslims of rejecting power-sharing agreements in order to carve out an Islamic fundamentalist state.[10] The only way he could possibly live with his order of "ethnic cleansing" was by justifying it as having a high moral purpose.

Our brains are good at making comparisons, so setting up a contrast to a worse situation is another way of making evil look good. People may compare their own behavior to more reprehensible behavior to make their own behavior seem acceptable. For example, Chechen terrorists justify suicide bombing as acts of selfless martyrdom by comparing the attacks with widespread cruelties inflicted by Russian soldiers on the Chechen people. The more flagrant the contrasting inhumanities, the more likely that one's own violence will appear benevolent.

Euphemisms, moral justifications, and comparisons, taken together, are powerful psychological mechanisms for disengaging moral constraints. Investing evil conduct with high moral purpose not only eliminates self-censure, it engages self-approval in the service of atrocity. What was once condemnable as unmitigated evil becomes a source of self-esteem and pride.

A second category of moral disengagement mechanisms has to do with reducing personal responsibility or distorting the consequences for evil. Our moral controls work best when we are able to accept personal responsibility for the harm caused by our actions. When we do not have personal accountability, our moral compass can be ignored. For example, individuals will deflect their personal accountability by shifting it to an authority figure or to subordinates. As we learned at Abu Ghraib, when atrocities are publicized, they are often officially minimized as isolated incidents arising from misunderstandings of what had been authorized. The blame is assigned to subordinates, who are portrayed as misguided or overzealous. In the Abu Ghraib scandal, the people who went to prison were teenaged army reservists, not the military officers or intelligence agents that set up the conditions for the abuse.

People will diffuse their sense of personal responsibility by looking to the group ("it's not my job," or "my team made the decision"). When everyone is responsible, no one really feels responsible. Social organizations go to great lengths to devise mechanisms for securing responsibility for decisions that will injure others. Psychological research shows that people act more cruelly under group responsibility than when they hold themselves personally accountable for their actions. People will also distort their personal responsibility by minimizing their evilness ("It's OK, everyone has to die sometime").[11]

The third category of moral disengagement mechanisms reduces identification with victims. When a person is seen in terms of common humanity, empathic emotional reactions based in the brain's mirror neuron system are activated through a sense of similarity and social obligation. We find it very difficult to mistreat humanized persons without suffering intense personal distress and self-condemnation because we literally feel the same suffering when our mirror neurons are activated. With dehumanization, people become unworthy of moral consideration because they are thought to be different, stupid, or not even human. Once dehumanized, they are no longer viewed as persons with feelings, hopes, and concerns, but as subhuman objects. Enemies become "satanic demons," "infidels," "sinners," "degenerates," and so forth.

Dehumanization has been established as an essential ingredient of evil, war, and violence. In one experiment, a team of supervisors was given the power to punish a group of problem solvers with varying intensities of electric shock when the problem solvers did not perform adequately. The punishment was administered either personally or collectively to the problem solvers. The problem solvers were characterized in humanistic, animalistic, or neutral terms. The supervisors treated the dehumanized individuals far more harshly than those who had been invested with human qualities.[12]

In the same experiments, personal responsibility and humanization had a powerful self-restraining effect. Those supervisors who assumed personal responsibility for their actions with the humanized problem solvers rarely justified the group decision to punish and almost always disavowed it. When the problem solvers were dehumanized, the supervisors had no interest in condemning harsh punishment. When the punishment intensity impaired the problem solvers' performance, the supervisors responded even more harshly.

When people in authority have power over others with few safeguards to constrain their behavior, they tend to dehumanize those over whom they wield control. Lord Acton expressed this principle in a letter to Bishop Mandell Creighton in 1887: "Power tends to corrupt, and absolute power corrupts absolutely. Great men are almost always bad men."[13] Even college students, who had been randomly assigned to serve as either inmates or prison guards, when given unilateral power in a simulated prison, quickly came to treat their charges in degrading, tyrannical ways.

Moral disengagement ties into moral development with an important, but rarely cited, study. Lawrence Kohlberg, who was Stanley Milgram's colleague at Yale University, interviewed some of Milgram's participants to assess their stage of moral reasoning using his developmental model. The subjects' level of moral decision-making maturity powerfully predicted their tendency to resist evil authoritarian instructions—almost none of the stage 1, 2, or 3 participants (14 percent) quit Milgram's obedience experiment and continued to administer electric shocks to the highest intensity available. Almost all of the stage 4 and 5 participants (83 percent) defied the authority and refused the command to administer higher-intensity shocks. What this tells us is that the lower a person's moral maturity, the more likely he will be able to disengage his moral compass, and the less likely he will be able to ignore the situational factors that permit evil. The power of humanization to counteract evil conduct has considerable importance in mediating peace in the face of evil, war, and violence. When people can recognize how they are linked together and how their interests in each other's welfare support them all, they are instilled with a sense of community. The affirmation of common humanity can bring out the best in others.[14]

MEDIATING EVIL, WAR, AND VIOLENCE

How does one mediate peace in the face of evil? This question has perplexed peacemakers, international leaders, and diplomats for millennia. The easy political answer is that there can be no negotiation with evil; it must be met with irresistible force. However, that emotionally satisfying and anxiety-reducing answer is inadequate. Superior military power simply does not eradicate evil, and the expenditure of blood and treasure is often futile against modern forms of violence.

Refusing to negotiate with people who are characterized as evil is no longer a luxury. Where military force is not working (see Afghanistan and the Lord's Resistance Army in the Congo), engagement through negotiation and mediation is all that is left. That does not mean that mediating evil is easy. It is just the opposite: mediating evil is the most difficult, challenging work a peacemaker will undertake.

The structural problems associated with the development of Africa show us the complexity of the problems associated with evil, war, and violence. Over the decades since independence from European colonial rule in the 1960s, African leaders developed a feeling of entitlement and privilege. While no one has surveyed the past and present African leaders on Kohlberg's scale of moral development, most of the leaders would probably fall within stage 1 or stage 2. As a group, they have demonstrated underdeveloped moral maturity.

Most of the African political leaders that took power in independent Africa were socialized under the colonial system of governance. In that governance system, African countries existed for the sole economic benefit of the imperial powers. Colonialism was not designed to benefit Africa or Africans. So when it was their turn to lead, African leaders copied the only model they knew. They made the African nation-state an instrument of oppression for their personal benefit to guarantee the well-being of their family, clan, and tribal groups at the exclusion of others.

After all, this was the European model, was it not? The state was seen as belonging only to those who are in power. This resulted in the "Big Man" syndrome. The most ruthless men became the despotic rulers of their African nations and maintained control through torture, rape, violence, and genocide. The list is long: Idi Amin of Uganda, Jean-Bedel Bokassa of the Central African Republic, Samuel Doe and Charles Taylor of Liberia, Foday Sankoh of Sierra Leone, Mengistu Haile Mariam of Ethiopia, Juvénal Habyarimana of Rwanda, Robert Mugabe of Zimbabwe, and Omar al-Bashir of Sudan, among many others, have been responsible for untold human atrocities in Africa.

The European concept of sovereignty coupled with the Cold War kept these men in power as they pandered to their Western allies or the Soviet Union. The Organization of African Unity that existed between 1963 and 2002 was widely regarded as a "dictators'" trade union, as it was composed of African "Big Men" interested in protecting their personal power, position, and privilege. When the "Big Man" was threatened by Marxist uprisings, he received support from the West. When the "Big Man" leaned left, he was supported by the Soviet Union. The "Big Men" were savvy enough to use sovereignty as an excuse to prevent intervention in their internal affairs, even when those internal affairs constituted genocide, war crimes, or crimes against humanity. In addition, they quashed the right of self-determination by large minorities within national boundaries. These minority groups, disempowered by international law to seek independent self-rule for themselves, were also systematically excluded from power sharing or civic participation in governance.

The leaders resented anyone that challenged their absolute authority. Evil started with a constriction of empathy and compassion toward the disenfranchised dissenters. In each country, as evil grew, it replaced trust with suspicion and confidence with fear. Identifying the opposition group as evil became a justification for violence. By defining "them" as bad, African leaders defined themselves as good. They gave themselves permission to act in ways that would appear evil to outside observers, but that seemed self-righteous. Every accusation directed to political opponents established the moral logic required to justify committing evil. Evil therefore became directly connected with the unequal distribution and adversarial exercise of power.

In Sierra Leone, leaders systematically privatized political and economic control to perpetuate their patronage-based networks. In Chad, Déby used the chaos brought about by the Darfur conflict and a domestic insurrection to renege on his promise to spend oil royalties on development. In Sudan, the northern al-Bashir government, which depends on the oil revenues generated in the south, has promoted chaos throughout Sudan to undermine the formal authority and functioning of the state while improving the relative standing of the northern Arabs. In case after case, African leaders have shown no interest other than protecting themselves and their supporters. In the most recent episode, Kenya invited Omar al-Bashir, under indictment for war crimes and genocide, to the inauguration ceremony of Kenya's new constitution. Under the Rome Statute creating the International Criminal Court, Kenya was required to arrest him and turn him over to the Office of the Prosecutor. Instead, al-Bashir was treated as an honored guest by President Kibaki and Prime Minister Odinga. The ICC indictment and order for arrest were publicly and flagrantly ignored. Of course, the ICC is investigating Kenya as well, and indictments for war crimes are expected to be issued against a group of Kenyan elites implicated in the massacres following the 2007 election.[15]

The endless wars have been about power. In these violent struggles, the "revolutionary" faction may claim to seek equality and democratic institutions, but the sad tale is that insurrectionist leaders are usually seeking to replace the current leader for personal self-aggrandizement. Charles Taylor replaced Samuel Doe in Liberia, and the bloodshed continued. Most insurrectionists are not schooled in constructing and sustaining a civil society based on the rule of law and governed by democratic principles. As a consequence, peace agreements are made, hailed, and almost immediately ignored because they do not deliver the wealth, power, prestige, and status that come with "owning" one's nation-state.

Nevertheless, within this understanding of evil lie the seeds of peace to be planted by a skilled mediator.

THE MOTIVATIONS FOR PEACE

The big question for any mediator is "Why are they here? Why mediation? And why now? What is driving people characterized as evil to negotiate? What do they expect to get from negotiation that they have not been able to get from war or terrorism?" Asking these questions frames the guts of the problem.

Invariably, evil leaders coming to mediation are hoping to improve their current situation. They typically want some form of amnesty for war crimes and human rights abuses, and they want to be paid off. They may or may not hold loyalty toward their soldiers and to their immediate followers and commanders. They may be operating under a number of cognitive biases that convince them that they are about to win. Certainly, they do not see themselves as evil or morally corrupt. They are completely disengaged from their moral compasses.

For the most part, these leaders are not capable of leading the development of civil society based on the rule of law. They are used to autocratic command and the perks that come with being the boss. They cannot be expected to govern effectively, so persuading them to share power will be a nonstarter. The government leader-in-power probably obtained his position through force or fraud or both and is likewise incapable of leading systemic reform. After all, had the leader-in-power led the creation and growth of a civil society with full transparency and accountability, the rebel leader probably would have become a legitimate opposition political leader.

While mediation properly conducted can produce amazing

results, its effectiveness is limited by the motivations of the parties. Sometimes, the most that can be expected is a mediated conversation between the parties, not a negotiated agreement. Sometimes, violence must be met with violence. However, responding to evil with violence is not justice and is also no guarantee of peace.

No one wants to negotiate from a position of weakness, and no one willingly gives up power. So, among the things that probably cannot be successfully mediated is relinquishing power. Likewise, power-sharing agreements between implacable enemies probably cannot be successfully mediated. Oh, a mediator might get parties to sign a power-sharing agreement. But as the Kenyan experience demonstrates, the performance of the agreement will be doubtful.

This leads us to a fundamental principle of mediation: do not mediate an agreement that cannot or will not be performed. Mediation is about the art of the possible. A small agreement performed by all parties is far more powerful than a massive, headline-making agreement that no one has faith in. Maybe the agreement can permit NGOs access to people in desperate need of humanitarian aid. Maybe the agreement can create neutral ceasefire zones or sanctuaries. Whatever the topic, mediate only that which the parties are willing to risk. By making mediation incrementally successful, trust in the process will slowly evolve.

REENGAGING THE PARTIES' MORAL COMPASSES

Where there is moral disengagement, the mediator must help the parties come back to their moral compass. The challenges are steep. Since moral disengagement is a pain-avoidance mechanism, people will resist accepting their moral responsibility out of a need to avoid self-censure. Dehumanization may mean that the idea of sitting across the table from your enemies is unthinkable—who would negotiate or even talk with satanic forces of evil? Mediators must help the parties move from diffused responsibility to personal accountability.

Assume you are mediating a conflict rife with evil on both sides. You are talking with the leader of the hypothetical country of Lubanga, Mr. Sbeke, in a private meeting. The conversation might go something like this:

"Tell me about the massacres."

"What massacres? There were no massacres!"

"Well, then how would you describe what happened?"

"What do you mean?"

"Mr. Sbeke, at some point in time, you will have to face the fact that thousands of people were killed by forces under your command. If you wish peace, acknowledging that fact will be necessary."

"Those people were not killed by my command. My military generals were out of control. It was not my responsibility."

"Tell me what happened from your perspective."

"I do not know the details."

"Did you ask for details?"

"Yes. No one gave them to me."

"So you are saying then, that you did not have control over your military generals?"

"Yes."

"They acted on their own without your knowledge or consent."

"Yes."

"Not your fault then?"

"Yes, not my fault."

"So would you be willing to make amends with those who suffered?"

"Those animals? No. Not possible. They are satanic demons!"

"How many women's bodies were ripped apart by AK-47 rounds?"

"I don't know."

"Have you ever seen a human destroyed by bullets?"

"Yes."

"Describe it to me."

"It is like an abattoir, very bloody."

"What does it look like when a child is torn apart by bullets?"

"They are animals and deserved to die."

"As we sit here, how does talking about this make you feel?"

"I am thinking that you are not a good mediator. You are obviously biased."

"How do you feel that I am biased?"

"You are accusing me of massacres and war crimes. I had nothing to do with it."

"Part of my job as mediator is to help you see other stories, other perspectives. When the stories are so unpleasant you do not want to listen to them, you call me biased. You would prefer me to listen and agree with your story?"

"Of course."

"Then what good would I be as a mediator? All of the stories will come out, and you will have to accept them for what they are—other stories."

"I suppose that is so."

"The question is whether you have the courage to look at those stories despite your strong feelings."

"Are you questioning my courage?"

"No. I am asking you to look inside yourself and decide what kind of a person you are."

"And if I decide that I am righteous in fighting the despicable vermin that started this civil war?"

"Then the war will continue. You will eventually have no country to govern. Your clan and tribe will continue to be victims of violence, ripped apart by bullets and grenades. Your tribe's children will scream in terror and agony for their parents as they are murdered. And your forces will continue to murder the children of the opposing forces, as they scream in terror and agony for their parents. That does not sound like noble leadership to me. What about to you?"

This conversation is tough, as the mediator respectfully but firmly does not allow Mr. Sbeke to morally disengage from the violence. At the end, the mediator rehumanizes both sides in graphic, emotional words to trigger the emotional centers in Mr. Sbeke's brain.

Through many conversations like this, the mediator will help both sides build empathy and will create the possibility of remorse or regret. During this difficult process, the mediator must help the parties save face by protecting their self-esteem. The mediator must create a container to hold all the anxiety and fear and give out the emotional tasks of confronting what has happened one piece at a time.

The mediator can expect many emotional outbursts as the pain becomes too great to face. The mediator will be personally attacked as incompetent, biased, disturbed, or unethical. These attacks must be viewed as deflections away from moral engagement, and the mediator must have the inner strength and fortitude to stand into them gracefully. Whenever possible, the mediator must reframe the language from euphemism to vivid emotion, from distortion to personal accountability, from comparison and justification to accountability. The mediator will consciously ask questions to tap into the part of the brain that processes ethics and morality. Using ethical language like *integrity*, *honesty*, *fairness*, and *propriety*, or asking questions about immoral behavior with words like *lying*, *cheating*, *killing*, *murdering*, and *stealing* will trigger moral thinking because these terms are attached to existing cognitive categories that have moral content. There will be powerful emotional resistance to this process, so the mediator must be patient and be committed to a long process of moral reengagement.

There are a wide variety of techniques and processes available to skilled and experienced mediators to help the parties come to grips with the atrocities of evil, war, and violence. The most important concept is that this evil must be confronted and accepted on both sides as one of many truths. As that occurs, the possibility for peace grows.

Epilogue

In the Native American tradition, the story is told of a boy who came to his grandfather, incensed at an injustice done to him by a friend. The grandson wanted justice, and vengeance filled his heart. It was so unfair!

Grandfather said, "Let me tell you a story. I, too, at times, have felt a great hate for those who have taken so much, with no sorrow for what they do.

"But hate wears you down, and does not hurt your enemy. It is like taking poison and wishing your enemy would die. I have struggled with these feelings many times."

He continued, "It is as if there are two wolves inside me. One is good and does no harm. He lives in harmony with all around him, and does not take offense when no offense was intended. He will only fight when it is right to do so, and in the right way.

"But the other wolf, ah! He is full of anger. The littlest thing will set him into a fit of temper. He fights everyone, all the time, for no reason. He cannot think because his anger and hate are so great. It is helpless anger, for his anger will change nothing.

"Sometimes, it is hard to live with these two wolves inside me, for both of them try to dominate my spirit."

The boy looked intently into his grandfather's eyes and asked, "Which one wins, Grandfather?"

The grandfather smiled and quietly said, "The one I feed."

The challenge for the twenty-first-century mediator is to learn how to feed the good wolf and starve the bad. We are not rational beings with feelings; we are feeling beings with the ability to think rational thoughts. If it were otherwise, there would be very little conflict in the world that could not be settled by logic and reasoning. Our world would be more like Vulcan, the world of Mr. Spock from the *Star Trek* series. However, we know that logic and reasoning have very little to do with peacemaking. Thus, mediators working in international conflicts must have a unique set of skills and experience that recognize the highly emotional, nonrational nature of intractable conflict.

So what will it take to develop these mediators? First, in the long term there is good news. There are now hundreds of graduate programs offering masters' degrees and doctorates in conflict resolution, peacemaking, and related fields. These academic programs are multidisciplinary, exposing students to the vast array of knowledge necessary to be an effective peacemaker. A least a few will rise through political and diplomatic ranks in twenty-five to thirty years to be the premier peacemakers and mediators of our world.

Most professional mediators in North America and Europe are committed to continuing education. As a result, each year there are dozens of conferences, training workshops, and academies where mediators go to learn the latest in the science and practice of peace. This model should be adopted for those diplomats and politicians who aspire to mediate international conflict. Obviously, these people have day jobs that keep them busy. However, taking the time to attend a three- or four-day training conference where they are the students, not the honored guests, could expose them to the nuts and bolts of mediation practice. In addition, these types of meetings, if developed in the right way, could foster cross-fertilization of ideas between scholars, full-time practitioners, and diplomats. One example of this type of meeting is the Oslo Forum cosponsored by the Norwegian Ministry of Foreign Affairs and the Centre for Humanitarian Dialogue. Launched in 2003, it provides an opportunity for senior mediators, diplomats, and political leaders to share their experiences in an informal setting. In addition to an annual gathering in Oslo, the process also includes retreats that focus on region-specific issues or particular themes. This type of forum can be replicated around the world.

Third, regional organizations are tending to take on more mediation work than the United Nations or individual countries. These organizations, if they can generate the political will to do so, can become the foundation for a cadre of professional mediators and peacemakers and the training and resource centers for those called to intervene as mediators who are not professionally trained. For example, the African Union, formerly the Organization for African Unity, while underfunded and fragile, could promote the development of professional African peacemakers dedicated to conflicts on the continent. Likewise, the League of Arab States could develop programs in mediation, conflict resolution, negotiation, and peacemaking that would create a cadre of Arabic peacemakers and mediators for disputes within the Arabic world.

Certainly the United Nations could direct more resources toward the professionalization of mediation. It would be the obvious sponsor, perhaps with several universities, of advanced professional education through workshops and training conferences. The UN has an opportunity to expand and grow its capacity for developing the skills of senior mediators, and this would be an important demonstration of world leadership.

Learning new skills when you are already accomplished in life can be an interesting exercise in humility. There may be some who resist the idea that they could use more training, more knowledge, and more practice. One way around this is for those who select mediators to demand higher standards of competency. Those mediators willing to sacrifice time, effort, and ego to learn should rise to the top of the short lists. The Big Names who do not invest in their professional development should fall by the wayside. I suspect that even Jimmy Carter, Desmond Tutu, and others like them could continue to grow and learn in the skill of mediation.

Finally, the United States is emphasizing the importance of dialogue and negotiation in dealing with Iran, Korea, the Israeli-Palestinian conflict, and others. While the Obama administration and Secretary of State Clinton still cast conflicts and negotiations in the terms of the old diplomacy, their actions show that they can listen, respond thoughtfully, and not impose American agendas on others. There is, for some, hope as patience and persistence seem to be overtaking, at least in this administration, the desire for vengeance and power projection.

In a *New York Times* opinion piece, Thomas L. Friedman noted that American foreign and defense policy will necessarily have to become frugal in the decades ahead. This could benefit the prospects for peace. As Friedman observed, "Europe is rich but wimpy. China is rich nationally but still dirt poor on a per capita basis and, therefore, will be compelled to remain focused inwardly and regionally. Russia, drunk on oil, can cause trouble but not project power."[1] Perhaps this is the dawn of mediation and peacemaking as a full force in the world; it's all anyone can afford right now. If we can prepare our leaders, diplomats, and international mediators to step up with the best tools, peace will not be so elusive.

Notes

INTRODUCTION

1. Alex Altman, "Middle East Envoy George Mitchell," http://www.time.com/time/world/article/0,8599,1873532,00.html (accessed October 17, 2010).

CHAPTER 1

1. http://www.warresisters.org/pages/piechart.htm (accessed February 11, 2011).

2. "The Treaty on the Non-Proliferation of Nuclear Weapons [July 1, 1968]," http://www.un.org/en/conf/npt/2005/npttreaty.html (accessed October 17, 2010).

3. Kenneth C. Cloke, "Copenhagen Diary: Reflections from Inside the Climate Change Conference," private e-mail to board members of Mediators Beyond Borders, December 9, 2009 (copy on file with author).

4. Private conversation and correspondence between Laurel Kaufer and the author, December 2010.

5. Thuycides, *On Justice, Power, and Human Nature: Selections from the History of the Peloponnesian War*, trans. Paul Woodruss (Indianapolis: Hackett, 1993), p. 93.

6. D. Gardner, *Thomas Hobbes and Niccolò Machiavelli: A Comparison*, http:www.e-ir.info/?=4892 (accessed February 11, 2011).

7. Augustine, *De Peccato Originali*, 13, http://www.earlychurch texts.com/public/augustine_pelagius_de_peccato_originali_13.htm (accessed February 11, 2011).

8. Robert O. Keohane and Joseph S. Nye Jr., "Power and Interdependence Revisited," *International Organization* 41, no. 4 (Autumn 1987): 728.

9. Antonio Damasio, *Descartes' Error: Emotion, Reason, and the Human Brain* (New York: Penguin, 2005).

10. Dan Ariely, *Predictably Irrational: The Hidden Forces That Shape Our Decisions* (New York: HarperCollins, 2008).

11. Bab Shiv and Alexander Fedorikhin, "Heart and Mind in Conflict: The Interplay of Affect and Cognition in Consumer Decision Making," *Journal of Consumer Research* 26 (1999): 278–92.

12. Ibid.

13. "Peace Treaty between the Holy Roman Emperor and the King of France and Their Respective Allies [October 24, 1648]," http://avalon .law.yale.edu/17th_century/westphal.asp (accessed October 17, 2010).

14. Ibid.

15. Ibid.

16. Harold Nicolson, *Diplomacy* (London: Oxford University Press, 1977), pp. 71, 77.

17. Charles W. Freeman Jr., "Why Not Try Diplomacy?" in remarks to the University Continuing Education Association, March 28, 2008, New Orleans, LA, http://www.mepc.org/whats/diplomacy .html (accessed October 17, 2010).

18. Clayton Swisher, *The Truth about Camp David: The Untold Story about the Collapse of the Middle East Peace Process* (New York: Nation Books, 2004).

CHAPTER 2

1. "53rd Weather Reconnaissance Squadron 'Hurricane Hunters,'" http://www.403wg.afrc.af.mil/library/factsheets/factsheet .asp?id=7483 (accessed October 19, 2010).

2. Roger Fisher, Willliam L. Ury, and Bruce Patton, *Getting to Yes: Negotiating Agreement without Giving In*, 2nd ed. (New York: Penguin, 1991).

3. Laurie Nathan, "When Push Comes to Shove: The Failure of International Mediation in African Civil Wars," *Track Two* 8, no. 2 (November 1999), http://webworld.unesco.org/Water/wwap/pccp/cd/pdf/educational_tools/course_modules/reference_documents/conflict/whenpushcomestoshove.pdfediation (accessed October 19, 2010).

4. Scott Lasensky, "Paying for Peace: The Oslo Process and the Limits of American Foreign Aid," *Middle East Journal*, March 22, 2004, http://www.accessmylibrary.com/coms2/summary_0286-214521 03_ITM (accessed August 19, 2010).

5. Clayton Swisher, *The Truth about Camp David: The Untold Story about the Collapse of the Middle East Peace Process* (New York: Nation Books, 2004).

6. Ernest H. Preeg, *Feeling Good or Doing Good with Sanctions* (Washington, DC: CSIS Press, 1999), p. 3.

7. Margaret P. Doxey, *International Sanctions in Contemporary Perspective*, 2nd ed. (New York: St. Martin's Press, 1996), p. 65.

8. Gary Hufbauer, Jeffrey Schott, and Kimberly Ann Elliott, *Economic Sanctions Reconsidered: History and Current Policy*, 2nd ed. (Washington, DC: Institute for International Economics, 1990).

9. Antje Herrberg, "Perceptions of International Peace Mediation in the EU: A Needs Analysis," November 2008, p. 11, http://www.initiativeforpeacebuilding.eu/pdf/Needs_analysis.pdf (accessed October 19, 2010).

10. Ibid.

11. Erica Ariel Fox, "Beyond Yes," presented at the National Academy of Distinguished Neutrals, Orlando, Florida, August 20–21, 2010.

12. Allen H. Kitchens, "Shape-of-the-Table Negotiations at the Paris Peace Talks on Vietnam," in *Crowding and Behavior*, edited by Chalsa M. Loo (New York: MSS Information, 1974), p. 244, http://books.google.com/books?id=XA8Ho_aITVoC&dq=vietnam+paris+negotiations+over+shape+of+the+table&source=gbs_navlinks_s (accessed October 19, 2010).

13. Fisher et al., *Getting to Yes*, pp. 3–5.

14. Mihaly Csikszentmihalyi, *Flow: The Psychology of Optimal Experience* (New York: Harper Perennial, 1991).

CHAPTER 3

1. Unless otherwise indicated, all quotations and information related to the Argentina-Uruguay conflict come from this source. Marcela Valente, "Christmas at the Roadblock," IPS News Service, December 18, 2006, http://ipsnews.net/news.asp?idnews=35890 (accessed October 21, 2010).

2. "Welcome to Uruguay: Fray Bentos," http://www.welcome uruguay.com/fraybentos/index_i.html (accessed October 21, 2010).

3. "Gualeguachú Carnival," http://www.argentinacontact.com/ en/conozca/carnavalGualeguaychu.php (accessed October 21, 2010).

4. "Argentina and Uruguay: Statute of the River Uruguay. Signed at Salto on 26 February 1975," http://untreaty.un.org/unts/60001 _120000/10/4/00018191.pdf (accessed October 21, 2010).

5. Tony Pagliaro, "Who Is Jorge Busti, the Man Endorsed by Kirchner Who Caused the Argentine Conflict with Uruguay?" http://vcrisis.com/index.php?content=letters/200603200634 (accessed October 21, 2010).

6. Carlos Malamud, "Pulp Mills Divide the River Plate," Real Instituto Elcano, April 4, 2006, http://www.realinstitutoelcano.org/ wps/portal/rielcano_eng/Print?WCM_GLOBAL_CONTEXT=/wps/ wcm/connect/elcano/Elcano_in/Zonas_in/ARI%2033–2006 (accessed October 21, 2010).

7. "Pulp Mills on the River Uruguay (Arg. v. Uru.) (Provisional Measures Order of July 13, 2006)," http://www.icj-cij.org/docket/files/ 135/11235.pdf (accessed October 21, 2010).

8. *Wikipedia*, "Pulp Mill Dispute between Argentina and Uruguay," http://en.wikipedia.org/wiki/Pulp_mill_dispute_between _Argentina_and_Uruguay (accessed October 21, 2010).

9. "Decision of the Mercosur ad hoc Arbitral Tribunal (Uru. v. Arg.) (Sept. 6, 2006)," http://www.mrree.gub.uy/mrree/Prensa/Laudo TribunalADHOC.pdf (accessed October 21, 2010).

10. World Bank, Compliance Adviser Ombudsman, Uruguay/

Orion-02/Gualeguaychú-Argentina, http://www.cao-ombudsman.org/cases/case_detail.aspx?id=152 (accessed October 22, 2010).

11. "Argentina v. Uruguay, Final Judgment," April 20, 2010, http://www.icj-cij.org/docket/files/135/15877.pdf (accessed October 22, 2010).

12. As conceived by MacDonald and Diamond, the nine tracks are:
   1. Government
   2. Professional Conflict Resolution
   3. Business
   4. Private Citizens
   5. Research, Training, and Education
   6. Activism
   7. Religious
   8. Funding, and
   9. Public Opinion/Communication

13. John Paul Lederach, *The Moral Imagination: The Art and Soul of Building Peace* (New York: Oxford University Press, 2005).

14. Matthew D. Lieberman et al., "Putting Feelings into Words: Affect Labeling Disrupts Amygdala Activity in Response to Affective Stimuli," *Psychological Science* 18, no. 5 (2007): 421–28, http://www.scn.ucla.edu/pdf/AL(2007).pdf (accessed October 22, 2010).

CHAPTER 4

1. Unless otherwise indicated, all quotations and information related to the Nassar family come from this source. Richard Boudreaux, "A West Bank Struggle Rooted in Land: A Palestinian Fights in Court for a Hill His Family Has Held Since 1916. But Jewish Neighbors Say the Farm Should Be Theirs," *Los Angeles Times*, December 27, 2007, http://www.latimes.com/news/nationworld/world/la-fg-hilltop27dec27,1,3375978.story?coll=la-headlines-world&ctrack=1&cset=true (accessed October 22, 2010).

2. Clayton Swisher, *The Truth about Camp David: The Untold Story about the Collapse of the Middle East Peace Process* (New York: Nation Books, 2004), p. 145.

3. Eitan Felner, "Apartheid by Any Other Name: Creeping Annexa-

tion of the West Bank," *Le Monde Diplomatique*, November 1999, http://mondediplo.com/1999/11/08israel (accessed October 22, 2010).

4. For a short history, see http://www.dismalworld.com/disputes/arab_israeli_conflict.php (accessed February 11, 2011).

5. Francis Bacon, "Novum Organum," 1620, http://www.constitution.org/bacon/nov_org.htm (accessed October 22, 2010).

6. Drew Westen et al., "Neural Bases of Motivated Reasoning: An fMRI Study of Emotional Constraints on Partisan Political Judgment in the 2004 U.S. Presidential Election," *Journal of Cognitive Neuroscience* 18, no. 11 (2006): 1947–58.

7. Ibid.

8. Ibid.

9. Emory University Health Sciences Center, "Emory Study Lights Up the Political Brain," *Science Daily* (January 31, 2006), http://www.sciencedaily.com /releases/2006/01/060131092225.htm (accessed October 22, 2010).

10. Ibid.

11. Ibid.

12. Ibid.

13. Unless otherwise indicated, all quotations and information regarding the interviews between Israeli and Palestinian students come from this source. Moises F. Salinas, *Planting Hatred, Sowing Pain: The Psychology of the Israeli-Palestinian Conflict* (Westport, CT: Praeger, 2007).

14. Swisher, *The Truth about Camp David*, p. 326.

15. Ibid.

CHAPTER 5

1. Since Kahneman and Tversky's seminal research in 1974, there have been thousands of research studies done on cognitive biases in nearly every conceivable form of human interaction. Just Googling the term "cognitive bias research" brings up 980,000 entries.

Take gender bias, for example. Here is a web bibliography just on cognitive bias and gender stereotype that has hundreds of studies: http://genderbiasbingo.com/gender_biasbibliography.html.

2. R. J. Robinson et al., "Actual versus Assumed Differences in Construal: 'Naive Realism' in Intergroup Perception and Conflict," *Journal of Personality and Social Psychology* 68, no. 3 (1995): 404–17.

3. D. Johnson, *Overconfidence and War: The Havoc and Glory of Positive Illusions* (Cambridge, MA: Harvard University Press, 2004), p. 21.

4. Irving L. Janis, *Groupthink: Psychological Studies of Policy Decisions and Fiascos*, 2nd ed. (Boston: Houghton Mifflin, 1982).

5. Ibid.

6. Akbar Khan, *Raiders in Kashmir* (Karachi: Pak Publishers, 1970), p. 191.

7. Benedetto De Martino et al., "Frames, Biases, and Rational Decision-Making in the Human Brain," *Science* 313, no. 5787 (August 4, 2006): 684–87.

8. Mahmoud Ahmadinejad, speech before the United Nations General Assembly, September 23, 2009, http://www.ironicsurrealism .blogivists.com/2009/09/23/transcript-ahmadinejad-speech-at-the-un -general-assembly-9-23–09/ (accessed April 18, 2010).

9. "Ahmadinejad Speech: Full Text," given at the Durban Review Conference, Geneva, Switzerland, April 20, 2009, http://news.bbc .co.uk/2/hi/middle_east/8010747.stm (accessed April 18, 2020).

10. "Iran 'Makes First Batch of 20% Enriched Uranium,'" *BBC News*, http://news.bbc.co.uk/2/hi/middle_east/8510451.stm (accessed April 18, 2010).

11. Nazee Moinian, "Is Iran the New Four-Letter Word?" *Huffington Post*, March 4, 2010, http://www.huffingtonpost.com/nazee-moinian/ is-iran-the-new-four-lett_b_484769.html (accessed October 22, 2010).

CHAPTER 6

1. Unless otherwise indicated, all quotations and information related to the Albanian blood feud come from this source. Scott Anderson, "The Curse of Blood and Vengeance," *New York Times Magazine*, December 26, 1999.

2. Henri Taijfel, "Experiments in Intergroup Discrimination," *Scientific American* 223:96–102.

3. Muzafer Sherif et al., "Intergroup Conflict and Cooperation: The Robbers Cave Experiment," http://psychclassics.asu.edu/Sherif/ (accessed October 22, 2010).

4. "Honour among the Pushtunwali," *Economist*, December 23, 2006; also found at http://www.sunniforum.com/forum/showthread .php?17302-Pushtun-tribalism-vs.-radical-Islam (accessed October 22, 2010).

5. "Mullah Omar—In His Own Words," interview with Voice of America, September 21, 2001, http://www.guardian.co.uk/world/ 2001/sep/26/afghanistan.features11 (accessed August 14, 2010).

6. Greg Mortenson and David O. Relin, *Three Cups of Tea: One Man's Mission to Promote Peace . . . One School at a Time* (New York: Penguin, 2007).

CHAPTER 7

1. George W. Bush, Address to the Nation, March 19, 2003, http://georgewbush-whitehouse.archives.gov/news/releases/2003/03/ 20030319–17.html (accessed October 22, 2010).

2. George W. Bush, "President Bush Outlines Iraq Threat," Cincinnati, Ohio, October 7, 2002, http://georgewbush-whitehouse .archives.gov/news/releases/2002/10/20021007–8.html (accessed October 22, 2010).

3. Thucydides, *History of the Peloponnesian War*, R. Crawley translation, http://evans-experientialism.freewebspace.com/thucydides 01.htm (accessed November 15, 2009).

4. J. S. Lerner et al., "Effects of Fear and Anger on Perceived Risks of Terrorism: A National Field Experiment," *Psychological Science* 14, no. 2 (2003): 144–50.

5. P. J. Shiromani, J. E. LeDoux, and T. L. Keane, *Post-Traumatic Stress Disorder: Basic Science and Clinical Practice* (Springer, 2009), p. 158.

6. Unless otherwise indicated, all quotations and information related to the Israeli-Palestinian dialogue process come from this source. Betwa Sharma, "The Manhattan Peace Process on Israel and Palestine," *Huffington Post*, January 15, 2010, http://www.huffington

post.com/betwa-sharma/the-manhattan-peace-proce_b_424478.html (accessed January 18, 2010).

7. A. G. Sulzberger and Matthew Wald, "Jet Flyover Frightens New Yorkers," *New York Times*, April 27, 2009, http://www.nytimes.com/2009/04/28/nyregion/28plane.html (accessed October 23, 2010).

8. Robert Gibbs, "Press Briefing by Press Secretary Robert Gibbs," April 28, 2010, http://www.whitehouse.gov/the-press-office/briefing-white-house-press-secretary-robert-gibbs-42809 (accessed October 23, 2010).

9. Jennifer S. Lerner and Dacher Keltner, "Fear, Anger, and Risk," *Journal of Personality and Social Psychology* 81, no. 2 (2001): 146–59.

10. J. R. Dunn and M. E. Schweitzer, "Feeling and Believing: The Influence of Emotion on Trust," *Journal of Personality and Social Psychology* 88, no. 5 (2005): 736–48.

11. Unless otherwise indicated, all quotations and information related to the COP15 proceedings come from this source. "Food Fight at COP15," COP Final Plenary Session, Copenhagen, December 17, 2009, http://skepticalbureaucrat.blogspot.com/2009/12/food-fight-at-cop15.html (accessed January 3, 2010).

12. Unless otherwise indicated, all quotations and information related to the 2010 Davos World Economic Forum come from this source. Associated Press, "Recep Erdoğan Storms Out of Davos after Clash with Israeli President over Gaza," *Guardian*, January 30, 2009, http://www.guardian.co.uk/world/2009/jan/30/turkish-prime-minister-gaza-davos (accessed October 23, 2010).

CHAPTER 8

1. Mildred Ngesa, "The Roots of Kenya's Crisis," *Development and Cooperation Journal*, February 2008, http://www.inwent.org/ez/articles/065121/index.en.shtml (accessed June 21, 2010).

2. IRIN Africa, "Kenya: It's the Economy, Stupid (Not Just Tribalism)," January 8, 2009, http://www.irinnews.org/Report.aspx?ReportId=76159 (accessed October 23, 2010). All of Mr. Annan's statements quoted hereafter come from this interview.

3. Ibid.

4. S. McCrummen, "No Quick Fix for What Still Ails Kenya," *Washington Post*, March 7, 2008, http://www.washingtonpost.com/wp-dyn/content/article/2008/03/06/AR2008030603766.html (accessed February 12, 2011).

5. Ibid.

6. G. Prunier, "Kenya: Roots of Crisis," Open Democracy-Free Thinking for the World, http://www.opendemocracy.net/article/kenya_roots_of_crisis (accessed February 12, 2011).

7. Ibid.

8. The Centre for Humanitarian Dialogue, "Interview: The Prisoner of Peace—Interview with Kofi Annan," May 9, 2008, http://www.hdcentre.org/files/Kofi%20interview%20(3).pdf (accessed October 23, 2010).

9. "Q&A: Githongo on Kenya Violence," *BBC News*, January 23, 2008, http://news.bbc.co.uk/2/hi/africa/7204987.stm (accessed October 23, 2010).

10. Private conversation with the author, March 29, 2010, Los Angeles, California.

11. Michael Kosfeld et al., "Oxytocin Increases Trust in Humans," *Nature* 435 (June 2, 2005): 673–76.

12. Ibid.

13. Paul Zak, "Oxytocin, Trust, and Negotiation," presented at the Master Mediator Institute, University of California at Los Angeles, October 30, 2009.

14. Beate Ditzen et al., "Intranasal Oxytocin Increases Positive Communication and Reduces Cortisol Levels during Couple Conflict," *Biological Psychiatry* 65, no. 9 (May 1, 2009): 728–31.

15. South Consulting, "KNDR Monitoring Project—Report by South Consulting (Progress Report for January–March 2010)," April 2010, http://www.dialoguekenya.org/docs/KNDRFebtoMarch2010Report.pdf (accessed October 22, 2010).

CHAPTER 9

1. United Nations Commission for Human Rights, "Impunity," Resolution 2003/72, April 23, 2003, http://www.unhchr.ch/Huridocda/

Huridoca.nsf/(Symbol)/E.CN.4.RES.2003.72.En?Opendocument (accessed October 23, 2010).

2. *Prosecutor v. Omar Hassan Ahmad Al Bahsir*, International Court of Justice, "Second Warrant of Arrest for Omar Hassan Ahmad Al Bahsir," July 12, 2010, http://www.icc-cpi.int/iccdocs/doc/doc 907140.pdf (accessed October 23, 2010).

3. Reuters, "U.S. Urges Sudan Cooperation on Bashir Arrest Warrant," July 13, 2010, http://www.reuters.com/article/idUSTRE66 C5C520100713 (accessed October 23, 2010).

4. "U.S. Special Envoy Unhappy about ICC Genocide Ruling against Sudanese President," *Sudan Tribune*, July 14, 2010, http://www.sudantribune.com/spip.php?article35657 (accessed October 23, 2010).

5. As quoted in "Uganda: Forgiveness as an Instrument of Peace," IRIN Africa, June 9, 2005, http://www.irinnews.org/Print Report.aspx?ReportId=54859m (accessed October 23, 2010).

6. Ibid.

7. "Warrant for the Arrest of Joseph Kony," International Criminal Court, issued July 8, 2005, as amended September 27, 2005, http://www.icc-cpi.int/iccdocs/doc/doc97185.PDF (accessed October 23, 2010).

8. "UGANDA: Amnesty and Peace Groups Urge ICC to Probe Government Army Too," IRIN News, February 3, 2004, http://www.globalsecurity.org/military/library/news/2004/02/mil-040203-irin03.htm (accessed October 24, 2010).

9. "UGANDA: ICC's Balancing Act on the Peace Process in the North," IRIN News, http://irinnews.org/InDepthMain.aspx?InDepthId=7&ReportId=59483 (accessed October 23, 2010).

10. Barney Afako, "Negotiating in the Shadow of Justice," Conciliation Resources, http://www.c-r.org/our-work/accord/northern-uganda-update/negotiating_justice.php (accessed October 23, 2010).

11. Ibid.

12. "Annexure to the Agreement on Accountability and Reconciliation," February 19, 2008, pp. 3–4, http://www.iccnow.org/documents/Annexure_to_agreement_on_Accountability_signed_today.pdf (accessed October 24, 2010).

13. Barney Afako, "Negotiating in the Shadow of Justice," Con-

ciliation Resources, http://www.c-r.org/our-work/accord/northern
-uganda-update/negotiating_justice.php (accessed October 23, 2010).

14. William B. Swann Jr., Brett W. Pelham, and David C. Roberts,
"Causal Chunking: Memory and Inference in Ongoing Interaction,"
Journal of Personality and Social Psychology 53, no. 5 (1987): 858–65.

15. Sukhwinder S. Shergill et al., "Two Eyes for an Eye: The Neuroscience of Force Escalation," *Science* 301, no. 5630 (July 11, 2007): 187.

16. Tania Singer et al., "Empathic Neural Responses Are Modulated
by the Perceived Fairness of Others," *Nature* (January 26, 2006):
466–69, http://www.nature.com/nature/journal/v439/n7075/abs/nature
04271.html (accessed October 24, 2010).

17. "Vengeance: A Male Game," *Aphrodite Women's Health*, January 23, 2006, http://www.aphroditewomenshealth.com/news/200600
23160245_health_news.shtml (accessed October 24, 2010).

18. Ibid.

19. Rome Statute of the International Criminal Court, effective
July 1, 2002, http://www.icc-cpi.int/NR/rdonlyres/EA9AEFF7–5752
–4F84-BE94–0A655EB30E16/0/Rome_Statute_English.pdf (accessed
October 24, 2010).

20. http://www.amicc.org/icc_activities.html.

21. OTP, "Policy Paper on the Interests of Justice," September
2007, pp. 1, 8–9, http://www.icc-cpi.int/NR/rdonlyres/772C95C9-F54
D-4321-BF09–73422BB23528/143640/ICCOTPInterestsOfJustice
.pdf (accessed October 24, 2010).

22. Ibid.

23. Luis Moreno-Ocampo, ICC prosecutor, address to international conference on "Building a Future on Peace and Justice," Nurem-
berg, June 25, 2007, p. 4, http://www.peace-justice-conference.info/
download/speech%20moreno.pdf (accessed October 24, 2010).

24. Private conversation with the author.

25. Mark Yantzi, *Sexual Offending and Restoration* (Scottdale,
PA: Herald Press, 1998), pp. 51–53.

26. John Mutamba and Jeanne Isabiliza, "The Role of Women in
Reconciliation and Peace Building in Rwanda: Ten Years after Genocide 1994–2004," National Unity and Reconciliation Commission of
the Republic of Rwanda, pp. 26–28, May 2005, http://www.nurc.gov
.rw/documents/researches/Role_of_women_in_peace_building.pdf
(accessed October 24, 2010).

27. Ibid.
28. Ibid.

CHAPTER 10

1. Oral argument before the Ninth Circuit Court of Appeals, *Humanitarian Law Project v. Gonzales*, December 14, 2004, http://www.ca9.uscourts.gov/media/view_subpage.php?pk_id=0000004506 (accessed October 26, 2010).

2. Oral argument before the United States Supreme Court, *Holder v. Humanitarian Law Project*, February 23, 2010, p. 40, http://www.supremecourt.gov/oral_arguments/argument_transcripts/0 8-1498.pdf (accessed October 26, 2010).

3. Nina Totenberg, "Does the Patriot Act Violate Free Speech?" National Public Radio, February 23, 2010, http://www.npr.org/templates/story/story.php?storyId=123993822 (accessed October 26, 2010).

4. Juan Williams, *Eyes on the Prize: America's Civil Rights Years, 1954–1965* (New York: Viking Penguin, 1987), pp. 147–48.

5. Unless otherwise indicated, all quotations and information related to Ralph Fertig come from this source. Doug Noll, "Interview with Ralph Fertig," *Doug Noll Show*, May 27, 2010, http://www.wsradio.com/internet-talk-radio.cfm/shows/The-Doug-Noll-Show/archives/date/selected/05–27–2010.html (accessed October 26, 2010).

6. Unless otherwise indicated, all quotations and information related to the *Holder v. Humanitarian Law Project* come from this source. Oral argument before the United States Supreme Court, *Holder v. Humanitarian Law Project*, February 23, 2010, p. 2, http:// www.supremecourt.gov/oral_arguments/argument_transcripts/08–1498.pdf (accessed October 26, 2010).

7. *Holder v. Humanitarian Law Project*, 130 S. Ct. 2705, 2721; 177 L. Ed. 2d 355; 2010 U.S. LEXIS 5252, November 2, 2009.

8. Ibid.

9. Adam Lipak, "Court Affirms Ban on Aiding Groups Tied to Terror," *New York Times*, June 21, 2010, http://www.nytimes.com/2010/06/22/us/politics/22scotus.html (accessed October 26, 2010).

CHAPTER II

1. L. Kohlberg, *Essays on Moral Development: Vol. 2, The Psychology of Moral Development* (Harper & Row, 1984).

2. S. Milgram, *Obedience to Authority: An Experimental View* (Harper & Row, 1974).

3. P. G. Zimbardo, *The Lucifer Effect: Understanding How Good People Turn Evil* (Random House, 2007).

4. William C. Crain, *Theories of Development* (Englewood Cliffs, NJ: Prentice-Hall, 1985), pp. 118–36.

5. Ibid.

6. Albert Bandura, "Moral Disengagement in the Perpetration of Inhumanities," *Personality and Social Psychological Review* 3, no. 3 (1999): 193.

7. Ibid.

8. John Darnton, "Revisiting Rwanda's Horrors with a Former National Security Adviser," *New York Times*, December 20, 1994, http://query.nytimes.com/gst/fullpage.html?res=940CE7D71230F933A15751 C1A9629C8B63&pagewanted=3 (accessed October 26, 2010).

9. Ibid.

10. Bruno Waterfield, "Radovan Karadzic: Bosnian War Was 'Just and Holy,'" *London Telegraph*, March 1, 2010, http://www.telegraph .co.uk/news/worldnews/europe/bosnia/7343731/Radovan-Karadzic -Bosnian-war-was-just-and-holy.html (accessed October 26, 2010).

11. A. Bandura, B. Underwood, M. E. Fromson, "Disinhibition of Aggression through Diffusion of Responsibility and Dehumanization of Victims," *Journal of Research in Personality* 9 (1975): 269.

12. Ibid.

13. The Phrase Finder, "Power Corrupts; Absolute Power Corrupts Absolutely," http://www.phrases.org.uk/meanings/absolute -power-corrupts-absolutely.html (accessed October 26, 2010).

14. Kohlberg, *Essays on Moral Development*.

15. P. Englebert and D. M. Tull, "Postconflict Reconstuction in Africa: Flawed Ideas about Failed States," *International Security* 32, no. 4 (2008): 120.

EPILOGUE

1. Thomas Friedman, "Superbroke, Superfrugal, Superpower?" *New York Times*, September 4, 2010, http://www.nytimes.com/2010/09/05/opinion/05friedman.html?_r=1&ref=thomaslfriedman (accessed October 26, 2010).

Index